TEN TOUGH TRIPS

Montana Writers and the West

TEN TOUGH TRIPS
Montana Writers and the West

WILLIAM W. BEVIS

A McLellan Book

UNIVERSITY OF WASHINGTON PRESS
Seattle and London

This book is published with the assistance of a grant from the McLellan Endowed Series Fund, established through the generosity of Martha McCleary McLellan and Mary McLellan Williams.

Library of Congress Cataloging-in-Publication Data

Bevis, William W., 1941–
   Ten tough trips : Montana writers and the West / William Bevis.
     p. cm.
   Includes bibliographical references.
   ISBN 0-295-96941-5 (alk. paper)
    1. American literature—Montana—History and criticism.
2. Authors, American—Montana—Biography. 3. Montana—Intellectual
life. 4. West (U.S.) in literature. 5. Indians in literature.
6. Montana in literature. 7. Montana—Biography. I. Title.
II. Title: 10 tough trips.
PS283.M9B48   1990
810.9'9786—dc20

89-77570
CIP

Endpapers: Dudes on skyline ride, Beartooth Mountains, Montana. Photo by F. W. Byerly *(courtesy of Montana Historical Society, Helena)*

To the memory of
Sarah Gardner Crump
1967–1989

"This was the last name west on charts.
West of here the world turned that indefinite white
of blank paper and settlers faded one at a time alone."
Richard Hugo, "Fort Benton"

Contents

Introduction

THE ISSUES ARE THE WEST: WHAT IS IT, WHAT WAS IT, WHO ARE we? The romance of the West may be misleading, but there is something special in the land, as anyone with a whole car and half a heart can see. Wallace Stegner tells of the thrill of crossing the Mississippi and entering the plains, coming home, and for the poet Richard Hugo and most of us here, driving Montana is an art. So although the old myths are crumbling, the land claims reverence; the trick is to figure out, when we think "West," what we really love.

My purpose is not to survey Montana literature, but to use ten authors—a dozen or so books—to bring up key issues of western identity. The Montana literature is so various and interesting, and the West is so intertwined with American national identity, that I thought many who do not usually read criticism or history might enjoy hearing a discussion of the books. These are personal essays, then, for a general audience. For a scholar, the writing has been a most enjoyable break from the objectivity and impersonality of professional publication.

To read these essays, you need not have read the books, though I certainly hope you will read them soon. I have chosen books readily available in paperback editions; this cuts out some very good writers. Fortunately, we have a new centennial anthology of Montana writers, *The Last Best Place*, to fill in gaps with at least excerpts from out-of-print authors, and to give readers an overall view of the extent and quality of our regional literature. Here, however, we want only a few good books and a chance to consider our lives.

The West. What is it? The West does not include California or any place with melons and beaches. The West, as moviegoers around the world know, is an immense desert (or grassland, if the film has a family) with shining mountains in the background, hardworking ranchers in the foreground, Indians preferably *way* in the background, hellacious winters, and no rain. Montana, for instance.

We can easily draw the borders of this mythic West. Exclude the coast. Exclude the Southwest, which has its own culture, literature, and "westerns." Exclude the Mormons, with their social visions of family, church, and empire. Exclude the eastern plains of Kansas, Nebraska, and the Dakotas; we are west of Willa Cather.

Include northern Nevada, western Colorado, Wyoming, southern Idaho, and Montana: the high plains, ranching West sprawled on either side of the Northern Rockies. Our region is reasonably coherent in history, ecology, and economy, the region of cowboys, Indians, miners, homesteaders, beaver, and cattle, and wheat and gold and snow. Montana has produced many of this region's best books.

Forget Texas, "hombre," "lingo," and other Spanish ruins; forget Pueblo Indians in cliffside towns. Think Cheyenne, Sioux, Crow, Assiniboine, Blackfeet, Nez Perce, fur traders, "Across the Wide Missouri," the Homestead Act of 1866, the blizzard of 1886–87, Butte— "The richest hill on earth," or as its chief of police said in the twenties, "An island of booze in a sea of easy money." Think American identity: wilderness, "Go West Young Man," freedom, beef, a fresh start.

The above three paragraphs deliberately parody the myth of the West as a place of colorful adventure. Now think instead of McDonald's buying cheap beef from razed rain forests in the Amazon. Think of two gas stations, a bar, a general store, and a failed bank, blank plywood nailed to the windows of an old ranching town. Two Dot, Montana, now. Think of a Chinese professor from Beijing sitting in the Two Dot bar discussing agricultural policy with a dancer and an English teacher from Missoula. That was us, November 1986. He was here to figure out why, when a country industrializes, it drives its people off the land. In Montana, twenty farms a week were going under. We took him to the Northern Plains Resource Council meeting in Billings. "We want to use tractors," he said to a group of men towering over and around him, "but we also want full employment." "How do you cut your wheat?" asked Wally McRae, rancher and cowboy poet. "Like this," said Professor Meng, making gestures of holding a fistful of stalks in one hand and cutting them with a sickle in the other. "You got troubles," said McRae, pushing his hat back with his thumb. "Yes," laughed Professor Meng, "and you?"

China, the Amazon, the West—more people, more industry—it is one world now. We cannot leave it for another. So *that* West, the West of escape, is gone, or at least it lies somewhere out in that other space, beyond our field of gravity.

This book has two centers: stories to ponder, and ideas to revise. Because "The West" and "western" are crucial categories in our national identity, the revisions are interesting. And when cultural history meets good stories head on, the discussion is fun.

You will find in this book many instances of conflict between East and West, and it is important to see East-West conflict in historical perspective. England opposed trans-Allegheny settlement, for the British feared that once over the mountains and into the Ohio valley, the colonists would break loose from England. Similarly, Jefferson doubted whether settlers past the Mississippi would keep their allegiance to a government in Washington. The day I arrived in Montana, in 1974, Governor Richard Lamm of Colorado half-jokingly suggested that the West secede from the union, because the West was becoming an energy colony of the East. That same day, a dour old man rang up my loaf of bread at the mom and pop grocery in the Rattlesnake Valley. Three days out of Massachussetts, I remarked that bread was ten cents cheaper back East. He looked up over his spectacles. "Then you better go back East to buy your bread."

Western resentment of the East is well founded, for it reflects the ways in which the western edges of colonial expansion have always been controlled, ignored, or abused by the centers of power to the East. That is, Europeans at the frontier are sometimes in the position of natives: their labors or resources are exploited by powers to the East, and they have little control over their land and lives. For instance, we have had four major economic booms in Montana: fur, 1825–45; mining, 1860–1920; open-range cattle, 1880–87; and homesteading, 1909–19. The first three booms were created by out-of-state capital for out-of-state markets, and most of the profits went to partners and shareholders back East. Whether the land is overgrazed is one thing to a locally owned family ranch and something else entirely to an international corporation which, when Montana grass gives out, can move its operations to Argentina. Anaconda Copper, with a little help from the U.S. government, had no trouble moving from Montana to Chile. The fourth boom, homesteading, was a national policy subsidized by a government which, situated next to the rolling farms of Virgina and Maryland, thought 160 acres was a fine spread for supporting a family.

The same patterns were true of the recent oil boom: companies owned somewhere else, reacting to international markets, came in and transformed small towns—such as Sidney, Montana—overnight. A man I met retired after a lifetime in Sidney, surrounded by friends and family, sold his house and moved into an apartment. Suddenly his rent went up five times in a year, he couldn't afford to rent or buy back into the housing market, and he had to move to another town and take a menial job. Two years later when the price of oil dropped, the companies left a shambles, and once again the local residents are trying to pick up the pieces. Who will pay off the bonds for the new primary school and sewer system? Let's face it: the money, power, and political clout lie to the East; people without money and power get pushed around; they resent it.

The economic and political colonialism which is part of Montana's history has a counterpart in what we might call cultural colonialism. People without money and power are often considered inferior by those with more, and indeed often judge themselves harshly. They may have trouble developing their own art if they have no powerful conception of themselves. Colonies from the Atlantic to the Pacific have often had a child's relationship to the eastern powers that spawned them; like a child, they can only imitate or rebel, until they have come into their own. Imitate: mining camps would erect false-front downtowns and grand opera houses with Parisian chandeliers. Or rebel: "western" must be anti-eastern—coarse, tough, drunk, anything but "classy." Unfortunately, rebellion, like imitation, keeps you subservient to someone else; *their* expectations are defining *your* behavior, whether through imitation or reaction. The history of Montana literature is the history of a region freeing itself from cultural colonialism, developing its own point of view, coming to know and trust a westerner's view of the West.

Our regional writings, like our economy, have gone through different phases. The nineteenth century produced many documents, often semiliterate and dramatic: Lewis and Clark's journals of 1805–6, several excellent trapper journals such as Osborne Russell's, cowboy reminiscences such as Teddy Blue Abbott's, and ranching memoirs such as Granville Stuart's. "There was only two things the old-time cowpuncher was afraid of," said Teddy Blue Abbott, Stuart's foreman, "a decent woman and being set afoot." There it is. Either he had read the dime novels, or they were reading him. These early memoirs, and some journalism, are fascinating, but Montana and western fiction in the nineteenth century is mostly sentimental, romantic, and boring.

In Part I of this book, "Treasure Islands of the West," we will look at three excellent and unusual stories set in that nineteenth century of empire and hope. First we will consider A. B. Guthrie's *The Big Sky*, written in the 1940s but set in the fur trade of the upper Missouri in the 1830s, then two reminiscences: Andrew Garcia's half-crazy (I may be too polite) memories of Montana in 1877–78, *Tough Trip Through Paradise*, and Nannie Alderson's reminiscence of homesteading in 1884, *A Bride Goes West*.

A second phase of Montana writing, from about 1900 to 1940, often followed Hollywood and popular fiction in romanticizing the West. The period was dominated by tales of exotic adventure such as Dorothy Johnson's "The Hanging Tree" and "The Man Who Shot Liberty Valance." I will not be discussing any of these books, partly because popular mythologies are already well known. John Cawelti's *The Six Gun Mystique* is a good survey of the popular "western." During that period a few people labored in different vineyards, but the realistic prose of Myron Brinig from Butte, of Grace Stone Coates and Mildred Walker, is largely out of print.

A third phase, 1940 to 1960, consisted of a "realistic revolt" by a handful of western writers. Guthrie was part of this conscious revolt against Hollywood romance, along with Wallace Stegner, Bernard

DeVoto, and Walter Van Tilburg Clark. Serious "westerns" began with those authors and others of their time, such as William Eastlake and Wright Morris.

By the late 1930s, Native American literature had come into its own. Frank Linderman, Chief Plenty-coups, and Pretty-shield had collaborated on their memories of the buffalo days, and D'Arcy McNickle had written both of his remarkable novels, which set the pattern for Native American fiction right up to James Welch and Louise Erdrich. Native American culture and literature, especially the fiction of McNickle and Welch, will be the subject of Part II of this study, "The Hearts of My People."

The final phase, 1960 to the present, is "modern," and will be considered in Part III, "Making Certain It Goes On." The shift from realism to psychological modernism arrived in Montana around 1964 when the poet Richard Hugo came to head the creative writing program at the University of Montana in Missoula. Since then, Montana writing has become increasingly sophisticated. All the recent authors here discussed—James Welch, Richard Hugo, Ivan Doig, and Norman Maclean—have received national and international recognition and numerous awards for their work.

Most important, a region has found its voice. I remember walking out of the locally written and produced movie *Heartland* in 1979, thinking that I had just seen the *first* western. No longer imitating eastern fantasies of what the West might be, no longer, for that matter, bothering even to react against Hollywood, the people of this region have begun to write honestly and seriously about growing up in Montana and about trying to find here what people everywhere need: dignity, love, a place, cash.

Readers will find in the chapters that follow some classic western books, myths, and revisions of those myths. Many scholars, especially ecologists, feminists, and Indians, have contributed to these revisions. I have occasionally included remarks by students in my course on Montana writers, English 375, at the University of Montana, for how the people of a region read their own books seems to me important. Student papers on regional books sometimes put professional articles to shame. I would not be printing my own views on many of these issues if a lot of westerners had not said those views ring true.

I was supported in this project by the University of Montana and by Toyo University in Tokyo, by grants from the State of Montana's Coal Severance Tax for research, by grants to Juliette Crump (professor of dance and my wife) for taking Chautauquas around Montana, and by many programs and opportunities made possible by Margaret Kingsland and the Montana Committee for the Humanities. I would also like to thank the most interesting group I have ever worked with, for their invaluable stimulation, goodwill, and companionship, my colleagues on the editorial board of *The Last Best Place*: Mary Blew, Bill Kittredge, Bill Lang, Rich Roeder, Annick Smith, Jim Welch.

Thanks are due to the following for the permission to reprint previously published material: the University of California Press for portions of Chapter 6, "McNickle: Homing In," and Chapter 8, "Welch's Winters and Bloods," which appeared in *Recovering the Word*, edited by Arnold Krupat (Berkeley and Los Angeles: University of California Press, 1987); the University of Montana for portions of Chapter 9, "Hugo's Poetry," which appeared in *Cutbank 20* (spring-summer 1983); and *Environmental Review* for portions of Chapter 12, "Cooper: Then and Now," which appeared in vol. 10, no. 1 (spring 1986).

Montana *is* special, and that special quality has some relation to being western. I recall our daughter Sarah, who had grown up in Montana and was a freshman at Hellgate High School, riding through the Danish countryside on her first trip abroad. Everything in Denmark is neat as a pin: cottages are perfect, the trees are planted in rows, even the factories have gardens and lawns and no litter. Sarah had been silent a long time. Finally she said, "I've got it!" "Got what?" "Something about Denmark is different, and I just figured it out." She was serious. "What's that?" "The stop signs," she said. "They don't have bullet holes."

Part I
Treasure Islands of the West

"Ten year too late anyhow." Uncle Zeb's jaw worked on the tobacco. "She's gone, goddam it! Gone!"

"What's gone?" asked Summers. . . .

"The whole shitaree. Gone, by God, and naught to care savin' some of us who seen 'er new. . . . This was man's country onc't. Every water full of beaver and a galore of buffler any ways a man looked, and no crampin' and crowdin'. Christ sake!"

—A. B. Guthrie, Jr., *The Big Sky*,
scene set in 1830

1

Guthrie's Big Sky

A man could sit and let time run on while he smoked or cut on a stick with nothing nagging him and the squaws going about their business and the young ones playing, making out that they warred on the Assiniboines. He could let time run on, Boone thought while he sat and let it run, and feel his skin drink the sunshine in and watch the breeze skipping in the grass and see the moon like a bright horn in the sky by night. One day and another it was pretty much the same, and it was all good. The sun came up big in the fall mornings and climbed warm and small and got bigger again as it dropped, and the slow clouds sailed red after it had gone from sight. There was meat to spare, and beaver still to trap if a man wanted to put himself out. In the summer the Piegans went to buffalo and later pitched camp close to Fort McKenzie and traded for whisky and tobacco and blankets and cloth and moved on to the Marias or the Teton or the Sun or the Three Forks for a little trapping and the long, lazy winter. (257)

EIGHTY STUDENTS SAT IN A CLASSROOM IN MISSOULA. "WHAT DO you think of this book?" I asked, because it is the first question, and the last, and the best. From a Blackfeet Indian in the back of the class came the shout, "Treasure Island."

Why had he said that? His tone was derisive, challenging, secure. Those are precious moments in the classroom, when different readings meet head on. In the first second of reaction, I was puzzled and angry. Puzzled because *Treasure Island* is a child's fantasy of adventure and escape, while Bud Guthrie had wanted "the day by day— the real guts" of mountain man life. I remembered Guthrie's gravelly voice speaking those words just a few months before. He had leaned forward on the kitchen table of his home above Choteau, above the open wash where the Teton River drains out of the Rocky Mountain Front Range, not more than a mile from where Boone Caudill had sat in the sun and let time run on, fresh married to his Blackfeet bride.

"No one had written honestly about the days of the fur traders," he said. "I hated those hero-type books that glossed over all the brutality." Guthrie had meant to set the record straight. "You had the romanticized version, but you didn't have the rough, tough, sinful, brave-heroic aspect. . . ." Sitting in his kitchen I had looked out the window, down toward Choteau and the plains, thinking of Bud growing up there searching for arrowheads and tipi rings. I tried to think back, as he had, to what it must have been like for Boone, in 1845, on this same old Blackfeet ground, by this same clear creek, October frost still under the sage at noon, and the plains below dark with buffalo.

The memory of Guthrie's home and of Boone by the Teton River lasted but a second. I was still standing in front of a classroom in Missoula. Here we were, reading a book that admired Indians, a book honest as it could be, a book carefully researched, tragic and tough, and this Blackfeet student was calling it *Treasure Island*. That's why I was puzzled, but not why I was angry. I was angry because I feared he was right.

It took me years to figure out how the student from Browning was right, and what the fantasy is in *The Big Sky*, but it's there, and what's also there is a moral for us all: we can be as honest as possible, and still be blind. The problems posed by *The Big Sky* are the problems of the West. Where Guthrie was blind, we are blind. I'm jumping ahead, however, to the end of this chapter, to why the white West is not the Indian West, and why a belt buckle reads, "Montana is what America was." There's a kind of longing in that slogan, and in *The Big Sky*, which the Indians properly see as a longing for escape. Was Boone in Indian country, or had he left one white world only to arrive at another? Escape from what, and to what, and why—that's the question. The story of Boone Caudill is "a classic," as Montana author Bill Kittredge said. "It had to be written." In writing it, A. B. Guthrie, Jr., gave Montana its central myth, and its slogan.

Harvard, 1944

Strange place for the son of the Choteau superintendent of schools, some might think, though a lot of Montana ranchers have taken their turns back East. After graduating from the University of Montana in 1923, Guthrie found no work in Montana and bounced from California to New York before settling in Kentucky as a journalist on the *Lexington Leader*. He worked there for twenty years. In 1944 Guthrie had a wife, two children, and the first drafts of a fur trader novel; he didn't like it and neither did anyone else. Then he received a Nieman fellowship to spend the year at Harvard. The family moved to Cambridge in the fall of 1944. The Nieman gave Guthrie the chance to escape deadlines and routines, to learn and to write, and that year "made all the difference," Guthrie said.

In the summer of 1945 he went from Harvard up to the Breadloaf writers' conference in Vermont, where he rewrote almost half the book. He was invited to a meeting with the famous publisher William Sloane. Sloane looked at the manuscript and offered a $5,000 advance on the spot. "Swinging on a star," Guthrie wired to his wife.

It was not only the right time for Bud Guthrie to write his book; it was also the right time for a westerner to write about the West. Before the Second World War, most works about the West had indeed been Treasure Islands. For over a century, eastern and European audiences had thrilled to romantic adventures set in the Rockies and Great Plains: sentimental stories of gold camps, homesteaders, and pioneers, or dime novels that grew up with the first cowboys and outlived them all. And then, movies. The first story-telling film, *The Great Train Robbery*, was a western. It came out in 1903, when Guthrie was two years old, and as Guthrie grew, Hollywood trotted out showhorse and showman one after another: Tom Mix, William S. Hart, Gene Autry, Roy Rogers . . . Those horse-heroes were not always in touch with reality. "Tom Mix?" said one student, at ninety-two the oldest college (elderhostel) student in America, and taking—or more frequently, teaching—the Montana writers course. "I knew Tom growing up, in Oklahoma. We all thought it so funny he wound up in the movies, 'cause at the County Fair when everybody was rodeoing, Tom was behind the stands, selling Coca-Cola. We'd never seen him on a horse, 'til those movies."

So when Guthrie wrote *The Big Sky*, westerns were still fantasies, agri-science fictions. At Harvard and Breadloaf in 1944–45, Guthrie met Bernard DeVoto from Utah and then Wallace Stegner from Saskatchewan, just north of the Montana Highline. Those three westerners had long read and seen the lies about their homes. Each resolved to tell the story better, and they did, Guthrie in fiction, DeVoto in history, and Stegner in both. The western realism movement, and westerners learning to tell their own versions of the western story, began with those three in exile in Boston and Vermont. In some ways they were like the Americans in Paris in the twenties—Hemingway, Stein, Fitzgerald—challenged by the atmosphere of art and learning, thinking of home.

It's All Gone Now

The book Guthrie pulled together back in Boston and Vermont was full of home, full of sweet longing for that "state of few people, entirely surrounded by space," in Joseph Kinsey Howard's words. Joseph Howard from Great Falls, the journalist and historian of Montana and the Metis Indians, was doing the same job at the same time as Guthrie, DeVoto, and Stegner, taking western history back from out-of-state interests and telling it from a Montana point of view. His *Montana: High, Wide and Handsome* is still a classic. He and Guthrie would become good friends, after *The Big Sky* was published in 1947 and Guthrie moved back to Montana to write. In 1951, Guthrie helped scatter Joe Howard's ashes from Flattop Peak above the Teton canyon.

Boone Caudill was Guthrie's hero, or anti-hero, set in the middle of Howard's high, wide, and handsome space. *The Big Sky* is a classic western story because it is about a young man who feels crowded and oppressed and strikes out into the West to start his life over. That part of the plot reflects the progressive notion of the West that is known to all America, Europe, and the world.

The first three fourths of *The Big Sky* is part history of the Missouri fur trade, part story of Boone growing up, and part chronicle of western optimism; but Guthrie added several twists to these tales. First, no one in the book worth his salt *wants* the West to progress. And second, Boone is a mean son of a bitch. We can quibble about why he is sullen and mean, and we can sympathize with the nasty background that created him, and we can even point to some positive qualities: his attraction to the land; his loyalty to his trapping partners, Summers and Jim Deakins; his love of Teal Eye, his Blackfeet wife. Near the end of the book, Boone does indeed seem to be changed as he settles down. He has found the West: a fresh start, room for a man to stretch, and the happiness quoted at the beginning of this chapter as he lies in the sun by the Teton River. Yet, as if to save us the trouble of arguing whether we like Boone or not, or whether he has changed, Guthrie has him destroy it all. On the slightest—and mistaken—evidence, Boone suspects that Teal Eye and Deakins are having an affair, finds them embracing (in friendship), and without demanding or begging a word of explanation, he kills his best friend. Boone then leaves his wife and child and western paradise to roam, broken and alone, among the settlements of the Mississippi frontier, the place where he began.

So *The Big Sky* is also a classic story of Paradise Lost. A young man of promise, with a steady aim and the guts to strike out for the West, marries the girl of his dreams and settles where it suits. Then he destroys what he loves.

His fall is not the only fall, however; this is not just a story of Boone being a chip off the old block, as stupid and violent as his father. Guthrie makes it clear that the entire West is going, and going fast. The settlers are appearing, the beaver and buffalo are disappearing, and the Indians are dying of smallpox. With or without Boone, this paradise is gone. One of the great passages in the book, or in all western literature, is spoken by Uncle Zeb when young Boone is first coming up the Missouri, in the spring of 1831:

> "Ten year too late anyhow." Uncle Zeb's jaw worked on the tobacco. "She's gone, goddam it! Gone!"
>
> "What's gone?" asked Summers.
>
> Boone could see the whisky in Uncle Zeb's face. It was a face that had known a sight of whisky, likely, red as it was and swollen-looking.
>
> "The whole shitaree. Gone, by God, and naught to care savin' some of us who seen 'er new." He took the knife from his belt and started jabbing at the ground with it, as if it eased his feelings. He was silent for a while.

"This was man's country onc't. Every water full of beaver and a galore of buffler any ways a man looked, and no crampin' and crowdin'. Christ sake!" (150)

There's more of the West in those words than we like to admit: the booze, the pervasive sense of loss, Zeb's random violence in response to this fading dream. He jabs at the ground with his knife "as if it eased his feelings."

It's all gone now. An endless refrain in frontier history. Andrew Garcia, looking back on Montana of the 1870s, says it was paradise then but it's all gone now; Norman Maclean, looking back on the Blackfoot River of the 1920s, says it was paradise then but it's all gone now; Ivan Doig, looking back on Montana of the thirties and forties, says it was paradise then (innocence, at least), but it's all gone now. Merrel Clubb, longtime English department chairman in Missoula, says the Blackfoot was paradise in 1965 but it's all gone now. Now is 1988 and last week the new department chairman and I floated and fished the Blackfoot. You know what we'll tell our grandchildren.

Something about the frontier, something about Boone's paradise, something about Montana *as we conceive it* is doomed. This is important territory. When a local belt buckle says proudly, over a carving of an elk in wilderness, "Montana is what America was," we feel, alongside of pride, a tinge of fear. How long can we expect to remain outside of America, outside of the future? The future, in our minds, clearly means progress, civilization, just as it did to Boone and Uncle Zeb in 1831. We have put a lot of eggs in one basket—the past—and set it in front of an unstoppable steam roller—the future. *The Big Sky* is a classic because it captures this western sense of tragedy, of an inevitable and awful end. We don't mind so much that Boone the thug is being kicked out of paradise, but we certainly mind that paradise itself is being destroyed by the civilized world.

No one likes being doomed. We do not enjoy loving a Montana that will disappear. We do not like bringing up children to expect a long, tragic decline. We Montanans are in an odd position. Despair is supposed to be foreign to the frontier (even as individuals fail, the frontier is supposed to march forward) and pessimism is certainly un-

American. Yet much more than, say, New Yorkers, Montanans have chosen or slid into a tragic point of view that Guthrie has perfectly expressed. Those who do not share this point of view, who represent the interests of civilization and the future, and who often argue for the necessity of destroying paradise, may be as bitterly resented as Peabody, the land-grabbing entrepreneur of *The Big Sky*. For years there was a billboard outside the Missoula County airport: "Keep Montana green. Shoot a land developer." It was funny, outrageous, important. What some people in this state perceive as an "anti-business" attitude is much deeper than that: Montanans have a profound distrust of progress and the future. We *are* Guthrie. We *are* Boone.

Neither Americans nor westerners have to be doomed. We do not have to be split into factions of developers (pro-progress) and preservers (anti-progress). There are enough problems facing us without compounding them by mistakes of consciousness. When I first taught *The Big Sky*, I knew it repeated some kind of mistake that I could never quite put my finger on. And that's why I knew the Indian student was right. It is a white inheritance, this idea of a western paradise and inevitable demise; it is both a Christian narrative of a fall from paradise and, more important, a nineteenth-century European conviction. "It's all gone now" is not the structure of the universe; it's a response to problems within *European culture*, and if those problems can be faced, we don't have to be doomed. Forty years have passed since Guthrie wrote *The Big Sky*, forty years of dramatic shifts in European and American thought, and we can now look back and see how "It's all gone now" depends on certain assumptions, certain expectations, that we need not accept and that were always disturbing. Besides, Boone's West was never paradise. Never.

This requires explanation. How can a tragedy of white expansion also be a fantasy of escape, like *Treasure Island*? Whatever is wrong in *The Big Sky* is also wrong in our heads and in our history, and Guthrie has laid it all out on the table where we can have a look.

Boone Caudill

Before we consider the problems Boone presents, or the trouble Guthrie gets himself into, or, to put it another way, the trouble we're all in, let's state the obvious about Boone.

Boone on the one hand is Guthrie's answer to Tom Mix: Boone is a mean, violent, unthinking mountain man deliberately created by Guthrie to correct romantic notions of how the West was won. When he leaves home in the opening pages he is already a tough young realist who gets in fights, keeps to himself, says little, has no religion, and thinks the world is out to get him. It is. He is treated badly by Pap and a thief and a sheriff as he runs west, and by others, and he holds grudges in the strong, silent way that Hollywood, too, at the same time as Guthrie, was beginning to define as "western." The shift from Roy Rogers to John Wayne to Clint Eastwood as western hero is disturbing, and that shift toward silence, loneliness, and violence appears in Guthrie's Boone.

Guthrie makes us feel sympathy, however, for this sullen young runaway: he is homesick for his mother and, in those rare instances when he does trust someone, he is robbed or cheated or framed. A tough kid in a mean world: the world of his family, of Kentucky society, of civilization. In *The Big Sky*, the East is always oppression. Only the West is free.

The West is free. That *was* our reputation, and it still is. *The New Yorker* magazine of November 10, 1986, contained a cartoon of a tenement apartment, filled with scruffy cats, the disheveled woman ironing in the kitchen with a frayed cord to the bare ceiling bulb, and her worthless, delightful old geezer of a husband lying in the tub in the background. They've been in this apartment, in these Booth cartoons, for years, and he's saying from the tub: "Hon, I feel like riding out into big-sky country." It's all there still: the romance of space, a horse, a fresh start under the Big Sky. The opposite of New York, of Louisville. Just another Boone.

So on the one hand, Boone is pushed west by a society that cramps and crowds and has already damaged him, and Guthrie's treatment of this character is in the realistic tradition, a journalist's uncovering of a nasty truth.

On the other hand, Boone is pulled west by a beautiful dream. That dream, the dream on the belt buckle, is what we will have to understand.

"Bigness, distance, wildness, freedom are the dream that pulls Boone Caudill westward," Wallace Stegner said in his introduction to Guthrie's book. That dream is grounded—literally—in land. Face to face with the West, Boone knows something final. Like a hundred movie heroes, Boone is a tough, lone sinner, but is redeemed by his relation to the land. Boone sees the West through Guthrie's eyes and loves it as Guthrie does, and he and Guthrie come to call the Teton River and the Rocky Mountain Front Range home. So Boone is a villain in a villainous society, a foe to most and traitor to his friend, but he is a hero on the land. Evil society versus the good land. Making room for antisocial outcasts, indeed forgiving them because they love God's country, is an old Montana and western tradition; as one westerner said, "You can't judge a man by what he does in town."

Guthrie, in this book, agrees with Boone. Civilization is not a place where a man—"leastways a man that could call himself a man"— would want to be. Boone sees a city on his way west. "Louisville was busy as an anthill and bigger than all the places, put together, that Boone had ever seen." The two runaway boys, Deakins and Boone, stand and stare. Guthrie makes it look worse than a Missoula inversion in winter:

> There were chimneys everywhere, all breathing out a slow, black smoke that came down in a regular fog, except that it bit at a man's lungs and set his nose to running.
> "Godamighty!" said Boone.
> "She's big," agreed Deakins, and spit over the wheel. "Twenty thousand, last count." He thought for a moment, then added, "I can't figger why folk'll do it, less'n they don't know no better."
> Boone shook his head. "I don't hanker to live in no anthill." (19)

Boone's judgment stands. Throughout the story Guthrie offers nothing to contradict Boone's impression of towns. Like his namesake,

Daniel Boone, Boone Caudill seems ready to move when he can see the smoke from his neighbor's cabin. What is the alternative to towns for both Boone and Guthrie? The West. The tendency of the frontier, as historian Frederick Jackson Turner noted, is antisocial. Out West, Boone is in nature, and is himself natural. And insofar as Boone is natural, he is in this book often forgiven and sometimes blessed. Now this gets tricky, but we can begin by saying that for Guthrie, as well as Boone, Nature Saves. The key to what's wrong in this book, and in our heads, is right there—in our concepts of "nature" and "natural"—and the lock into which the key fits is "civilization." We will have to rethink those terms, which is not easy to do because they are so simple and central to our culture. Nature and civilization—to a remarkable degree, Americans live and speak within those words. In *The Big Sky* the East is identified with civilization, the West with nature, and Boone seems happy out West until for some reason his paradise falls apart. For some reason. Who *are* these white men from the East? What do they want? While readers may think Indians believe that Nature Saves, that's not quite right, and the difference defines who we are.

Let's back up and consider some problems in Boone's story, and as we go we can keep two simple questions in mind: Why did Boone kill Jim? And, without that shot, was Boone happy out West? You can see the importance of these questions: is this a story of one man's tragic "mistake" made in a moment of passion, or is Boone's relation to the West inherently flawed, with or without the killing of Jim? Is his relation to "nature" and to "civilization" our relation, and Guthrie's, and is it a mistake that dooms us to inevitable decline? The trouble is that the more we look at Boone, the more we see Guthrie's mythology, and the more we think about it, the stranger—and the more like us—it becomes.

The Trouble

Why Boone fired the shot that destroyed his life is complicated and not absolutely clear. Boone's obsessive love and his domination of

Teal Eye may indicate some sexual insecurity and fear. Even though Guthrie treats the obsession as healthy and the domination as typically Indian, he also plays up Boone's jealousy in the pages before the murder. Boone considers his sexual satisfaction with Teal Eye "like a weakness in him, like a secret that has to be kept in his own skull" (336). So the door is open for Freudians to say he is Samson, scared that women and passion rob him of his strength, and for Californians to say that he should learn to communicate. We know that Boone is disturbed by his baby's red hair (Deakins is red-headed). We know also that Jim has strong feelings for Teal Eye, though Jim's kindness prevails.

The Big Sky is not primarily about jealousy, however, or recessive genes, or even Boone's personality. It is about the West, and a dream. Guthrie thinks Boone is a son of a bitch, but he accepts his dream. The dream itself, however, may be the trouble. If Boone had not fired the shot, would he have been happy out West? Yes, Guthrie implies, if he didn't do some other fool thing. Until it all disappeared anyway. But I believe Boone was never happy. Boone not only fails to achieve his dream—the dream itself fails to serve his interests, or ours. The interesting question is not so much why Boone fired the shot as why Guthrie had him fire it. Apparently Guthrie knew, however instinctively, that the book was becoming Treasure Island, some kind of escape. Boone blows up his life, as Guthrie intends, but also Guthrie blows up his own plot, since he shared with Boone faith in the dream and since the dream as well as Boone's character is the foundation of the plot. Neither Boone nor the reader nor Guthrie need quite understand why the plot explodes. After all, Summers doesn't stay out West either—he returns to the frontier to farm—and Deakins is dead. For various reasons, everyone's western paradise fails. The constant element, failure, shows that Guthrie, while he sympathized with Boone's quest to escape to a western paradise, felt that paradise had to be lost.

Why? Why is the classic western story a tragedy? The answer is clearly not in Boone's character alone; Guthrie is following a narrative structure that links a natural paradise to inevitable decline. This particular dream contains its own demise. "Montana is what America was," and, by implication, Montana will someday be what America is now. It's all going fast. To understand that tragic narrative structure, we have to understand the mythology on which it is based.

Boone, repeatedly, is presented in *The Big Sky* as a real mountain man, even more so than his mentor, Summers. Let's look at what a real mountain man, our original western hero, is to Guthrie, and therefore what kind of trouble the original westerner is in, from Boone to Grizzly Adams to Robert Redford in *Jeremiah Johnson*.

As he travels up the Missouri with Summers and Deakins, the young Boone is learning the mountain man trade, and part of that learning is a hardening of the heart: "When he thought about leaving home and the tears coming into his eyes and the lump aching in his throat, he wondered if he was still the same body. It would take something to make him cry now. It would take something to make him worry, even . . ." (125). Boone is being freed not only of his past and of adolescent sentimentality. His reactions, feelings, and associations are being reduced; he is becoming less sensitive. In an extraordinary passage, Boone prepares to kill a trapped beaver, while just below the surface of his mind he associates her eyes with the eyes of Teal Eye, dark and fluid. But Boone is learning to deny what lies below the surface—that's how to become a mountain man:

> He saw now that she had been at work on her leg. A little bit more and she would have chewed herself free. There were just the tendons holding, and a ragged flap of skin. The broken bone stuck out of the jaws of the trap, white and clean as a peeled root. Around her mouth he could see blood.
>
> She looked at him, still not moving, still only with that little shaking, out of eyes that were dark and fluid and fearful, out of big eyes that liquid seemed to run in, out of eyes like a wounded bird's. They made him a little uneasy, stirring something that lay just beyond the surface of his mind and wouldn't come out where he could see it.
>
> She let out a soft whimper as he raised the stick, and then the stick fell, and the eye that had been looking at him bulged out crazily, not looking at anything, not something alive and liquid anymore, not something that spoke, but only a bloody eyeball knocked from its socket. It was only a beaver's eye all the time. (184)

In three paragraphs of prose clean as a peeled root, Guthrie leads us past thoughts of the "wounded bird's" eyes of Teal Eye, the soft whimperings of things that speak, to Boone's conclusion: "It was only a beaver's eye all the time." Associations, feelings, imaginings, rememberings—whatever goes on in the mind and heart—are being purged from Boone's experience. They do not belong. Not here. Not now. Not out West, where things are just things.

In an obviously parallel passage, Summers responds to an Indian's eyes, and kills him with regret. Interestingly, Summers himself believes that his response—that responsiveness itself—proves he is not a real mountain man. We are thus prepared not only to observe Boone's process of hardening, but to approve it.

> The Sioux's fingers lay loose around the handle of his tomahawk. Summers thought his eyes were like a dog's, like a pitiful goddam dog's. He had to let him have it. The eyes followed Summers' arm up to the knife, waiting for it to come down. The far-off part of Summers' mind told him again that he wasn't a real mountain man. (121)

The idea of Summers not being a real mountain man is a little surprising, since he is so competent and experienced out West. But the theme has been developed by Guthrie for several pages. The French boatman on the Missouri, Jourdonnais, "was glad that Summers was an easy man, without the dark strain of violence that ran so often in mountain men" (116). That ran in Boone, for instance. Unlike Boone, Summers also likes his own people, and his own food, and even an occasional town:

> He knew he wasn't a mountain man as some men were. He liked to get to St. Louis once in a while and sleep in a sure-enough bed, with a white woman that smelled of perfume instead of grease and diamond-willow smoke. He didn't mind farming, too much. It was still getting outside. And he hadn't lost his taste for bread and salt and pies and such. (119)

Now some things are beginning to clarify, and notice that we're talking not so much about Boone's character as about Guthrie's mythology. Boone is called the truer mountain man because he is violent and insensitive, far beyond the scenes I've quoted: "a sudden man, acting first and thinking after," as Deakins says (189). Boone kills without regret and never wants to sleep with women of his own race or eat his own food or go back East.

Two considerations undermine Guthrie's vision of the pure mountain man (though we don't expect Guthrie to have known this in 1944). First, the historian William H. Goetzmann discovered in the 1960s that out of 800 mountain men, we could follow by name the careers of about 400. Out of those 400, half died in the field, and out of the remaining 200 whose subsequent lives he traced, only five stayed out West. If it was such a paradise, why did only five remain? And why have we come to see the Boones as typical? In reality, most made money as fast as they could and returned to St. Louis to buy a big house and marry a white woman. Like the miners and the first ranchers, most mountain men were businessmen, entrepreneurial explorers, not sleeping in skins to be saved by a return to nature.

The second consideration is so obvious it hurts. Indians were not like Boone. They preferred their own wives and food, wanted to stay in their own villages with their own families, killed animals with a regret often formalized in prayers, and indeed encouraged their youth to perceive the beaver as their sister rather than treat it as an object divorced from humankind (although they killed each other with considerable gusto). This is crucial, for at times Guthrie and some readers want to understand Boone's character, and excuse it, as a necessary adaptation to life in the harsh, wild world of the West. Stegner in his introduction suggests this "survival of the fittest" interpretation: he calls Boone a "killing machine," and "what the logic of his ferocious adaptation demands, the action of the novel fulfills." But are we really reading about the logic of adaptation? Is anyone going to stand up and claim that the Sioux and Crow and Blackfeet were not adapted to life on the plains? That their extraordinary sensitivity and tenderness (Chief Plenty-coups took his advice from the chickadees), their willingness to honor parents, to stay at home and weep, left them less able to survive in the West? The Indians could be vicious and brutal to each other, but they hunted, killed, and survived without reducing themselves to a part of a man, and without hating their own society.

The original westerner, the mountain man, as represented by Guthrie and Boone, cannot be understood as either a fact of history or as the product of some kind of Darwinian natural law. Whatever Boone dragged with him from the East made him what he was. The Big Sky was his vision, not a natural reality, not an adaptive necessity, and not an Indian paradise. In attempting to escape his past he had, by becoming increasingly blind and ignorant and impatient, wrapped himself in his own psychic culture until everything, ironically, was a figment of his imagination.

I am suggesting that Guthrie's idealizing of the emptiness of western space, an idealizing which actually began in the eighteenth century, has its counterpart in the ideal of an empty psyche. A man who is a man just does, without thinking or feeling. Both ideals—the ideals of an empty space and of an empty psyche—represent a pursuit of innocence, a longing for a virgin land inside and out. Uncle Zeb: "God, she was purty onc't. Purty and new, and not a man track, savin' Injuns', on the whole scoop of her" (150). Summers: "A river wasn't the same once a man had camped by it. . . . There was the first time and the place alone, and afterwards there was the place and the time and the man he used to be . . ." (194). We often take it for granted that our cherished dreams are universally shared; actually, our American desire for a trackless wilderness, very possibly a fearful response to the overpopulation and industrialization of Europe in the nineteenth century, was quite puzzling to the Indians. We wanted an empty space for starting over, and wanted to arrive there with an empty mind. No complexities of civilization and its discontents, no ties that bind, no feelings and ideas, "no crampin' and crowdin'. Christ sake!" But that was not what the Indians wanted; it was not their dream. And it was not an adaptation to environment.

Sometimes, I think, Guthrie shares Boone's hope of escape. You see that we are approaching the shores of Treasure Island. I said that Guthrie seems to believe Boone was happy, for a while, out West. Deakins, Guthrie's most trustworthy observer of Boone, says, "All

Boone hankers for is fat meat and a fire and to be away from folks" (169). And later on, Deakins says that Boone's reduction to some pre- sumed animal simplicity has worked: "Take Boone, now. . . . He was like an animal, like a young bull that traveled alone, satisfied just by earth and water and trees and the sky over him." Boone is presented as simple and innocent, even in his brutality, and therefore happy. "It was as if he talked to the country for company, and the country talked to him, and as if that was enough" (185). Boone sums it up: "Here a man lived natural" (201). But buffalo bulls don't talk to the country any more than Indians run from their past or avoid their own kind. Are Indians unnatural? Are elk unnatural, because they like the company of elk? Something is phony.

Guthrie, it seems, presents both psychologies: on the one hand, Boone is repressed and violent and this is a story of human neurosis; on the other hand, Boone is simple and natural and in some ways innocent. Guthrie *knows* Boone fits the first description, but seems to share Boone's hope that a man might achieve the second. For a few pages in the Blackfeet camp, before the shot, we think that Boone might have made it.

Boone is a mean man: "He'd as soon kill a man as look at him." I have yet to know a mean man—as opposed to a tough one—who is simple. Boone's feelings in running from his abusive Pap, his long seige of Teal Eye, his nurtured revenges, his fierce pride in resenting any attempts by Indian brothers or even Teal Eye to suggest what he might do, portray not a simple man but a driven one, obsessive and fearful. His notion of freedom is a child's notion, a pure license to do what he wishes without anyone hassling him. But of course, in this childish state, instead of being free he is a slave to his heart, to his past, to his father's blind rage passed on to him, to circumstances, to accidents like his baby's red hair.

When Boone kills Jim, "He knew what he had to do. No use to talk or think or wonder. No use to ask or plan. A man's body acted for him" (340). Here is the West of the imagination indeed; here, ex- plicitly and technically, the mind and psyche have been bypassed, short-circuited. Boone is hot-wired. His body, Boone would believe, acts in pure innocence without any central nervous system corrupting it. Man and nature are split; man and his works are social and evil. Following those assumptions, Boone has finally achieved the goal of leaving behind both all civilization and all humanity. "Shoot first and ask questions later." At this moment, Boone's mind is open space, "not a man track . . . on the whole scoop of her," unsullied by any need to consider motives or consequences, to converse, to think, to feel. Boone has run west to escape not only Pap and external civilization, but also his own mind and heart, internal civilization. The shot rings so perfectly through the book because the escape totally fails; at the moment of murder Boone is least simple, least natural, least free.

What Boone embodies, then, is a European fantasy of escape from civilization, from complication, from responsibility. We will set out for a more simple, empty space, and arrive there with a more simple, empty psyche. "Get away from it all." Guthrie knows that Boone is a son of a bitch, but he can't figure out what's wrong with his dream. If he just hadn't shot Jim . . . he seemed so happy. Thoreau tried the same dream, moving out to Walden Pond the same year Boone settled on the Teton, and Thoreau's escape is as full of holes as Boone's plot. It ought to work, it seems. We're still trying to make it work.

Like Boone, we won't be free until we face what we want, and why we want it. The West as an escape from civilization, the West as we know it, as Guthrie knew it, and as Boone knew it, was invented about 1800. Guthrie fired the shot at Boone. It is time to fire the shot at Boone and Guthrie's dream. The West was never paradise. But it may have been real nice, and even with man tracks on her, she may be real nice still.

2

Guthrie's Dream of the West

MEN HAVE HAD GREAT DREAMS: GOLD, VIRTUE, FAME, IMMOR-
tality. One of those great dreams was the West. To understand that
dream, and how it holds Guthrie's hand as he holds Boone's finger
on the trigger, we have to go back, past the invention of the West
in 1800, to William Bradford stepping off the *Mayflower* at Plymouth
Rock, Massachussetts, in 1620, and recording in his journal that he
had come to a "hideous and desolate wilderness."

All wilderness, to Bradford and his compatriots, was hideous and
desolate. Their world was the opposite of Boone's world, and of ours.
To the Renaissance mind, God was associated with man and with the
kind of ordering that man brought to nature. *The City of God* by St.
Augustine had been a favorite book for over a thousand years. Imagine, now, thinking of heaven as a city; imagine people with wings
and harps on 42nd and Broadway. This is not easy. Conversely, try to
picture the wilderness—Bradford did—as complexly evil, the home
of Satan and opposite of the divine, a chaos needing to be improved
by man. In the last 400 years, the connotations of the words "civilization" and "nature" have become perfectly reversed. In that reversal,
which occurred about 1800 as Thomas Jefferson was telling Meriwether Lewis to explore the new Louisiana Purchase from the Mississippi to the sea, the West was born. So it happens that the period of
American expansion into the vast prairies and mountains and deserts
of the inland West coincided with a shift of thought that prepared us,
for the first time, to see those trackless wastes as the home not of
Satan but of God. A place where we are not damned but saved. To
this day we have that double inheritance: we are the ones who use
and control nature; we are the ones who worship it.

Bradford's Renaissance mind had been following a logic that many
scholars have traced back to the Bible, indeed all the way back to

Genesis. There man is made "in God's image"; nothing else is. Man, shaped like God and by Him from the mud, is entirely different from the rest of nature. God pointed out to Adam all the conveniences of paradise, all the birds and animals and plants waiting in corners for his use, like animated appliances. "Subdue and have dominion," He said to Adam: bring a Man-God's order to the wild chaos, put it all in your store. The world as inventory. Apart from man, who has spirit, things are just things. Adam was the first consumer in God's mall.

God's moral imperative to develop—that is to explore, conquer, subdivide, exploit—had by 1620 hardly been followed. Europe was just emerging from the feudal Middle Ages. World population had barely doubled between the time of Christ and 1500. Ships to sail the open oceans and the navigational instruments to take them there were being constructed for the first time. Copernicus and Galileo had set the stage for global exploration and, incidentally, had begun to take man away from the center of God's universe. The old split was being redefined: man and nature would still be divided, but if the sun, not the earth, was the center of the universe, perhaps man was no longer at the center of God's garden. Perhaps nature was.

This tendency to take the "divine" away from man and push it toward nature continued for two hundred years, until it reached its extreme as Lewis and Clark were pulling pirogues up the Missouri River to stand in awe, as once men stood in a cathedral, face to face with Boone's West. Nature was no longer Satanic. It was holy.

Take one story, told in Roderick Nash's *Wilderness and the American Mind*, as an example. In 1336 the Christian scholar Petrarch ascended a small mountain in southern France. At the top, he and his brother had what climbers call a summit experience: "The great sweep of view spread out before me. . . . I stood like one dazed." But he happened to look at his copy of St. Augustine's *Confessions*, always in his pocket, and found an admonition not to take pleasure in scenery but to work for eternal salvation. "I was abashed . . . that I should still be admiring earthly things . . . nothing is wonderful but the soul." He hurried off the mountain, feeling that his experience in nature had seduced him away from the divine. But by 1750, mountain climbing had begun in the Alps and entire new theories were associating God with "the sublime," a feeling of awe and grandeur in confronting natural immensity. Barren vistas—on the ocean, in deserts, above treeline—began to be prized for the quasi-religious feelings evoked in their presence. As in a cathedral, one feels the effect of awesome space.

It was the perfect time to discover the West, and our legacy of holy landscape continues to this day. Consider a cartoon by Montana illustrator Stan Lynde. The cowboy character Hipshot is riding, on Easter Sunday, up into the mountains. As he goes he thinks of preachers all over the world talking of "how to live in this life, and what's waiting for us when it's over . . . heaven . . . what it's liable to be like . . . and if, as some say, it's a place of beauty, peace, and happiness" —Hipshot dismounts in a high mountain meadow, stream in front, snow-covered peaks behind—"then we've come to the right place, old horse, for a sort of preview." Petrarch's values have been perfectly reversed; the mountains, instead of being associated with the flesh and Satan, are associated with the spirit, and with God. Boone came West to live in Hipshot's paradise.

It seems paradoxical to us now, but our love of nature was fueled by the rise of science. The telescope and microscope, for instance, became common between 1500 and 1800. They were a way to focus attention on the natural world. Just in the act of looking through them a person asserted curiosity about this world, the world of the flesh, versus the world of the soul. The new instruments undermined "otherworldliness," although it still survives in vestigial hymns and prayers left over from ideals of the Middle Ages. My grandmother in Tennessee used to sing the Baptist hymn, "This world is not my home," and "I've got a home that's so much better, I'm gonna go there sooner or later, I don't want to get adjusted to this world." But such otherworldliness has long been belied by our behavior. We are the people of the world, and largely through science, empirical method, technology, we have since William Bradford explored that wilderness, studied, pondered, and manipulated it, split its atoms, taken it away from Satan, and made it our home. Under the microscope, that world is indeed beautiful, and ordered, and easily associated with divine design. That was noticed as early as 1691, by John Ray in a book entitled *The Wisdom of God Manifested in the Works of Creation* (instead of in the works of Spirit). Many thought the book heretical at the time.

During the same years, we were inventing a civilization that seemed an invitation to Satan and his chaos. It took fifteen hundred years after the time of Christ for population to double, but then it doubled again between 1500 and 1800, and again between 1800 and 1950, and again between 1950 and 1980. As Europe was bursting at the seams, as London was going from the town of Shakespeare's day, less than two hundred thousand, to ten million, we were also inventing the industrial revolution to execute—really for the first time—the imperative to subdue and have dominion. London by 1750 had "killer fogs," black with soot from burning coal; by 1845, Thoreau was both delighted with the new "choo-choo" going by his pond and simultaneously frightened at the power, at the assault on nature, it represented. Not to mention weapons: that was really the shock of the First World War, the Great War. After 400 years of invention, we finally had the armaments and transportation to slaughter ourselves and innocent bystanders on a scale previously unimagined. And with the population boom, and the industrialization, and the new cities, came a new loss of control. The poor, the homeless . . . Remember the Statue of Liberty pedestal, given by France in 1886 and emblazoned with an American pledge: "give me your tired, your poor, your huddled masses yearning to breathe free." The statue was literally a sign of the times, promising a western freedom on American shores, escape from the evils of civilization, a fresh start.

Those masses were no longer fed; indeed the hungry were no longer even known to the neighbors, the village, the leaders, the church. Innumerable and nameless, the urban masses began to take on the characteristics of chaos—complex, unknown, infinite in extent, and to be feared—characteristics that once had belonged to the woods. By 1900, the old metaphors for untouched nature were commonly applied to the cities: *The City Wilderness* was one popular book at the turn of the century, along with Upton Sinclair's book on Chicago meat-packing, *The Jungle*.

It is quite possible that the image of women in the late nineteenth century also reflected this growing industrialization, that the "feminization" of women represented not just some deep, dark male fantasy or power play, but also a need, felt by everyone, for some place to escape to: the woods, or home. Both were increasingly sacred alternatives to the cold, cruel world of man. Both offered a retreat from the jungle of the marketplace, to a place of purity and innocence. The ideal woman became the proprietress of all that was contrary to the street; she was soft, chaste, caring, sweet. Women were losing occupations to the industrial revolution; the house was no longer a workplace, a scene of "cottage industry." By 1860, Charles Dickens was the great realistic novelist of the new cities, but as one Kentucky professor used to say, "When it comes to home and fire and hearth in Dickens, you can pour it on waffles."

Never mind that all over the world women had for thousands of years been going out into the village, to the marketplace, to the well, washing their clothes together in social groups that often *ran* the village, that *were* the society; in the nineteenth century we decided to exempt something from the harsh new reality we were creating, and that something was women. Women and, of course, children, who were seen as having many of the same qualities. Over here would be the rough reality of work and product; over there would be its virtuous opposite: women and children. This description of our new world, however, never fit western ranch life. Nor did it fit working-class people in town, as Dickens well knew.

But it does fit Teal Eye. She is the opposite of the troubles of this world:

> When Jim came back from a trip he was full of talk about new forts along the river and new people moving out from the settlements. . . . Boone cut him off, not wanting to be bothered with fool talk that stirred a man up inside. . . . Teal Eye was the woman for Boone. . . . Teal Eye never whined or scolded or tried to make a man something else than what he was by nature, but just took him and did her work and was happy. . . . What she cared about most was to please him. (259–60)

Here Guthrie deliberately places Boone's need to escape progress (even the Indians are amazed that he thinks the buffalo will return) next to his need for a hassle-free wife. Unfortunately, we never get Teal Eye's point of view, so the book has the effect of endorsing Boone's idea of the perfect woman. The passive Teal Eye and the empty West are Boone's final retreats from the problems of this world.

Whatever the pressures of the new civilization, by 1800 there was hardly any reason to fear the woods; the "hideous and intolerable wilderness" had been tamed. With the gun, Lewis and Clark could shoot almost every grizzly they met as they moved upstream. Individual adventures—running away, jumping into the river to escape a bear—could not obscure the greater truth: we would take the land from the great bears, push them to the mountains or the sea. Nothing was beyond our control. Satan was gone. With the natural world tamed, we could enjoy the luxury of loving it. And why stay back East? Town was getting more crowded every day.

Take one example, crucial to our American identity and to the West: Thomas Jefferson. By 1800 Jefferson had visited England and had seen the new cotton mills and manufacturing cities. He was appalled by the working conditions, the long days, the low wages, the child labor. Like many observers of his era, he felt that America would not and should not become a manufacturing nation. John Adams thought we would not supply our own manufactures for at least a thousand years; the Frenchman Crèvecoeur thought us lucky to have "no aristocratical families, no courts, no kings, no bishops," and also "no great manufacturers employing thousands." Jefferson concurred: "Those who labor in the earth are the chosen people of God . . . let our work-shops remain in Europe." To Jefferson, farming was an alternative to, and a denial of, European industrialization. All of America was once the West, and Montana is what America was.

In addition to being an alternative economy, farming was associated with nature. Not only was nature becoming more respectable every day, but in America the new worship of nature was especially welcome, for nature was what we had always had, while civilization was scarce. American national pride, ever since colonial days, had strained to admire that wilderness which Bradford had despised. By 1800 we were sitting pretty, because much of Europe was deciding that a forest is as good as a museum: "Il n'y a de vieux en Amerique,

que les bois . . ."—"Nothing is old in America but the trees . . . and liberty . . . these are worth as much as monuments and ancesters" (Chateaubriand). Jefferson inveighed against "European luxury and dissipation," and urged avoiding "the voluptuary dress and arts of the European women," admiring instead "the chaste affections and simplicity of those of his own country." Abigail Adams thought the birds sang sweeter in America. Nature, and innocence, were alternatives to civilization. Virgin Land.

So a national need to extol nature, and a growing international need to value what was being lost, had by 1800 become complexly interwoven with an emerging American identity that saw itself as natural, innocent, and simple, as opposed to the industry, corruption, and complexity of Europe. Boone, in his dream of escape, his woods, his Indian wife, and his lack of self-knowledge, is a part of this movement.

Jefferson went only half way, admiring the half-natural, half-civilized, "pastoral" condition of the farmer. The "primitivists," however, like Boone, went all the way. "A sort of delirium" seized Chateaubriand in upstate New York in 1792, in the absence of roads, towns, laws and kings. "In this deserted region the soul delights to bury and lose itself amidst boundless forests . . . to mix and confound . . . with the wild sublimities of nature." Civilization was directly opposed to happiness. Beyond the last farm lay the empty and untracked wilderness, the antithesis of civilization, the abode of God. Once in those woods, people imagined, one might live in a "state of nature," in "primitive" simplicity and innocence. William Bartram camping in Florida, 1775: "Our situation was like that of the primitive state of man, peaceable, contented and sociable." Society was admired only as long as it stopped at the edge of the firelight. Both the pastoralists and the primitivists criticized civilization from the point of view of a superior nature, and wished to avoid an urban future by remaining within a "natural" past.

After Lewis and Clark came back in 1807 to tell Thomas Jefferson what they had found, and especially after Biddle's account of their trip was published in 1815, the empty plains and vast mountains of the West became a mecca for primitivists. By the 1840s, as the beaver were trapped out, it sometimes seemed that European landscape painters outnumbered mountain men beyond the wide Missouri. By the end of the century, the history of the West was typically seen from a primitivist point of view, even when the realities were consistently social, political, mercantile, and exploitative. For instance, few realize that several famous "mountain man" explorers reported to Congress, and that many saw their own travels as an important contribution to the new government as well as a way to get rich in the fur trade. It's not surprising really, but their political and mercantile activities are suppressed in our mythology in favor of the idea of the lone male living in a state of nature.

Behind the primitivist lay not just the pull of nature and simplicity, but the push of the teeming, sooty cities of Europe. As Boone said, "I don't hanker to live in no anthill." Like Chateaubriand, Boone longed to be beyond law as well as beyond town: "It wasn't fair, bringing in the sheriff, just because a body did what he had to" (8). All of this had to be most puzzling to the Indians, who wanted only their own law, their own society, their own civilization which to them was inseparable from natural order, while among them settled these strange escapees fancying themselves "primitive," "natural," "Indian," "free."

Guthrie, writing in the 1940s, on the one hand corrected Hollywood notions of western pioneers by means of a "realist" or "naturalist" novel, gutty as the hard-hitting turn-of-the-century realism of Dreiser or Sinclair, focusing on strong, even stupid people following natural law. That was his antiromantic intent. Yet we can see on the other hand that Guthrie—so loving the West—could easily fall prey to a different romanticism, a primitivist dream. That dream described (or created) the awesome beauty of the West and offered the West as an antidote to a civilization Guthrie and Boone and we, too, distrust. Until very recently, pastoralism and primitivism have had to bear all the weight of criticizing European progress. Those theories offered the only discourse of dissent. Boone might be a son of a bitch, but Guthrie shared his dissenting dream.

Consider the models which primitivism (and in many ways pastoralism, too) offers us as alternatives to "civilization." Oddly enough, primitivism, for all its ecstatic worship of western expanse, is largely a negative model, for it demands that we reject our own past, our own people, and the most advanced aspects of our species: thought, especially abstract thought, language, complex societies. Freedom, perhaps, is the primitivist's greatest dream, but that freedom is often a childish desire to be left alone. Such an antisocial freedom, carried to its extreme, can result in the loneliness and isolation that we have idolized in the western hero, riding off into the sunset. His songs are sad.

Let me illustrate what I mean when I say that primitivism is negative. In 1982 I heard a local panel discussing the topic "Missoula the Beautiful." The mayor and several leading Chamber of Commerce representatives, all interesting and intelligent people, stood up and praised the beauty of Missoula. Mind you, these were not outfitters or environmentalists, but downtown businessmen. One after another, they pointed to the mountains, but not to a single street; to the sky, but not to a single building; to the river and even to the fish in it, but not to a single one of our five bridges. Now ask a Parisian about Paris the Beautiful, and she will enumerate streets, buildings, and bridges lovingly built, lovingly maintained, lovingly inhabited day after day, and lovingly lit at night.

Missoula is ugly—or at least we seem to think it is—because we see it as man's work set in the midst of God's splendor. So we remain polarized: we look for beauty in the Selway-Bitterroot or Rattlesnake wilderness right on the edge of town, but we remain demoralized about our streets, gas stations, and architecture because deep down we believe that man's works are, well, hopeless. Except for a few civic heroes, no one tries to control our western towns. That's not healthy, for a people to give up on their own society, to turn against their own kind. But to varying degrees, it's in all westerners. An Alaskan geologist in the Montana Writers class the year of the Alaska Lands Bill, an older man who loved the land but who was also very pro-development and anti-wilderness, said one day he wouldn't mind all Alaska being locked up for wilderness—his voice was shaking—on one condition: no one would ever be allowed to set foot on that land. "God, she was purty onc't. Purty and new, and not a man track . . ."

Uncle Zeb's tearful, probably drunken memory of a virgin land brings us to the most troubling aspect of a pastoral and primitivist model of thought (and feeling and action). The pastoral-primitivist is always looking back to a golden age, a paradise that was lost, an earlier point in a curve of sure decline: "We seen a sight of rivers, clear and purty rivers. We had us a whole world to play around in, with high mountains in it and buffler and beaver and fun, and no one to say it was his property and get the hell off" (306). For all its appeal, this is the voice of a child, the gospel according to Dennis the Menace. "Let me do what I want." Yet all species live within territorial, ecological, and social realities. Doing what you want is not natural. For that matter, our wants themselves are as much cultural as natural. The pastoral-primitivist concedes the future to civilization, then washes his hands of it, drops out to an imagined and inaccurate past. Even Jefferson, instead of wrestling with the problems of the new industrialization, its working class and their relation to democracy, said America should avoid it all. Thus the pastoral-primitivist model predicts a sure decline, refuses to do anything about it, and advocates hiding out or playing around until the end comes.

It may well be that as long as the human population increases— even at a slower rate—we shall all have worse lives, and it may be that technology and the speed-up of change pose tremendous problems. The paradox, after all, is by now evident: empirical technology gave attention to the natural world and attention became respect, which led to understanding, then manipulation, then destruction of what we loved. The basic story Guthrie follows is profound: it is *the* western story of killing what we love, the story we must rewrite. But the specific problems generated by our specific culture—even if insurmountable—do not make society innately evil, nor do they make civilization the opposite of nature. When we consider the contrast between European and Native American culture in Part II, these points will become obvious.

Even if we feel, with Boone, the most extreme disgust with civilization, the greatest suspicion of progress, the worst fear of the future, his answer is not the only course we could take. In Part III, we will consider how the ecological movement in the last forty years has redefined our categories in such a way that we can now criticize progress on empirical grounds instead of on pastoral-primitivist grounds. One thing is sure: the rancher won't hold on to his land by telling Congress that he wants to live in the nineteenth century, when things were better. Nor should he. The pastoral-primitivist response is regressive: it advocates a return to a lost past of simplicity and innocence, a virginity of the psyche, a childhood of the mind. We need better conceptual models to explain our love of land and fear of industrial progress. To be outrageous (a western tradition I much admire), let's say the country could be talking mandatory birth control instead of buying second homes.

The land was never virgin; this was never paradise. Remember that the Northern Plains Indians themselves had recently arrived; that the plains buffalo culture was greatly changed by the horse, available after 1700, and that most northern Indians were pushed onto the plains by whites. Amidst this rapid and forced change, the very first whites often found not a timeless paradise, but tragedy, even by 1804. Before they reached the first Pawnee villages, Lewis and Clark passed an old French fort and village exterminated, they assumed, by Indians, and a factory abandoned by a St. Louis merchant. The Pawnees themselves were hardly living in a stable paradise. In Biddle's version of the Lewis and Clark journals: "This people were among the most numerous of Missouri Indians, but have gradually been dispersed and broken, and even since the year 1797 have undergone some sensible changes" (July 22, 1804). Another neighboring tribe, the Kaninaviesch, have "degenerated from the improvements of the parent tribe, and no longer live in villages, but rove through the plains."

The true tragedy is revealed, however, on August 11, 1804, when they near the creek called "Great Spirit is Bad":

> The Makas had a village, and lost 400 of their nation by the dreadful malady. . . . The accounts we have had of the effects of the smallpox on that nation are most distressing; it is not known in what way it was first communicated to them, though probably by some war-party. They had been a military and powerful people; but when these warriors saw their strength wasting before a malady which they could not resist, their

frenzy was extreme; they burnt their village, and many of them put to death their wives and children, to save them from so cruel an affliction, and that all might go together to some better country.

And so on up the river: the Poncaras who "once numbered 400 men, are now reduced to about 50," and by October 1, when they reached the Cheyenne, Lewis and Clark had learned the litany: "Their history is the short and melancholy relation of the calamities of almost all the Indians. They were a numerous people." It doesn't sound like Uncle Zeb's paradise to me. Temporary fun, perhaps, for whites with immunities and guns, and lots of animals that stand still at fifty yards, but is that paradise? Easy kills? Rushing into a new ecological opportunity, living in temporary ease and greed? Being thoughtless, self-centered, and certain you will bequeath to your children a world worse than your own? Are we sure that brings out the best in us? Even if we were there, is that what makes us happy?

The primitivist fantasy mocks both society and experience. The primitivist rejection of adult learning in favor of some "natural" childhood of impulse parallels its rejection of society: in both rejections one retreats to an imagined, innocent past. Those who have children may judge for themselves the innocence of the child, and its happiness. Do we really wish to repeat the obsessive selfishness and crushing disappointments of a two-year-old?

These issues are still with us. A fifteen-year-old boy drunk at party after party is not simply a good old boy in a state of nature; he is an awkward, uncomfortable child who cannot talk to girls or even to his own friends any more than Boone could talk to Teal Eye. When children are not encouraged to develop themselves in thought and language, their culture is letting them down by offering no interesting, useful, respected models of "society" and "civilization." And "natural," as they are taught to conceive of it, is a lie. Raising the drinking age won't cure this.

The dream of escape from European civilization, of escape to a West that opened up at just the time we needed that fantasy, was powerful and beautiful. I have no doubt that Guthrie shared that dream with Boone, who headed West through "country that kept getting freer and bigger until sometimes, looking out over it from a rise, Boone felt he was everywhere on it, like the air or the light."

"Goddam, Jim!" he said.
"What?"
"It's slick, ain't it?" (127)

Whatever the troubles involved, whatever the silliness of the fantasy, it is one of our oldest American dreams. An Ozark mountain song:

I heard my neighbor's rooster crow,
  early in the day.
I heard his ax beyond the hill,
  and I must be away.
For some folks love the city life,
  others love the town.
I'll pack my goods for the Arkansas woods
  and I'll be homeward bound.
Fiddle and a bow and a firelight glow
  you can hear that lonesome sound.
I'll leave behind my troublesome mind
  and go the whole world round.

"Leave behind my troublesome mind." Wrong.

Guthrie's novel was one of the first serious fictions to deal with the old West in a realistic manner. His style, and his success, I believe, had an important and healthy impact on writers to come. Hemingway had praised Mark Twain for writing in his local dialect, the language of the tribe, and one can say that Whitman and Twain allowed us to imagine American speech as the medium of great art. In a similar embracing of the local, Guthrie wrote in a western vernacular, partly regional and partly literary, stretching back to the mountain man talk of G. F. Ruxton's *Life in the Far West*, 1848. Guthrie's idiom is vivid and graceful. On the first page, Boone's mother is watching her husband limp from his old war injury. "It was a time ago, a right smart time, for a man still to have misery from a wound." Guthrie's trust in the Kentucky and western dialects he knew so well takes us into the characters' heads, for in diction Guthrie tries to keep the author off the page and to offer a language roughly appropriate to each person's thoughts. This language can be eloquent; we can be moved. So the language itself, used seriously and beautifully, assures Guthrie's neighbors and successors that the West can generate art. We need not imitate British speech or French manners. We can speak in our own voice.

Guthrie's craftsmanship, as well as his dialect, was a kind of pioneering: the western stereotype, though it may allow for a few words well chosen, does not allow for many words well chosen. Guthrie's seriousness about fiction and language, in a book that was also aggressively male and coarse ("the real guts," as he said), helped other western writers, especially men, imagine that sophistication in language was no disgrace.

In the last pages of *The Big Sky*, Boone has wandered back to Dick Summers's cabin on a Missouri farm. "I kilt Jim," he tells Dick. "It's like it's all sp'iled for me now, Dick—Teal Eye and the Teton and all. Don't know as I ever can go back, Dick. Goddam it! Goddam it!" Boone finally has achieved awareness; he has discovered language and himself; he has fallen from innocence, or rather has realized that he never had it. But this is the last page of the book. Will Boone ever go back? Guthrie leans on the kitchen table of his Choteau home, several years before writing *Fair Land, Fair Land*, his sequel to *The Big Sky*. "That's the question I'm always asked. I get calls from Florida in the middle of the night." The answer? "I don't know." Does he think Boone has finally accepted responsibility for his actions? Has the child grown up? "Recognition, regret—yes," says Guthrie. "Responsibility —I don't know."

It is significant that the book takes place, and ends, within Boone's ignorance, though on the last page he seems to be waking up. Guthrie shared with Boone that primitivist, escapist vision. Guthrie knew it didn't work, but couldn't figure out *why* it didn't work. So the book, properly, remains in a kind of darkness. If we return to our central questions—why did Boone fire the shot, or why did Guthrie have him fire it, and would Boone have otherwise been happy out West?—the answers *within* the book are murky. No, the book is not about jealousy, but yes, Boone seems to have spoiled it all, and neither he nor Guthrie can figure out why he shouldn't have been happy out there. On the other hand Guthrie knows the shot must be fired; this must be a tragedy.

In classical tragedy the reason for the fall is always clarified. Oedipus violates the order of the gods; Lear commits a tragic error of stupidity and pride. But in *The Big Sky* the reason for the fall is never made clear. Somehow, all just gets spoiled.

I've tried to show the reason for that fall, unconsciously imagined by Guthrie but not fully clarified by him. Like Boone, Guthrie believes with all his heart and soul in a narrative structure of inevitable decline; this story begins with exploding population and industry far to the East and ends with shrinking islands of virgin innocence out West, awaiting corruption. "Montana is what America was." Boone could be a saint, and still "It's all gone now" would be the only end.

That story holds Guthrie in its grip. Boone is its child. Guthrie is fascinated by Boone's obsessions, his hatred of his own kind, his various escapes to a mythic West. And so *The Big Sky* is Guthrie's best book. In later books, when Boone is off the page, and healthier, more adjusted, more social characters take his place, the pages don't crackle. Boone, or Boone's dream, even though Guthrie will later see its limitations (*Fair Land, Fair Land*), is the central obsession of his work. That dream is dark and doomed, and its dreamers remind us of D. H. Lawrence's frightening comment: "The essential American soul is hard, isolate, stoic, and a killer."

I have tried to come to the core of the book, to Montana as Paradise before the fall, and to our lingering love of a land for which humans seem unfit. These are *our* problems, responses to *our* European culture; these are our dissents and escapes. And so the Blackfeet student was right: "Treasure Island." And that's why, standing in front of the class, I was angry as well as puzzled. I knew he was putting his finger on some dream I had always had of another place, another time, some dream that pervaded the book, some dream, as I considered *The Big Sky*, that I was about to lose.

Guthrie's Dream of the West

Guthrie is a great poet of that dream. In October 1972, he addressed the Western Literature Association in Jackson Hole, Wyoming.

West is another word for magic. Long before the beginnings of our nationhood, a Spanish explorer of the continent, bravely lost in the wilderness, said, "We always held it certain that, going toward the sunset, we should find what we desired."

3
Garcia's Tough Trip

When we were packing up, I knew that I should have shot him down while I had the chance. What Red said was so; when La Brie got the chance, he would have shot me in the back if he had to. But I had not the heart to do it that way. This killing business may seem easy to do on paper, but no one whose heart is any good wants to stain his hands with human blood if it can be avoided. I know that according to blood and thunder writers, who write from a deranged brain back East, and manufacture such stuff, that I ought to have pulled my gun at the start, and at the crack of both our guns, the villain La Brie would lay dead on the ground. (35)

WHAT A WONDERFUL AND CRAZY BOOK. IMAGINE ANDREW GARCIA sitting in his ranch house near Alberton, on a benchland above the Clark Fork gorge west of Missoula, writing his memoirs in type, in ink, in charcoal, and stuffing the thousands of pages into dynamite packing crates. He started writing in 1923, when he was seventy years old, and kept writing until 1943, when he was ninety. The old man used to show up at meetings of the Sons and Daughters of the Montana Pioneers dressed as he is photographed in the book: wide-brimmed hat, buckskin shirt, and angora chaps. His memoirs were about his youth, especially about the years 1877–78, when he first came to Montana and married an Indian bride. Because it was a long time ago, the memories are suspect; because it was Garcia, the memories are fun. His heart was good, and a better storyteller would be hard to find.

No one knows what kind of mess the manuscript is, or just how much the editor, Ben Stein, has revised it. Stein lives near Wilsall; he acquired the manuscript in 1948, soon after Garcia's death. Although he has kindly answered a number of my questions, he has not allowed anyone to look at the original copy, leading to speculation that the book is a hoax. Until Stein allows someone to compare Garcia's manuscript to the book, no one can know for sure what's going on. But we can guess. Stein has told me that there was a great deal more manuscript, and that he chopped at least 300 or 400 pages from within the story as printed, including hundreds of pages of "squaw squabbling" in the middle, which in my opinion could be cut further. Stein also said that he cut several hundred pages of poetry. Other parts of the manuscript cover other stories and years. Stein said that Garcia never made a "continuous narrative" of his life.

K. Ross Toole, University of Montana historian, told me that Stein stayed at the Florence Hotel in Missoula after picking up the manuscript. Toole said he saw the dynamite crates but was not allowed to look at the pages. One old rancher who asked to remain nameless said he knew Stein and had seen several pages of the manuscript, which was a mess—nearly illegible and nearly illiterate. But it did tell stories.

So what do we have? Either Stein is a genius, or the manuscript exists. You could imitate Hemingway, but could you imitate a seventy- to ninety-year-old man writing fantasy reminiscences of Indian women fighting over his young body? For hundreds of pages? Could you imitate the crazy style, the unpredictable shifts, the strange combination of awkwardness and grace? *Would* you? I think not. Ed Gallagher, Missoula horsebreaker and historian, said when I interviewed him and Ross Toole on the book's accuracy, that we have a delightfully human reminiscence by someone who was there. I believe him.

However, whether that reminiscence is centered on the beautiful love story that shapes this book, whether the manuscript has chapters, whether it has pacing, is another matter. I suspect that Stein has pulled the central love story of Garcia and In-who-lise out of a chaotic manuscript and, using mainly Garcia's sentences (too zany to invent), has made a book worth reading. So call it edited or co-authored, we have here a unique, irreplaceable tale of Montana before the disappearance of the buffalo, told by two talented, irascible, uncooperative old coots. What could be more western?

The Voice of the Coot

"Voice" refers to the way style suggests a certain person speaking. Reading Garcia is so much fun partly because he has a number of voices of which he seems unaware, but which have their own personalities and points of view. He slides from wise man to kid, from moralist to renegade, from infinitely fair to sexist and racist.

My favorite is the Grand Retrospective voice. Garcia will be telling a story from his youth when all of a sudden the voice of old age will interrupt, echoing down the hallways of sixty years, snapping us from the "squaw kid" of Montana in 1877 to the grizzled sage of Alberton scribbling by lamplight on the ranch: "The Squaw Kid learned much that day, fifty-two years ago." One such passage:

> Sitting here tonight, many years later, with more time than money, I think about those faces that pass before my eyes like it was yesterday. They remind me of the chances and temptations to become an outlaw. I sure came through a tough mill. I see those men as they stood in those old days of the Golden West—some of them in the springtime of their manhood, so beautiful and strong that it makes you wonder, because their hearts are as black as night, and they are cruel, treacherous and merciless as a man-eating tiger of the jungle. Others are ruffians, with the stamp of evil so plain on their whiskered faces that they make you shiver.
>
> All of them died some kind of a violent death. It seems more real and horrid, because I knew them, and now stand like the sexton in the funeral train, for they have gone—all—all—all. (40)

I love it. First of all, Garcia, as far as we can tell, knew very few criminals and probably was close to few people who died a violent death, although at over seventy he must have outlived most of his friends. He himself was most unviolent, and after his few years in the army and wandering in the Musselshell, settled to ranch in the Bitterroot and then near Fish Creek. It is easy to believe that the western romance of violence and danger has affected these paragraphs. He did not run with a rough crowd, and his book proves that he was never one of their kind.

But what this man can write, he can believe. The grand sense of

38

"It's all gone now" floods his prose with bittersweet nostalgia, and legions of unnamed desperadoes lie scattered like buffalo carcasses across the plains. In the background, Garcia, alone on the hill, hat in hand.

After the dash in the first paragraph, he changes verb tense from past to present. He does this all the time; he will begin a memory in the past tense, and then as he warms to the subject he will switch to the present: "I see those men as they *stood* . . . their hearts *are* as black as night." Garcia doesn't remember his past; he relives it. Then, the memory over, he changes paragraphs and returns to the past tense.

This is not a matter only of grammar. In narrating his past, Garcia actually returns to the point of view of a young man, which is very different from the point of view of the old man writing the grand retrospective passages. We get the voice of an old man, and the voice of a young man, and the voice of the old telling of the young. For instance, we hear the voice of a wise old man telling of callow youth: "But I was of the age—just coming twenty-three years old—when a fellow thinks that he knows it all, and in reality he doesn't. This is the time in life when a fellow ought to have a guardian—one of the good old-fashioned, short-arm kind that will kick or pound the conceit out of him" (3). But this voice of the "writer," the eighty-year-old writing of the twenty-three-year-old, is not consistent throughout the book. As Garcia warms to his tales he not only returns to the present tense as if it were happening right now, he also returns to the innocence, arrogance, and conceit of youth. This is not just a story *about* the Squaw Kid; this is the Squaw Kid himself telling the story, and for pages the old man in Alberton, his years, his wisdom, his perspective simply do not exist. Sure he was an innocent fool back then; the miracle is that he can write like one now.

The result is that the story shifts from a rejection of Spanish Catholicism (the old man) to an embracing of it (the Squaw Kid), from sophistication to naiveté, and back again, sometimes within the same sentence. This is not grammatical; this is not legal; this is wonderful.

One of the zaniest voices is that of Garcia the Writer. When he decides to really turn it on we are treated not only to classical allusions and French phrases, but also to an entire set of racist, sexist attitudes that have nothing to do with Garcia the man (a kinder husband to his Indian wife is hard to imagine). These attitudes do, however, remind us of the colonial centers of power that wrote high literature back in England or on the Continent, and of parodies of high style by Americans such as Twain. When Garcia puts on the dog, watch out: "He had a young Crow squaw of magnificent girth and beauty. She looked like a large sack of flour with a string tied in the middle. This Amazonian prairie Juno went under the poetical and soul-stirring nom de plume of Leather Belly" (17).

In another passage (132–33), Garcia describes the tipi-creeping affairs of the "dusky amourites" along the Musselshell. Make no mistake: Garcia is one of the fairest, most open writers we have on Indians and women in 1877 (or one of the Garcias is), but when he uses a term like "dusky amourites," sure enough a "dusky Beau Brummell" chasing a "fairy nymph" is only a half page away. Again the classical allusions and French language trigger an entire colonial point of view in which the Indians (or women) are inferior and their patterns of sexuality are to be mocked as clumsy and dusky imitations of French (i.e., perfect and white) affairs. This from a man who within that year would love, respect, and treat as an equal the Nez Perce woman In-who-lise.

Here is another in Garcia's boxful of voices: Who is speaking this passage?

> Sow-set said, "Lovely Squis-squis, how comes your day? Why does not your voice ring out with laughter and song? Sweet life to us is short, and the night soon to come is long."
>
> Squis-squis said, "Oh, that I should have to say it, she, whom the warriors greet with songs, now smiles no more. The white-faced warrior, An-ta-lee, his heart is dead to me." Kat-a-lee called out to the two young bucks ahead, . . . "Stay, brave warriors. Why hurry on your way? A race, a race, to liven up the day, when the night is still far away, and the sweet prairie was made for play." (p. 143)

This is Henry Wadsworth Longfellow, even if it is in the middle of Garcia's women fighting for his (An-ta-lee's) body. Suddenly our hero is surrounded by voices from "The Song of Hiawatha."

And who wrote phrases like "One of the bunch was on the square"? Dashiell Hammett or Raymond Chandler? Actually the major dialect of the book is this kind of 1930s detective lingo, which makes Garcia sound like a tough guy talking out of the corner of his mouth. What was Garcia reading in Alberton from 1923 to 1943? The result of these shifts of voice is a delightfully puzzling, ambiguous atmosphere, uncontrolled, undesigned, and spontaneous. The dominant tough guy, detective-story dialect is at curious odds with Garcia's character, and this tension between tough talk and soft action establishes the central tone of the book. For instance, he tells us, sounding like Spillane's Mike Hammer, that he "had been taught down on the Rio Grande never to ask a man his name, religion or politics" (14). Yet this is exactly what Garcia does on pages 19, 24, 34, and 123, to name a few. By bad luck, he and Beaver Tom have met up with the La Brie gang. Garcia knows perfectly well that La Brie is a murderer stealing horses. La Brie says, "We will pull out in the morning. . . . We want to trade for a horse or so more to use for trapping." Garcia pipes right up: "Funny trappers you are, who use whiskey for bait and carry no traps with you" (19). If this guy lived to a ripe old age and died in bed, there's hope for all of us.

Garcia was hopelessly impractical and beautifully sensitive. His passages on the greed of trappers (55), on the Spaniards versus the Indians (63), on his beloved bride, In-who-lise, and on the defeated Nez Perce being herded into boxcars (127) establish him as a remarkably sympathetic, trustworthy, and acute observer of the scene in 1877. He actually borders on the timid; his friends have to intervene for him to accept a profit on his buffalo robes (267). This is one nice guy, and here he is talking tough about the tough old West and what a hard mill he came through. The best single-sentence summary of this book came from a student in class who called out: "Charlie Chaplin playing John Wayne."

Is This Book True?

It seems to be, amazing as that sounds. Let's review the dates: Garcia claimed to have come to Montana in 1876; the events transpired in

1877–78; he wrote the book from 1923 to 1943 in Alberton; Stein acquired the manuscript in 1948 and printed it in 1967, almost a century after the events. A whole lot can happen to a story in a hundred years.

Ross Toole and Ed Gallagher joined me on KUFM radio to discuss the authenticity of *Tough Trip Through Paradise*. Their opinion was emphatic: Garcia was there. Many of the details, people's names, and Indian languages seemed persuasive (although Stein also was expert in both Montana history and Indian language). They wondered about the photographs; later I asked Stein, who did not know when they were taken and simply said Garcia carried them around and claimed they were his wives. Ed Gallagher gave a delightful analysis of Garcia's outfit and tack in the picture with his horse, calling the style "early Tom Mix." They wondered why the abduction of white tourists during the Nez Perce retreat was not mentioned by In-who-lise, but then how was her entire twenty-page story of the retreat remembered by Garcia? A student analyzed it and found the style less various and material more continuous than the rest of the book, and he speculated persuasively that the retreat story was written by Stein or paraphrased by Garcia from sources.

But apart from such minor objections, the historians gave the book high ratings. I asked if it suggested a wilder Montana than existed in 1877, but Toole said that beyond the centers of trade in Miles City, Bozeman, Missoula, etc., places like the Musselshell country, where most of the action takes place, were still quite wild. Most Indians were not on reservations, the buffalo were still numerous, the cattle had only begun to arrive, and the railroad was years from crossing the state.

We discussed whether Garcia was a typical trader or mountain man. Remember that the fur trade took place roughly from 1825 to 1845. Garcia was an Indian trader in 1877–78, a totally different era; army forts were numerous and the frontier was on the edge of closing forever. Garcia, we all agreed, was an exceptionally sweet, sensitive, and impractical type; that may not be unusual among the writers and painters of his period, but most historians think the earlier mountain men were a much rougher bunch, more like Boone Caudill. Osborne

Russell's journals of being a mountain man in the 1830s sound more like Garcia than like Boone; yet, as Toole pointed out, Russell could and did write, and this itself was unusual and perhaps indicative of a rare sensibility. We cannot solve it; most who kept journals were indeed interesting men, far from the Boone stereotype.

How unusual Garcia was among white men of his generation, we will never know, but I suspect that our primitivist myths push us toward the strong, silent type as a frontier norm, and delay our appreciation of the number of artistic, verbal, and loose-wired folks who came West for fun. We love to think of pioneers as practical men of action, but Granville Stuart, a pioneer Montana rancher, was a dreamer and in many ways a failure, and Montana by 1885 had many sensitive observers of a fading "scene" (painters Charlie Russell and Frederic Remington, writers George Grinnell, James Schultz, Frank Linderman). Guthrie's Uncle Zeb, too, spoke of the land as if he were George Catlin, who came out in the 1830s to paint the West before it was gone. So alongside the fence building, sodbusting, and barnraising that popular film and literature enshrines, the West always contained a good deal of watching, done by spectators, men and women not of action but of expressiveness and sadness. Nineteenth-century romantics saw themselves as witnesses to the fall of a natural paradise. Romantic primitivism *postulated* a simple, natural hero, but was often *perpetrated* by a complicated, tragic, and highly sophisticated observer. Which brings us to the story, as Garcia tells it. What was the Squaw Kid doing in Montana of 1877?

The Book

As presented by Stein, *Tough Trip* is a love story: Garcia comes up from the Rio Grande, falls in love with In-who-lise, and marries her. The story is so appealing partly because Garcia, like Chaplin, identifies with the underdog. He himself has no inclination to grab land or carve out economic territory; he is appalled by the traders' and trappers' greed and brutality. He easily sees the Indians' point of view and becomes one of them. Garcia is not an empire builder, and in this

way he is not at all typical of whites out West in 1877, unless spectators of the old indeed outnumbered builders of the new. He meets,
marries, and loves the people being wiped out.

From there on, things get a bit more complicated. Garcia often sees
his own story through a Spanish Catholic lens, although what he sees
tends to flicker. He keeps interpreting his story as one of innocence
and guilt, but he can't always decide who plays which role. He is apparently at first a virgin, and nearly a hundred pages trace the agony
of whether he will give in to the passionate advances of a number of
Indian women. When he finally "falls" into sin and guilt, he is ex-
traordinarily happy (beginning of Part Two). In this plot, Garcia is the
young innocent, and the Indians are the wicked heathens bringing
him into the world.

On the other hand, in all matters except sensuality he keeps presenting a primitivist scenario in which he is the wicked and sophisticated European who has escaped to the innocent paradise of these
noble savages, and he has twinges of guilt at sullying their pure life. In
that plot, he is wicked and they are pure. So innocence and guilt, and
the traditional Christian story of a fall from paradise, shape Garcia's
narrative, though he can't always decide just how this story should
be applied to real life.

A rough rule of thumb can be applied: in the first half, when Garcia
is resisting advances by various women, he is innocent and they are
devilish. Once he meets In-who-lise, she, as both woman and natural
savage, becomes the center of innocence, and Garcia is the wicked
European. He insists that they be married by a priest, and hopes that
he will not "ruin" her.

Garcia's story is certainly primitivist: a romance of escape from
wicked civilization to a natural paradise, a place wild and free and
pure. This plot is appropriately excerpted for the blurb on the back of
the book: "Little did I know . . . that I was leaving the white man and
his ways forever, and that I would become innoculated with the wild
life of the old-time Indian and be one of them, to live and run with
them, wild and free like the wild mustang" (5–6). It was not "forever."
After a few years with Indians he lived the rest of his life as a farmer
with a white wife, but no matter, the dream is clear.

Garcia himself is certainly wild and free. He has run away from home, just like Boone, away from a father who threatened him:

> While my people may have been bitter and revengeful in their hates and would think nothing of sticking a knife in a person in anger, still there were some things they did not tolerate, and they were drunkenness and stealing. I can remember just a few years ago when as a small boy going through El Paso one day with my father we met several drunkards —desperadoes with some women that were no better than they were. After they went by, my father grabbed me by the arm and shook me, saying, "Say it, *muchacho*, that you will never be like those vile men, for I would rather see you lying dead at my feet; and so *Cristo* I would do it with my own hands, rather than see you grow up and be like one of them." (27)

Good Heavens. This violent morality, "the respect for God that my people had pounded in me with a club" (73), seems to have pushed Garcia West (in his case, North) just as Boone was pushed by Pap and laws that scared and shackled him. When he speaks of his own people, Garcia is not too kind:

> The English and French were not any too good either, and under the names of Christianity and civilization always gave the Indians the worst of it. Bad as they were, however, they were angels compared to the people I came from.
> The Spaniards, in brutality, cruelty and treachery, outshone them all, and were known, hated and feared more than all others by the Indian. (63)

So Garcia is following the classic primitivist plot, escaping a corrupt, cruel, and frightening civilization to run wild and free like the Indian and the mustang on the western plains.

This plot demands, of course, that his Indian wife be wild and free, while his nineteenth-century Christianity demands that she be pure. Garcia maintains these illusions against all evidence. Who was In-who-lise? She was Nez Perce, and tells the story of the Nez Perce retreat first-hand, from their home on the Snake River to their battle in the Big Hole, where her father and brother were killed and left without proper burial. Then the band escaped through Yellowstone Park and north toward Canada. They were caught just short of the border by the U.S. Army, most of them killed, the survivors captured and taken away. In-who-lise was one of the few who escaped, and when we meet her just a few months after the battle she is living uneasily with a friendly but alien tribe on the Musselshell, not far from Chief Joseph's last battlefield.

What is she going to do with her life? She is 500 miles from home, a young girl, alone, separated from her tribe. Her father and brother not only lie dead 200 miles away, but they lie dead without the rituals that will help them in the next life. Her own position in another tribe's camp is uncertain.

Enter the Charlie Chaplin of the plains. All In-who-lise has to do is play the little flower girl. I am not mocking the love story, for I'm sure Garcia loved her and I suspect she was genuinely touched by the kindness, fairness, and devotion of this strange young man. But what did they do after they were married? They went back to the Big Hole, found and buried her father and brother, and headed toward her home. For her, this may have been love plus: love plus strategy, diplomacy, the sweetest manipulation. For her, it was certainly a convenient marriage.

Savage? Wild and free? She is thinking socially, politically, tribally. *Garcia* is wild and free, but In-who-lise, and the mustang, and most of the people on earth for most of recorded time prefer the hierarchical society and traditional customs of their own kind. Garcia shows no sign of recognizing this aspect of his wife; to him, all is freedom and romance. Once again, the white escapee from civilization has projected his own primitivist plot onto the animals and Indians.

In primitivist and colonial mythology, the European is complex, sophisticated, experienced, civilized. The Indian, or any non-European native, is simple, childlike, innocent, natural. Double it for European men versus native women. Who in this partnership is the scheming adult, and who is the innocent child? It is one of my favorite moments in the book, over three fourths of the way through, when they get married:

I was greatly surprised when I asked Father Landre, who did not understand Pend d'Oreille or Nez Perce, if I would have to get an interpreter
to make In-who-lise understand what he was saying to her. He said, "I
have talked with her and she can speak English as well as either you or
I can, and has been to the mission school at Lapwai." I could not get
her to say a word in English as long as she lived. (261)

All during their courtship in camp, she could understand whatever
Garcia said to his white and Indian friends in English, but she never
let on. If you have ever been in this situation, you know what power
a hidden command of language gives. In-who-lise innocent?

The essential Christian narrative structures the book. The story is
about a fall from grace, and Garcia makes clear that his later life of
farming never compared to the happiness of being young and free in
the open country of his youth. The West, here as in Guthrie, functions
as a powerful image of a paradise that must be lost:

Those men, once free trappers, had roamed the prairies and hills, free
and untrammeled, most of them fierce and savage as the Injuns they
ran with. . . . Those men read the writing on the wall, and knew by the
way the settlers were pouring into the country, even the buffalo would
soon be gone. They bitterly resented the encroachment of the settlers on
what they claimed with the Injun as their own boundless prairies. (56)

While this history has its truth, it was never the "boundless" aspect of
the prairies that the Indians admired; they were losing the "bounds"
of a civilization they loved. Luther Standing Bear, a Sioux, said it quite
clearly:

We did not think of the great open plains, the beautiful rolling hills,
and winding streams with tangled growth as "wild." Only to the white
man was nature a "wilderness." . . . When the very animals of the forest began fleeing from his approach, then it was for us the "Wild West"
began.

Once again, even though in this case Garcia was there, and married
to an Indian, the story we get is a white story of escape to "the wild

life of the Indian," to be "wild and free like the mustang." Yet such a story has nothing to do with horses or Indians, and indeed overlooks the point of view of Garcia's beloved In-who-lise almost as thoroughly as Guthrie overlooks Teal Eye. Behind this story is Europe; ahead is Paradise Lost.

But no theory should blind us to Garcia's accomplishments as a storyteller. He subordinates everything to the telling of a tale. Near the end, he and his In-who-lise fall in with Rock Creek miners, and Garcia tells the tale of the Nez Perce murder of three Philipsburg men: the John Hays murders. It's a horrible massacre, to hear Garcia tell it. Has he turned against his wife's own tribe? Then, enter white greed. A new interpretation? No, he's just willing to play up any angle that heightens the drama. Skulking Injuns, greedy miners, raging bears— and himself as the fool while In-who-lise calms him enough to shoot the grizzly—anything to tell a tale, especially a good old-fashioned tale of "blood-stained gold dust and nuggets."

I know of no other book like *Tough Trip Through Paradise*. The crazy combination of history, fairmindedness, ignorance, and blarney leaves your head spinning. But behind it all is a kind man, a man who looked back on what he'd had and lost, who laughed at his own silliness, and who could write:

> We had a sumptuous repast of dried buffalo meat and straight coffee. It sure tasted good to us, who were young, had good teeth and didn't know any better. (293)

4
Alderson's Bride Goes West

EACH OF THEM CAME TO MONTANA WITH A DREAM: BOONE IN
1830 and Garcia in 1876 with dreams of escape, and Nannie Alderson
in 1883 with a different dream, more like the original *Treasure Island*.
Nannie and her husband Walt came to get rich.

1883

It was the best of times, it was the worst of times. Nannie had been a
lonely child in West Virginia, fatherless and abandoned by her mother
to a grandmother's care. On a visit to relatives in Kansas she met Walt
Alderson, a tall, handsome cowboy. The year they were engaged,
1882, the favorite book west of Kansas was James Brisbin's *The Beef
Bonanza; or How to Get Rich on the Plains*. The West was being liberated
from its burdens of Indians and buffalo, while people were discovering that cattle could be wintered on the Northern Plains instead of
trailed up from Texas in the spring. The old grass was still lush. Railroads were pushing in, linking from the south, east, and west in 1882
and 1883. Montana had been opened: "There a poor man can grow
rich while a rich man can double or even treble his capital" (Cincinnati
Gazette, 1882). After a year or two on the plains, five-dollar cows were
expected to sell for fifty dollars. The resulting "bonanza" mentality
clearly imitated the values and expectations of the mining camps. Forget Jefferson. Forget primitivist or pastoral notions of the sanctity of
earth and husbandry. The beef boom was a cattle rush, a mercantile
not an agrarian frontier.

To young Walt Alderson, who as a boy had run off to Texas and
had done his share of driving cattle, who had no money and a "wild
reputation," and who wanted to marry an eastern girl named Nannie
Tiffany, Montana was the answer. He came out to Miles City on one

of the first trains, in 1882, located a homestead, and went back to claim his bride. Her relatives "all thought the ranching business had a wealthy future" (14). Nannie and Walt in *A Bride Goes West* did not come like Boone to be close to the land, or like Garcia and the later homesteaders to settle down; they came to get rich and get out:

> We didn't mind the hard things because we didn't expect them to last. Montana in the early Eighties was booming just like the stock market in 1929, and the same feverish optimism possessed all of us. I believe the same thing was true of many other frontier communities. . . . We didn't expect to live on a ranch all our lives—oh, my no! We used to talk and plan about where we would live when we were rich—we thought of St. Paul. It all looked so easy; the cows would have calves . . . (54)

To Boone, and perhaps even to Garcia, Nannie and Walt would have been the enemy. They represented not only white settlement, but the westward advance of a European business and capitalist mentality that would exploit Boone's sacred space, the last retreat of the buffalo, grizzly, and God. The artist Frederic Remington had come West in those same years to paint what was left before the Aldersons did it in; he bemoaned the coming of "the derby hat, the thirty day note."

Nannie's book, then, chronicles the beginnings of the modern West. She came out in 1883; by 1884, the old West had ended. The buffalo had disappeared, the Indians had been forced by hunger to reservations and handouts, barbed wire was going up and the railroad had arrived. "She's all gone now." Nannie and Walt were part of that change.

> That year [1882, along the Tongue River] the buffalo were still so thick that Mrs. Lays had only to say: "Mr. Alderson, we're out of meat"; and he would go out and find a herd and kill a calf, all just as easily as a man would butcher a yearling steer in his own pasture. Yet when I came out, one year later, there was nothing left of those great bison herds, which had covered the continent, but carcasses. I saw them on my first drive out to the ranch, and they were lying thick all over the flat above our house, in all stages of decay. So wasteful were the hunters, they had not even removed the tongues, though the latter were choice meat.

The summer after I came out [1884] Mr. Alderson killed the last buffalo ever seen in our part of Montana. A man staying with us was out fishing when he saw this lonesome old bull wandering over the hills and gullies above our house—the first live buffalo seen in many months. He came home and reported it, saying: "Walt, why don't you go get him?" And next morning Mr. Alderson did go get him. (16–17)

Nannie's comment on the incident is interesting for its naiveté: "I am afraid that the conservation of the buffalo, or of any other wild game, simply never occurred to the westerner of those days" (17). But that's not true. May 6, 1882, the year Mr. Alderson arrived, the Yellowstone *Journal* reprinted on the front page this piece from the Bozeman *Courier*:

Friends of Montana everywhere are becoming seriously impressed with the fact that the large game of the country is being rapidly exterminated, and that a few years more of such wholesale slaughter as has characterized the operations of "hunters" during the past two years, will result in the almost, if not total, extinction of most of the valuable species of game in the territory. . . . The wholesale destruction of buffalo . . . can hardly be considered in any other light than that of a great wrong, whether viewed from the savage or the civilized standard of justice.

After such ringing trumpet calls, the paper takes a curious turn and chooses to accept these abominations in the name of progress, thus accommodating both its primitivist sympathies and its advertisers in one column: "We may, however, be compelled by the force of circumstances to accept the theory that the buffalo, like the Indian, is doomed; that it cannot survive the march of modern improvement and progress." The column then goes on to wish that at least we might not exterminate the antelope, deer, moose, and elk—which leaves us where we are today.

One can see here, in miniature, the terrible moral bind we were in by the end of the nineteenth century. All virtue seemed opposed to all reality; Huxley in England was calling ethics the opposite of civilization and evolution; "natural law" was assumed to be a mean law, guiding the self-interest of individuals and societies. "Progress," of course, was part of this inevitable and nasty evolutionary law. The good, and the true (Dickens's home, and the street), seemed hopelessly split. That is a terrible position for a culture to find itself in. The "realist" must then be amoral. The virtuous person is "idealistic"—or as we saw in chapters 1 and 2, a woman or a child.

Only industrial cultures, as far as I can tell, have adopted the position that earning one's daily living is a nasty business, a necessary evil. Other cultures may indeed pillage or kill for a living, but they seem to enjoy it, even make it sacred. Hence our "romantic" envy of cultures that do not think or act with our constant irony or guilt. So in the Bozeman *Courier* of 1882, we find the writer accepting "a great wrong." Now when should you ever accept a great wrong? He accepts this wrong in the name of "modern improvement and progress." He does not argue that progress is right, only that it's coming. But if progress isn't good, why are we doing it?

On both sides of the Atlantic in the 1880s, progress seemed out of control. Industrial change was taking its own course, quite independent of human needs. We could only hope that the new reality and some kind of good would coincide. By the time I was growing up after the Second World War, this faith was expressed by the concept of a "higher standard of living." We convinced ourselves that an industrial nation with cash and consumer goods offered a better life; that a washing machine united the good and the true; that "underdeveloped" nations were to be pitied and developed (into new markets). But of course we still face the issue, with our money and leisure time, of what the "good" is. More consumer goods? Individual freedom? Individual growth and accomplishment? Time with the family? A shared sense of national or social purpose? A tribal religion? The Aldersons wandered into the West of the 1880s only to face a situation that remains with us: European industrial culture was moving fast, destroying every way of life in its path, but where it was going, and why, and who was in charge, no one seemed to know. And any attempt to talk about values, or "a great wrong," was just whistling in the wind. The buffalo were gone. And that same rapid and apparently mindless change would hit the Aldersons as well.

People certainly did know what was happening. As early as 1880 the trader Joe Kipp at Fort Conrad was worried about rumors of buffalo depletion, and his friend James Willard Schultz at the mouth of the Musselshell received letters that summer from Locust Grove, New York, that expressed concern about the reported slaughter of the buffalo. Granville Stuart, that same spring, spoke of rotting carcasses from Forsyth to Miles City. So from 1880 until the end, in 1883, observers both local and national could see the trend. It was not a simple mistake.

The extermination of the buffalo was both a profit-making enterprise and a national policy aimed at subduing the Indians. General Philip Sheridan, addressing the Texas legislature in 1873, said that the buffalo hunters

> are destroying the Indians' commissary; and it is a well-known fact that an army losing its base of supplies is placed at a great disadvantage. . . . Send [the buffalo hunters] powder and lead, if you will, but for the sake of lasting peace, let them kill, skin, and sell, until the buffalos are exterminated. Then your prairie can be covered with the speckled cattle, and the festive cowboy, who follows the hunter as the second forerunner of advanced civilization.

After 1871, new tanning processes made the robes valuable for leather. The army, which wanted Indians subdued; the railroads, which wanted sportsmen, sightseers, towns, and cattle ranches needing freight lines; and individual entrepreneurs combined in ten years to bring thirteen million to sixty million buffalo (we will never know), which in passing would darken the prairies for days, to less than 200 in the entire West by 1884. Most of the slaughter occurred between 1878 and 1883, when Nannie arrived, and was intimately connected in both intent and effect with the establishment of the cattle empires on the old Indian lands. The policy was no accident, and the result of the policy was apparent to many Montanans and their newspapers by the time the Aldersons arrived.

I dwell on the buffalo slaughter partly for its intrinsic importance as a watershed moment in the history of the plains, equal to the coming of the horse or of irrigation, and partly because it leads us to one of

Nannie's problems. She saw very little in historical, social, or political perspective.

Nannie, like many Victorian women, had been trained to think that she need not bother with historical and political realities, and certainly communication of catastrophes was more crude in 1884 than now. But surely many pioneers knew that the buffalo were making room for their cows. Cattle and sheep ranchers understand grazing competition. Unfortunately for Nannie, by overlooking historical context and depending on a southern "innocence," she tended to take everything personally. That, as we shall see, did not make homesteading any easier. When hard times came, she saw it as her own failure, not the failure of a system. Many, by the winter of 1886–87, were in the same fix.

Nannie's ignoring of buffalo policy, or of any policy, was characteristic of both men and women in the West. Like farmers and ranchers of the present day, she was encouraged to see herself as a ruggedly independent individual, while at the same time she was thrown into an economic situation determined by governmental and historical forces beyond her control. This paradox of independence and dependence characterized the frontier.

One of the finest examples in Montana writings of pioneer individualism combined with political ignorance is the memoir of Pearl Price Robertson, published in *Frontier* magazine in 1933. She and her husband Alec came out in 1910 in the second homesteading boom. She and Alec "were young then, . . . and life was full of promise." Much like Nannie and Walt, they had not liked the "bread-and-butter sort of existence" back East, "so smug and safe and comfortable . . . growing up, living and dying, all in the same cramped space. There must have been an adventurous streak in the make-up of both Alec and me. Anyway, a restlessness of spirit made us both long to get away."

They got away to Judith Gap:

In a few weeks Alec went in search of a homestead; I could scarcely wait for his return, so eager was I. Pride of possession and joy of ownership seized me when I learned that we had claim to three hundred twenty acres on Lonesome Prairie in northern Choteau county—to us the first step in the accomplishment of our cherished dream. Long we sat by the fire that night of Alec's return, as he related to me the details of his trip and described the grassy prairie stretching westward twenty-five miles or more from Big Sandy to the Marias River; how three weeks after the land opening every foot of the land had been taken for twenty miles out; how the land locator had taken him out with a party of others who would be our neighbors; of the young Norwegian and his sweetheart but lately arrived from Norway who could not speak a word of English; of the genial old German who, when he found this broad stretch of fertile soil so much to his liking, and a whole section to be had for the taking, hurried back to the telegraph office and sent this telling message to two grownup sons and a daughter: "Come Henry; come Johnnie; come Mary; come quick!"

Pearl invites us to share again, so vividly, the immigrants' dream. They each seemed to be acting as individuals, adventurous, resourceful, loving freedom and opportunity and not shirking hard work. All that is true. But there is another truth. Lonesome Prairie was Blackfeet land, given by treaty. Three times the treaty had been violated and the reservation had been shrunk (1874, 1888, 1896). What did she think, what do *we* think suddenly made those sections open for the taking in 1910? The last shrinking of the reservation. And who did that? The government, with its army. Then the government surveyed, and recorded the pioneer claims in the land office, and in three weeks the "new lands" were gone.

Nothing in western traditions by 1910 had prepared Pearl to acknowledge that the government had finally made Lonesome Prairie "smug and safe and comfortable" in spite of pioneer hardships, and that if she had been "adventurous" enough to take Blackfeet land without government support, her adventure would have been short lived. True, she was able to "get away" from cramped space, but she had not gotten away from government, which had created the space, was handing out the land while it lasted, and was encouraging foreign and domestic immigration to make this new country settled and strong. From the fur trade, through laws encouraging mineral extraction during the mining booms, through the homestead acts and the railroad land grants after the Civil War, development of the West was a national policy. Pearl and Alec stood on Lonesome Prairie by government design. That policy had brought the Indians to their knees and had given Nannie a homestead in the middle of Crow and Cheyenne range; thirty years later that policy was continuing with shrinkings of Indian lands and continued subsidization of settlement. And a bursting Europe was gobbling up any parcel the government would give away.

The entire western mythology of rugged individualism must be seen in a larger context of governmental control. The first New England settlers in 1620, for instance, were truly without government support. Did they strike off into the woods alone? Of course not; they lived inside a stockade at Plymouth, in a tightly knit society with a third of the buildings owned in common. By 1880 a central government had sent its army west to erect, in effect, a stockade around the entire region, an invisible fence that ensured security. From Lewis and Clark on, exploration, treaties, battles, and land development were managed by central government, making possible the luxurious illusion of an empty earth made for the use of autonomous individuals, each moving farther West when they could see the smoke from their neighbor's chimney. But had they really come alone, they would have been wiped out. The Indians accepted trappers and traders out of self-interest, but they were not, and are not, interested in giving away land.

The West was won not by six-guns, but by taxes. The government raised the revenue, and spent it securing western land. In a daily way, fighting the weather and the awesome space, the rancher is still a rugged and self-reliant individual. But politically and economically, he and Pearl and Nannie and all the other whites west of the Mississippi have always been part of society, even international society, whether they liked it or not. No other part of the country is so indebted to government and so disdainful of it.

Nannie's innocence is only the tip of an iceberg; in the West, individual choices have always been made within a context of national policy (as now choices are made within management policy on Bureau of Land Management or Forest Service lands, or within water rights or water apportionment or farm or nuclear arms policy) no matter how blind to that truth we may wish to be.

Both homesteading booms—1882 and 1909—followed a dramatic shift in perception of the West at mid-century. Until about 1850, the West was presumed to be a desert wasteland, and therefore unfit for settlement even if ripe for economic exploitation. Then about 1850, the stereotype of a desert West gave way to its equally absurd opposite, the stereotype of a garden West, an agrarian paradise. The exploration had already been done by trappers and miners, and after the Civil War the new nation was primed for the adventure of meeting its manifest destiny across the wide Missouri. An editorial in the New York *Tribune* on February 5, 1867, when Nannie was seven, was typically optimistic: "If you strike off into the broad, free West, and make yourself a farm from Uncle Sam's generous domain, you will crowd nobody, starve nobody, and . . . neither you nor your children need evermore beg for Something to Do." Behind the words lay, as we have seen, a Europe of crowding, starving, and unemployment (begging for something to do), and ahead lay total disregard for Indian claims to the land.

By 1880, the railroads had built the means for bringing out numbers of people and were advertising all over America and Europe, extolling the virtues of the western garden. Northern Pacific brochures issued by Jay Cooke describe the virtues of "the Fertile Belt" of Montana: "seldom any difficulty experienced on account of the cold or snows of winter. . . . Cows pass the winter season with no other food than they clip from the grazing field, and although regularly milked, come out in the spring in excellent condition." The towns along the Highline were named by the railroad: Havre, Harlem, Malta, Glasgow. The story goes (Roberta Cheney cites old newspapers) that Great Northern officials in St. Paul would spin a globe and, blindfolded, finger a spot. But the spots are all European, and I suspect the profit motive outweighed chance as the railroad courted various nations and ethnic groups. Foreign capital invested heavily in the ranching business; in reaction a law was passed in 1887 prohibiting aliens from owning land in the territories. Most of the big outfits from Texas to Montana in the eighties were corporate ranches, some of them selling stock on international exchanges. Small operations like Walt Alderson's often had several partners. As historians Michael Malone and Richard Roeder have pointed out, the tremendous losses of the winter of '86–87 were due partly to a range already overstocked, with little hay put up for the winter. At the last minute ranchers decided to carry over extra animals in hopes of higher prices in the spring. That is what I mean by a mercantile, not agrarian mentality, and the disastrous result was pictured by Charlie Russell in "Waiting for a Chinook" in the spring of 1887. That same spring Granville Stuart, after surveying his range and finding 30,000 cattle carcasses rotting in the coulees where just a few years before he had seen all the buffalo dead, gave up forever a mercantile point of view, saying, "I never wanted to own again an animal I could not feed and shelter."

On April 4, 1883, Nannie Tiffany and Walt Alderson were married in Union, West Virginia. Within hours they were on a stagecoach, then a train: Chicago, St. Paul, Mandan, South Dakota, Miles City, Montana, "every other building was a saloon . . . a pretty hoorah place" (21). There's a fine Huffman print of Miles City in 1884, as Nannie saw it. April 17, just two weeks after they were married, they were on a stage out of Miles City, headed south for their homestead where Lame Deer creek joins the Rosebud. The Aldersons had jumped right into the middle of the cattle boom.

> That night we stayed at a second road ranch on the Tongue River. We had a comfortable room to ourselves with a good bed, which the hostess must have given up to us, since the ordinary accommodations consisted of a kind of bunk room which was occupied that night by fully fifteen men. They were all young, nearly all seemed to be Easterners, and they were all going into the cattle business. Next morning at breakfast we all sat at one long table, and they talked of nothing but cattle, horses and prices. Everyone, it seemed, was making fabulous sums of money or was about to make them; no one thought of losses; and for the next year my husband and I were to breathe that air of optimism and share all those rose-colored expectations. (25)

One year. Not much of a honeymoon. So much happened to Nannie and Walt in that year, they were so young and energetic yet so enslaved to fate that it makes your head swim. They built their dream house and their herd, lasted the winter, and in March Nannie's first baby was born. That same day her house was burned to the ground. Never again would she live so well. Never again would she have the same young dreams of freedom and easy wealth. Nannie, incredulous and resentful, tells her own version of the story; let's consider it from the Cheyenne point of view.

Black Wolf

Black Wolf was a Northern Cheyenne. According to John Stands In Timber, who was born the year the Alderson house was burned, Black Wolf would have been in his mid-thirties when he came into the Alderson yard that spring of 1884. To Black Wolf it was not Tuesday, March 18, but the Drying Up Moon at the end of the worst winter in memory. The summer before, the buffalo carcasses lay thick on the flats above the Alderson homestead. For the first time, the Indians had entered winter without dried buffalo meat, and the Starvation Winter of 1883–84 was now nearing its end. Spring had come again, but for the first time without buffalo. What would the future hold?

Black Wolf was a young man in his prime. He was a warrior, and by the way of things would soon be an older and respected chief. He was proud, and had a right to be, and hungry, as he stood in the yard that morning facing Hal, the Alderson hired hand, and one other cowboy. Black Wolf said they offered him breakfast; Hal said he begged.

Black Wolf had seen a lot. The past ten years had brought to him and his people a deluge of disasters that seemed to have no end; and in the last few months, he had watched so many die. But they were not the first. Black Wolf could remember a good deal of death, including death with honor.

He was almost certainly standing with Spotted Elk in the crowd around the fire in June 1876, the night before the fight with Custer. A Crow scout for Custer, White Man Runs Him, had told the Indians the soldiers wanted a fight, and both groups knew where the others were. So in the camp that night, packed with Sioux and Cheyenne, there was much anticipation of a battle. Some Sioux boys took the death vow, to fight the next day until dead, and four Cheyenne youths joined them: Little Whirlwind, Cut Belly, Closed Hand, and Noisy Walking. Black Wolf was part of Spotted Elk's band, and that night they gathered with everyone else to watch and honor the "dying dancing" in the big clearing at the upper end of the camp, beside the Little Big Horn river. Maybe someone was singing the Cheyenne warrior song: "My friends, only the stones stay on earth forever. Use your best ability."

Spotted Elk said that no more than twenty danced. Black Wolf would have been part of that firelight circle, and he would have watched the parade in the boys' honor the next morning—"Look well at these boys," the old men sang, "for none will come back this day." The parade wound through the Cheyenne camp and was returning to the Sioux lodges when Custer's men struck.

So Black Wolf had seen that too, would know which painting is correct of that last stand on the buffalo grass hills already in late June turning from green to yellow. It was a great day for the plains tribes, but an especially sweet revenge for the Cheyenne. The Sand Creek massacre of Southern Cheyenne women and children by an ambitious and vicious officer in 1864 had rankled for twelve years. They had not forgotten Colonel Chivington, who had defended the killing of children by saying, "Nits make lice." Everyone knew of Sand Creek; most Northern Cheyenne had lost relatives there. John Stands In Timber said there was not really much scalping after the Custer battle, adding casually, "The ones who had relatives killed at Sand Creek came out and chopped the heads and arms off, things like that." After the victory no one slept: all night they were singing, dancing, telling the stories of that day and other days, back to the beginning of time.

In a few days the Cheyenne split up for summer buffalo hunts, and many regrouped in Dull Knife's camp on the Powder River, where they were found by soldiers and suffered a disastrous defeat. The U.S. Army, too, had a memory. Black Wolf was probably there, and so was Two Moons, whom Nannie later came to know.

Two Moons, after the Dull Knife defeat, became a chief of the Tongue River band, leading in the Birney fight and then convincing his fellows to surrender to General Miles at Fort Keogh, arguing, as Plenty-coups did among the Crows, that cooperation with the whites would be the only way to secure a decent reservation in the future. Once they had surrendered, those Cheyenne with Two Moons gladly became army scouts, delighted with the opportunity to chase down Chief Joseph in 1877. This may seem to us traitorous, but General Miles simply offered them a chance to do what they had always done and liked: war on other plains tribes. Perhaps they had not yet made the transition to thinking "white versus Indian," instead of "Cheyenne versus Nez Perce." They continued to find honor in battle, in whatever uniform.

Two Moons was active in locating and defeating the Nez Perce at Bear's Paw, when In-who-lise escaped. By then he was a valued leader in both war and strategy. But after the buffalo went away, he would be a "steady visitor" at Nannie's, in her eyes "just an old beggar who came around to our house asking for coffee. He was absurd and squalid-looking, with his dirty cotton shirt turned wrong side out, and his white man's pants with the seat cut out, which he wore like a pair of leggings over a breech clout" (47). This sounds like a description of the proverbial "shuffling nigger," and in fact Nannie's condescension stems from southern roots:

> I looked, unconsciously perhaps, for the same affectionate relationship with the Indians that had existed in my old home between the colored people and the whites. One of the hard lessons I had to learn in Montana was that the affection I sentimentally wanted just simply was not there. (133)

Someone forgot to hand out banjos to the Cheyenne.

Black Wolf went southeast with the Dull Knife and Little Wolf people who surrendered at Fort Robinson, in Sioux territory. Little Wolf later became close to the Aldersons, and a powerful influence on Nannie. Little Wolf and Black Wolf became part of the infamous southern exile. All the Northern Cheyennes at Fort Robinson were sent down to the Southern Cheyenne reservation in Oklahoma, where they began to sicken and die in alarming numbers. The next summer,

1878, they told the agent they were going back north, with or without army permission. He said no. They left, fighting skirmishes with the army and terrifying white settlers all the way. After fording the Platte, they split in two, Dull Knife returning to Fort Robinson and Little Wolf wintering in the sand hills of Nebraska, where there was plenty of game and no army. Black Wolf stayed with the Little Wolf band, and in March 1879 they came back to the Powder River and struck a deal with the army to come into Fort Keogh with Two Moons's band. The deal was the reservation of their choice. The reservation of their choice included the land that, within three years, Walt Alderson would choose to ranch.

The reservation was not yet on paper, not yet an act of Congress. Colonel Miles let Two Moons and his scouts hunt in the Tongue and Powder drainages from 1880 on; it was understood this might become their reservation. There were still buffalo there, and no white settlers until 1882. Then Brewster came, and Rowland to Muddy Creek, and Walt Alderson came to Lame Deer Creek, choosing a place for his Virginia bride in the heart of the juniper-pine forest in the sheltered valleys far up the Rosebud. He knew almost nothing about Indians. She would arrive the summer of '83 even more naive: "Hot rolls, plus a vague understanding that petticoats ought to be plain, were my whole equipment for conquering the West" (19). The summer of 1880 or 1881, Two Moons met with Little Wolf to choose the reservation they had been promised, the reservation for which they had surrendered. They met at the mouth of Lame Deer creek on the Rosebud, less than a mile from where the Aldersons were to build the house of their dreams.

The year of the Aldersons' arrival was the year of the Indian nightmare. That summer of '83 the buffalo were gone. The tribes were going into winter without meat; in addition, the whites were bringing in the spotted buffalo, the cattle that roamed the unfenced range on the Indian reservation. But if an Indian killed one of these cattle for food, longhorns now walking where the buffalo had walked, eating the buffalo grass on lands promised to the Cheyenne by Colonel Miles, the army was set on them. All around the Alderson house that winter the Cheyenne starved.

One January night the dog barked so long and loud that my husband decided to go out, to see if a wolf or coyote could be nearby. He found two Indians in the angle of the house, slumped in their saddles and almost frozen. They were afraid of the dog and, in their stolid way, just sat there, not making a sound. They had started across the divide, but the snow was so deep their horses floundered till they were worn out, and I suppose the lights from our windows attracted them. (91)

The Aldersons took them, fed them and the horses and put them on the floor. They spoke no English. "In the morning they went on their way."

Other Indians told us [later] that one of the bucks who set fire to our house was one of the two whom we took in and fed and sheltered that stormy night. Somehow words fail me at this point. (131)

It is hard to imagine the gulf between those two pairs of people. But the Cheyenne were not scared of the dog.

Just what Black Wolf thought of the Aldersons, their spread, the soft-talking, fair-skinned woman, we cannot know. By that spring there were camps of starving Cheyenne just above and below the Alderson ranch on Lame Deer creek, and Black Wolf walked frequently past the house to visit his friends in the upper camp. He must have known by sight all the hired hands, especially Hal, who had slugged a Cheyenne the previous summer while branding over on the Tongue. Hal, whom Nannie considered a "strange character, warm-hearted, reckless and wild," was her favorite of the cowboys, full of fun. Perhaps he reminded Black Wolf of the undisciplined young braves, always trying to sneak out the night before the battle to count coup. Or perhaps Hal just seemed ignorant and loud.

Tuesday, March 18, Black Wolf asked for or was offered breakfast or a cigarette or both as he headed back to his family through the Alderson place about noon. The Aldersons were away; Nannie was having a baby in Miles City; a few hands were around. Black Wolf sat down in the yard, a man who had fought Custer, a man who had been through the southern exile, a man who had seen the buffalo disappear like smoke in the wind. A man who, as one of the younger chiefs, would have to counsel his people on what to do next as their world fell apart.

Hal saw an Indian in a tall black hat. "I'll bet you five dollars I can put a hole through that old Indian's hat without touching his head," he said to Reinhart, another hired hand. "I'll bet you can't." Hal, "that scamp," as Nannie called him, pulled a six-gun and fired (101). Black Wolf keeled over. The cowboys, scared of a Cheyenne uprising, jumped on their horses and took off for help.

Black Wolf came back to consciousness, creased in the head. He walked and crawled toward camp; soon someone found him and took him in on horseback. Both Indian camps were enraged. They thought the cowboys had tried to kill Black Wolf. But the truth was probably worse to a Cheyenne: the arrogance, the condescension, the shame. The young men could not stand it. Who did these people think they were? As John Stands In Timber tells it, "they rode in close and shot the windows out, and then broke in and took everything they wanted and set the house afire. They burned the whole ranch down—all the buildings and improvements, even the hay stacks and corrals. When they got through there was not much left." Nannie was incensed; they took her mother's heirloom silver and "worst" of all, "shot our dog out of pure meanness" (100).

Hal got away; four Indians went to prison (Nannie says two), including the father of John Stands In Timber. For Nannie, it was the end of all those western dreams that had begun back East with railroad brochures and the *Breeders' Gazette*. She never again had a house so fine, or so well furnished, with muslin and flowered paper on the walls, and a fireplace that burned five-foot logs. By the end of 1884 the beef prices were already falling, and as they moved from ranch to ranch, from house to cabin, she became burdened with children and work. The devastating winter of '86–87 froze the hopes that were left. For the Aldersons and the others down on the Powder, the Tongue, and the Rosebud, the dreams of a beef bonanza on Cheyenne lands were gone. But the buffalo did not come back.

Nannie

Who was she? What really happened? The answers are not perfectly clear. Historian Clyde Milner has shown that contemporary *diaries* of a given week on the frontier may be uneventful, while the *reminiscences* of that same week are full of Indians and hair-raising tales. Furthermore, Nannie's is an "as told to" reminiscence, and Helena Huntington Smith was a sophisticated listener and writer quite capable of sculpting the material herself. We seem to have a reminiscence in which Nannie, at eighty-two, laid bare more than she intended, more than she was willing to face. To put it bluntly, she keeps saying the hardships were worth it, which may be true when she is looking back, while at the time she may have been crushed. Later, after the events of the book, she apparently rebounded and found her place in Montana.

A Bride Goes West is so interesting because this is not the little house on the prairie, and reader reaction varies from those who see Nannie as a brave prairie Madonna surviving incredible hardship, to those who see her as a whining southern belle who could not, and did not, make it. I have received papers on this book entitled "Ninny Alderson" and "A Bride Goes Bonkers." In my classes, women of Montana pioneer descent have been Nannie's most extreme supporters and critics (usually critics). So this story both documents a fascinating, brief period of change—the open-range cattle boom—and touches to the quick our notions of what it is and what it takes "to pioneer in earnest," as Nannie called it after she and Walt had lost all illusions of getting rich enough to leave.

Certainly her life got worse after the house was burned in the spring of '84. She came back from Miles City with the baby in the fall, and they built a new, inferior house over on the Tongue River. In the spring of '86, Nannie went East to visit family and have her second child, because she had had such a hard time in Miles City with her first. The trip was quite a luxury. Her seven months boarding in Miles City, and the new house, had cost a lot; the firm was borrowing at 18 percent; beef prices were falling; they were no longer getting "fabulous offers" from rich easterners for their operation. Walt joined her in West Virginia that fall, and then reports of the winter of '86–87 began filtering back East. As soon as Walt figured they could reach the ranch, in March, they returned, across North Dakota where houses were buried in snow, then digging through drifts, day after day, the hundred miles in an open sled to the ranch. Nannie huddled beneath buffalo robes with two children between the trunks, and couldn't help contrasting this trip with her first, four years earlier: "I was a girl then, and every little hardship was a game, but now it was all grimly serious" (157).

Walt was a good rancher, had put up a lot of hay, and his strong cattle were better off than most. Yet it was still disaster. Across Montana, the frozen carcasses were piled. Three years of overgrazing had changed the range; not only the buffalo, but the buffalo grass was gone. Walt's partnership broke up, he and Nannie moved for the third time in four years, and then "I began to pioneer in earnest . . . no longer borne up by the belief that our trials were temporary" (165). She was back to two rooms and board floors, now with two children, then three, then four. No cash. No trips. Four walls. "There were weeks, in our long winters, when I scarcely left the house except to hang clothes on the line" (170). In the fall of 1893, ten years after coming West to get rich, Nannie and Walt gave up ranching and moved to Miles City. "How rejoiced I was at this decision" (249).

Just why they quit ranching we will never know; they had their pick of reasons. Conditions were bad, but they were equally bad for those who stayed. This reminiscence is valuable partly because it is a story of leaving the land. Think how many journals we have from those who stayed, and how few from the half who quit the homestead or returned to the East. Those whose lives did not fit the western notions of progress and optimism were less likely to tell their stories, or their children were less likely to publish them. Here we seem to have the rare story of someone who was busted, or who simply wasn't cut out for ranching. But you may not agree.

I will make the argument that Nannie was breaking down; a fact that I would guess Mr. Alderson knew, and that must have entered his decision to move to Miles City.

Certainly we can be sympathetic with Nannie. Her background could hardly have been worse as a preparation for homesteading. She had never farmed or worked. Her father died in the Civil War just after she was born. Her mother, a decadent and cold southern belle as Nannie portrays her, remarried when Nannie was four, and Nannie "kept an impression of being underfoot, and not wanted" at the wedding (4). The "kept" is important, for Nannie's continued resentment at her abandonment runs throughout the book. Sure enough, after the honeymoon her mother does not send for her child. Nannie visits her mother at her new home five miles away, and then is sent back to live with her grandmother. In the following pages, Nannie makes clear that she could never please her mother; she also dwells on this in a way that indicates it still rankles. Nannie displays, apparently, two standard consequences of early abandonment: she resents the parent, yet paradoxically cannot outgrow a desire to seek her approval. So her entire life—this is quite evident in the book—she is both rebelling, living a life of her own out West, yet still curiously concerned about what her mother would think and about how to please her.

Given her mother's values, any attempt to homestead in a way that would please her would be a problem. It was. Just for beginners, consider the world of slaves, ease, and grace to which her mother was born and which Nannie was led to expect:

> For a guide to housekeeping in the West I had brought a cook book and housekeeping manual which our dear old pastor at home had given me for a wedding present. This book, written by a Southern gentlewoman for Southern gentlewomen, didn't contain a single cake recipe that called for fewer than six eggs. I now opened it to the section on laundry, and the first sentence that met my eye was as follows: "Before starting to wash it is essential to have a large, light, airy laundry with at least seven tubs." (38)

Nannie was ready to leave the South and her mother's ways; she loved Kansas City and its western freedom, its lack of class and pretense, the possibility of single girls working and yet "being invited to the nicest homes" (8). But Nannie seemed always to swing back and forth between western practicality and her mother's refined ideals. So even though she knew the seven laundry tubs were absurd, she confesses that she wore the most "ridiculous" silk dresses with long trains trailing on the dirt floor of her cabin instead of sending to Miles

City "for a few yards of calico" to "make some plain washable clothes" (42). Later, even after years in the West, she would dress her girls in petticoats that reached the dirt floors, and then wash, and wash, and wash. She claims she was "not very bright" (43) about such things. But given the number of times she wonders what her mother would think of this or that, I think it was not a matter of brains. She was still trying to deserve that lost parent. In 1940, speaking of 1889 when she had been married and homesteading for six years, Nannie was still saying "Mother never understood the conditions of life out here." She wrote her mother proudly of a dance they mounted for the Tongue River ranchers, with leveled outdoor dance floor, lanterns in the trees, and "sweet, new mown hay" in the stables for the men's dormitory (once those folks had ridden to a party, they stayed awhile). Her mother wrote back, "My daughter, I can't understand how you can invite people to your house when you can't make them comfortable" (194).

Her mother's response is no surprise, but why is Nannie at eighty-two still seeking her approval, and remembering the response, and ending Chapter 16 with her mother's stinging reply? Nannie's ability to adapt to the West was severely hampered by her continuing need to please her mother.

There is considerable evidence in the book that the deteriorating economics and the daily strains of ranch life were taking a toll on Nannie. She is unusually harsh on herself about impatience and fatigue with the children, as if she had not been a good mother. Given their support of her later, I tend not to believe her charges against herself, but her illusion, at least, that she could not give the children enough time or energy must have hurt her. As the strain of life increased, especially after the winter of '87, she says her "outlook on life was affected." She became more withdrawn and stoic, keeping her feelings to herself. Throughout the book, her isolation from other women seems a burden and eloquent testimony to the difficulty of her role; she is also, however, quite critical of most women she meets, and a case can be made that to some extent she isolated herself.

In the last fifty pages, before the move to Miles City where the story ends with Mr. Alderson's sudden death, Nannie offers a tale of growing nervousness and discomfort. One cause was constant toothache, on top of everything else; one effect was fear of snakes and Indians, a fear partly unjustified by her own admission. Beyond that, all is arguable, but I keep finding, in as well as between her lines, a person creeping toward the edge of breakdown, increasingly unable to cope with daily life. Partly because many westerners consider a breakdown shameful, she may not have been able to admit what happened. Few others in such circumstances have. Indeed, Nannie may have re-written her life exactly as Laura Ingalls Wilder rewrote hers, severely editing and transforming a difficult and complex frontier background into *The Little House on the Prairie*.

Many did not and could not make it, psychologically as well as financially; we have suppressed that story, as Nannie does, bury-ing it under American optimism and frontier myths of ennobling en-durance. But remember where we started this chapter: Nannie's suc-cess or failure on the homestead is not necessarily a measure of her individual "character." Her government had sent her there. The rail-roads had sucked her in. She was part of a movement with its own history and intention. Had she been able to get angry at the move-ment, she might have taken less out on herself. My purpose then, is not to criticize Nannie but to point out how thoroughly the frontier could crush people. Yet often, neither those crushed nor our histo-ries hold to account the systems creating this pain: in this case, the government, the railroads, laissez-faire capitalism, and the Aldersons' own high hopes.

Chapter 18 is the beginning of the end for Nannie. She begins by giving thanks for her good health during those years, then confesses to headaches, "everlasting trouble" with her teeth, and "I had suf-fered from neuralgia all my life." Within a few pages, she tells us (this is 1889 and after): "I was haunted by a demon of fear." She does not speak of well-grounded fears, but of growing illusions, especially when left alone. "But now I was nervous about one thing or another all the time" (211). After six years in the West she was not adjusting; she was going the other way.

By Chapter 20 this theme has come to dominate the book: ". . . the years I spent on Muddy I was afraid most of the time." The tone has become quite serious and personal: "overworked . . . worn out . . .

constant, nagging misery with my teeth. . . . For five or six years, after my children started to come, I had every kind of wretchedness that teeth are heir to." Then comes an extraordinary passage:

> In time I came to have an obsession of unattractiveness because of them [teeth], so much so that I wouldn't even kiss the children. Mr. Alderson thought I was undemonstrative. He did not understand the real reason. (238)

He did not understand, apparently, because he was not told. There's a lot going on here, even if this is a coauthored reminiscence. If she wouldn't kiss the children because of unattractiveness, I certainly question whether she would kiss her husband. And she would not tell Mr. Alderson the reason, even though it was simply her teeth, and she could watch him drawing the wrong conclusions. Even in a nineteenth-century marriage, this seems an extreme of reticence and loneliness.

At about thirty years old, having borne four children, Nannie suffered increasing headaches, pain, fear, and isolation. "Indeed I was almost an Indian when it came to concealing my feelings," she says, and then: "I found I was taking dislikes to people." Who, for instance? Next sentence: "Mr. Alderson's boundless hospitality often rubbed me the wrong way" (242). Next page: "I would keep thinking of the same things over and over, until they nearly drove me crazy." All the ranch hands knew Mrs. Alderson could not be left alone. The pace keeps quickening: After the murder of neighbor Bob Ferguson "I was worse than ever. I was terrified" (247). One night Mr. Alderson didn't come home for dinner. "I couldn't go to bed. I couldn't even sit down. I was more nervous than I have ever been before or since" (248). Finally, at the age of thirty-three, "The whole thing became a nightmare which never left me until we decided, in the fall of 1893, to give up our ranch and move to Miles City. How rejoiced I was at this decision" (249).

Nannie was not making it; every tendency was toward a worsening crisis, not toward adjustment; surely Mr. Alderson could see the pattern, and surely that is one of the many reasons he gave up the ranch. This is not just a story of hard times in the beef industry; this is a story of coming apart on the ranch. Nannie might have been a lot better off getting angry, angry at her mother, at the hype of the beef boom that had brought her out, at her own ignorance, at Mr. Alderson, at the absurd expectations that she should prosper in this environment. Later she was aware of systems, and traced her sons' struggles on ranches to economic conditions, not to their characters. In her own case during those first years, however, she turned mainly inward in an unfortunate way. How many, I wonder, found the harsh life, the remote coulees, the absence of companionship and society completely intolerable. And yet we have so few stories of being driven off the land, and Nannie bravely tries to pretend that hers, also, is a tale of pioneer success.

Nannie and the West

As well as documenting the expected—loneliness, hard work, broad-mindedness, cowboy chivalry, cowboy racism and cruelty, trust, and generosity among strangers—Nannie's book presents a few surprising glimpses of the pioneer West.

Her own occasional embarrassment at being western versus eastern, her sense of cultural inferiority, was not just a matter of her relation to her mother. She quite vividly recalls how widespread this sense of inferiority was:

> I was struck by the number of people who thought it necessary to apologize for being in the West. With the first breath they would explain that they were, of course, out here for their health, and with the next they would tell you all about *who* they were, and how rich and important and aristocratic their connections were back East. (109)

Apparently the classless and democratic West, which exists to this day in Montana, is an invention of those who stayed. It did not arrive from the East. The absence of status and the consequent emphasis on self-reliance produced the same effect then as now. Montana children are often like city kids, "street-wise" in the sense that they are realistic, independent, not looking for others to take care of them. A visitor to Nannie observed the same phenomenon, but he speaks here of upper-class "city" children who have been protected, that is, who are from eastern money. "He said: 'You know, western children are more self-reliant and smarter than city children. They can look after themselves earlier, and they know so many things about life that city children don't learn until later—and then learn the hard way'" (223).

This is one way in which Montana still seems more "frontier" than "rural": it has a resourceful, energetic population, many of whom came through "the school of hard knocks." In some ways, many Montana children grow up in an environment more like the lower East Side of New York than the South. But what circumstances can give, circumstances can take away: the advent of towns, a middle class, television, shopping malls, and every other part of contemporary America is bound to affect us. If we admire self-reliant qualities, we have to find ways to embed them in our culture even when our daughters need not chop the ice in the dark before dawn, at fifteen below and blowing, to let the cattle drink.

One quite surprising and interesting remark in Nannie's book suggests that something like humility is at the center of Montana culture, in spite of frontier traditions of rugged individualism and "where there's a will there's a way." The passage (190) is too long and complex to quote here, but in it Nannie describes the two people, Mrs. Rowland and Little Wolf, who most impressed her because they had one impressive trait in common; a "quiet resignation to 'the inevitableness of things.'" It first seems she might envy them because their attitude is the opposite of frontier willfulness. But she then goes on to say their attitude helped her "'keep my chin up' when things were hard." Then she apparently recognizes that believing life to be a bad lot with nothing to be done about it is heresy on the American frontier, and she fudges: "I don't want to be misunderstood; I wouldn't have exchanged my lot for that of any other woman on earth. But, perhaps just because the rewards were great, the going at times was proportionately rough."

Now "a quiet resignation to the inevitableness of things" could hardly be further from popular notions of what it is to be western. It sounds more like Arab or Indian fatalism. It's un-American. But as we will be seeing toward the end of this book, something like humility, realism, and endurance are at the core of the Montana experience, and Nannie seems to voice this truth, even though she's a little embarrassed and vague about its implications. John Wesley Powell warned, just before Nannie came out (no one was listening), that areas west of the 100th meridian receiving less than twenty (or in Nannie's case, ten) inches of moisture a year had better look out: not everything was possible in that cold, dry climate. Especially not everything being promised by the "Garden of the West" promoters. Nannie, and many others, found out the hard way. The result was more quiet resignation to the will of things, more submission to earth and weather, than the movies have cared to record. So I find Nannie's remark early evidence of truths that are only now beginning to be recognized.

As a woman's book, presenting a woman's West, Nannie's account is both valuable and misleading. She gives a vivid picture of the burden of children, of washing and cooking in such situations, and, poignantly, of being excluded from the outdoors action down by the corral, where she felt the most interesting part of ranch work took place. She offers the classic opinion, voiced by T. R. Roosevelt, that Montana in 1884 was great for men and horses, but hell on cattle and women (221).

In using her book as a document, however, we must recognize that she was not well suited to ranch work. A number of older women have told me they are amazed at all the help Nannie got in the kitchen from the cowboys, and they are appalled that the men had to run a ranch without ever leaving her alone. She seemed willing to play the helpless female. Unlike many female pioneers, she had no farm or work experience at all and was used to being waited on. Many women find her account maddening exactly because it plays to sexist expectations of women as a kind of fifth wheel on the frontier, when in fact many women were more useful, more physical, and happier in their work than Nannie. Compared with Elinore Stewart of the memoirs and of the movie *Heartland*, Nannie is something of a belle. But then, Elinore was a widow cooking for a railroad crew before she came to Wyoming.

Recent research indicates that ranching women were indeed quite free and "western." In turn-of-the-century Colorado, for instance, there was "gender crossing" in ranch roles, the children were more free than eastern children of stereotypes, the literary societies—all male in the East—were mixed, Grange and Farmers Alliances had strong women, and the countryside supported suffrage for women (Jameson). In Teresa Jordan's recent book, *Cowgirls*, one gets a fine picture of western women who were and are integrated into a supposed "man's world." On the other hand, wealthy mining camps often preserved sex roles, at least for the rich. In Virginia City, Montana, in 1870, 95 of the 103 women were "keeping house" and 76 had children (West).

The place of women on the frontier is now receiving a good deal of attention. One conclusion is that the West was a working-class frontier, and those with working-class expectations could handle it best. The desperate accounts of mining camps are often from genteel women; similarly, genteel women were more likely to have been "dragged" west, resenting it, while the poor looked forward to opportunity. Scholar Norma Milton tells a quite funny story of a female journalist sent by the British Women's Press Club to the Canadian plains for six months in 1911, to check out the conditions of domestic servants by working as one. She was fired or left, job after job; the hours (on a Saskatchewan farm, 4:30 a.m. to 8 p.m., cooking, washing, canning, one hour off, no room of her own), the toil, the isolation were too much. Yet girls without her opportunities in Britain were flocking to the plains, and indeed the journalist recommended it—for lower classes. Certainly the frontier, past and present, seems to have offered to those ready for work a rare equality of the sexes and a remarkable number of strong, independent women. At meetings of the Northern Plains Resource Council, a group of concerned Montana ranchers, one sees a tradition of strong women taking prominent roles.

One other consideration may put Nannie's story in a different light. It is easy to look down on her willingness to play the belle, but Melody Graulich's excellent work on violence against women on the frontier makes it clear that while many frontier women found freedom in the West, many others were servants and victims of tyrants, often drunk and failed tyrants, in remote coulees, and that these women had no recourse in public opinion or law. With severe mistreatment of indentured women as an alternative, with no vote and no property in one's own name, it is easy to imagine a woman gladly mounting the pedestal. What a relief it might have been to find your husband was a gentleman; how grateful you might have been; how much you might wish to remain an ideal of womanhood. One option for the unempowered is to seek to please.

So here is one report from the mythic West. In Nannie's ten years of ranching the buffalo disappeared, the Indians starved, the railroad and the barbed wire came, and the market crashed. The winter of '86–87 blew the pieces into corners, where many lodged to become founding families of Montana. Her old West was wild and free, but much of the wildness was in the market, and the free were often alone. It was a beginning, for Montana, that finally rewarded not European dreams of open space where "a poor man can grow rich," but endurance. And endurance is still our most dependable crop. Endurance, and pride.

Part II
The Hearts of My People

"I have not told you half that happened when I was young. . . . I can think back and tell you much more of war and horse stealing. But when the buffalo went away the hearts of my people fell to the ground, and they could not lift them up again."

—Chief Plenty-coups

5
Linderman and Plenty-coups

WE WILL APPROACH THIS SECTION QUITE DIFFERENTLY. INSTEAD of proceeding book by book, we will talk generally about Native American culture, about white knowledge or ignorance of it, and about Native American literature. Even in contemporary Indian literature, the tribal contexts and general qualities of Native American works can be as important as the distinguishing characteristics of individual artists.

Chapter 5 will consider Frank Linderman and his relation to the Crow chief, Plenty-coups, and open the question of white and Indian knowledge of the old days. Chapter 6 will look at the remarkable career of D'Arcy McNickle, and see how the plots of Native American novels differ from white plots. In Chapter 7, "Chickadee Jive," we will take a brief look at the unusual handling of nature in Native American novels. Finally we will consider the important, contemporary Blackfeet novels of James Welch: *Winter in the Blood*, *The Death of Jim Loney*, *Fools Crow* (Chapter 8). This will bring us to the literature of our time, which will be the subject of Part III of this book.

Linderman

Remarkable events brought Frank Linderman to Plenty-coups's cabin in 1929, and equally remarkable events had prepared Chief Plenty-coups to receive him. The cabin stands to this day on the cottonwood flat beside Arrow Creek, west of Pryor, the stately trees wide-spaced and tall as they were when Plenty-coups and Linderman met day after day beneath them. Across the creek the bluffs rise sharply to a bare skyline where horses graze and coyotes keep watch in the evening.

The dark old log cabin is bequeathed to the tribe as Plenty-coups wished. Plenty-coups had visited George Washington's Mount Vernon and wanted, like Washington, to leave his people something: the house, the tradition, the book. All his life he had chosen, with regret and tragic awareness, cooperation with the whites. As a young man in the 1870s he had helped shape and execute the Crow policy of scouting for Custer and the U.S. Army; he had thereby helped secure the beautiful Crow reservation on ancestral lands. As an older man, he had preached to his tribe the necessity of white education, and had led the delegation to Washington, D.C., after 1912, in a seven-year fight against Senator Thomas Walsh's bill to sell half the reservation to homesteaders.

Robert Yellowtail was a member of that delegation, and in the excellent film *Contrary Warriors* he recalls how, the night before their crucial meeting with Congress, the Crow men attempted to perform the right ceremonies. They needed buffalo chips, no longer available in their homeland, much less in their hotel. Then someone remembered there was a zoo in Washington. They went to the zoo that night and the caretaker gave them six or seven pounds of dried buffalo chips. They brought the chips back to the room, put live coals to them to make smoke, sang songs, and prayed for victory the following day. They won. Senator Walsh withdrew his bill.

Plenty-coups had seen much. Now, in 1929, at over eighty, he decided to trust the white man's written word. He knew of no other way to preserve his tradition. The young ones were straying and forgetting so fast; the old culture was being lost. He seemed to have only two choices: lose the tradition, or tell the tales to the white man.

Not to any white man. Frank Bird Linderman had also been preparing most of his life for this meeting beneath the cottonwoods. At least since he was a boy in Ohio:

> I had found a large map of the western states and territories, and that night, for the hundredth time, I spread it upon the floor in my own room to pore over it as I always had, flat on my belly. Long before this I had decided where I wished to go, but now that my dream was coming true I needed to be sure I had made no mistake in my choosing. I had to have unspoiled wilderness, because I secretly intended to become a trapper. I remember that I felt glad when the Flathead Lake country in northwestern Montana Territory seemed yet to be farthest removed

from contaminating civilization. I'd go straight as I could to Flathead Lake.

The year was 1885 and the boy was sixteen years old. That night his parents had given reluctant permission for him to leave his Ohio home and have his "fling" in the West. "And how I feared that the West of my dreams would fade before I could reach it!"

It very nearly had. The young boy in Ohio had no idea that one year before, the hearts of Plenty-coups's people had fallen to the ground, and they could not lift them up again. The primitivist paradise of his dreams had just seen the barbed wire and railroad arrive, the buffalo disappear, and the Indians gather on reservations. When Montana became a state in 1889, Linderman agreed with his trapping friend who said, "Now she's gone to hell."

Frank Linderman was one of those men who came from the East in the 1870s and 1880s to see the West before it was gone. And though some, such as Frederic Remington and George Bird Grinnell, came and went, remaining mainly outsiders, some stayed. Three in particular, all in Montana, were unique and important observers: Charlie Russell, James Willard Schultz, and Frank Linderman. All three were important because they saw, they cared for, and they reported the West "before it was gone." The ties of these white men to the Indian life were slim in some ways; Schultz really lived with the Blackfeet only two summers, taking notes, and he returned East in the winter; his title, *My Life as an Indian*, is misleading. Yet all three had what we might call purity of heart. The Indians apparently sensed this and welcomed them, and spoke to them in ways that rendered ethnological credentials irrelevent. The result was a wealth of information, stories, drawings, and paintings of Indian life, a life all three men genuinely loved, a life that would otherwise be very nearly lost.

These romantic observers of the past knew and supported each other. Grinnell, as editor of *Forest and Stream*, encouraged Schultz, printed him, and introduced his work. Grinnell did his own collecting and writing among the Blackfeet and Cheyenne. Linderman's first book, *Indian Why Stories*, was dedicated to Russell and Grinnell and illustrated by Russell, and Linderman's *Recollections of Charley Russell* was edited by the next generation's leader, H. G. Merriam of Missoula, after Linderman's death.

The boy of sixteen bought his one-way, $67.50 ticket to Missoula and never looked back. For seven years he did indeed trap in his beloved wilderness near Flathead Lake, and as so often happens in western history, those few years became a Golden Age in his life by which all else was measured. He married, then became an assayer, then newspaperman, then state legislator. In 1905 he moved to Helena and was Assistant Secretary of State. But in his heart Linderman must have believed that he, like the territory, was going to hell in that direction and after making some money selling insurance he moved, in 1917, to Goose Bay on Flathead lake, to write. He was forty-eight years old with a family, and he was not rich. The move was a conscious and risky rejection of business and politics in favor of writing.

Between 1915 and his death in 1938 Linderman published—among other books, articles, and poems—five volumes of traditional Indian tales, two trapper novels (*Lige Mounts* and *Beyond Law*), and two Indian autobiographies. Maxwell Perkins, editor of Hemingway and many others, said, "It would be hard to write a better story than *Lige Mounts*."

Frank Linderman faithfully recorded the tales and customs of the Indians; he was their friend, and in politics he did all he could to help, especially in establishing the Rocky Boy reservation when the Cree were starving. Yet his name is hardly recognized outside of Montana.

In what we now call Native American Studies, which is sympathetic and accurate knowledge of Native Americans (overlapping, sometimes in harmony, sometimes in discord, with academic anthropology and ethnology), there was a seminal period from about 1880 to 1930. During that time, from the Indians' losing the battle for the West until the deaths of the last men and women who had known a pre-white West, much crucial work was done. Linderman was one of the last of a whole host of whites (including Schultz, Russell, and Grinnell) who gathered evidence and testimony during that time when direct knowledge of the old ways was still possible. This was especially important because not only time but reservation life, loss of self-esteem, and Christianity were being interposed between the Indians and their old ways. Even memory itself can change under such pressures, so the record was in every danger of being lost.

From about 1930 to 1965, knowledge of Indians in both popular and academic circles declined and often disappeared. Since about 1965, a boom in Native American Studies has produced fresh scholarship and, among Indians, fresh politics. Yet even now, when coverage of issues such as Navajo-Hopi disputes is expected, the general public has little awareness of the basic issues: threats of dereservation, how the Indians feel about it, what the Dawes Act and allotments mean and how they have been used, water rights, mineral rights. And in scholarship, much of the recent activity is discovering just how good the old work was and, now, how irreplaceable.

For instance, the Native American poetry translations by Natalie Curtis and others at the turn of the century were excellent, and were printed with interlinear translations of texts, comments by Indian informants, and musical notations. By comparison, the new "Indian Poetry" texts printed in the early 1970s had sloppy translations, no commentary, and no background information. We now realize that we can hardly do better than to reprint Curtis's 1907 book, informed as it was by direct knowledge, accurate fieldwork, and living Indian commentary. For Indians, as well as for whites, such volumes offer a precious glimpse into the past.

It is not always easy for a tribe, much less a white anthropologist, to find the past. The editorial board of *The Last Best Place* sought the best versions of traditional Native American stories. We began with a desire to avoid, whenever possible, white ethnologists and translators, since they are often suspect to the Indians. In going directly to tribal sources, however, we found that contemporary versions of stories offered by the tribes often seemed more "white," more Europeanized and Christianized, than turn-of-the-century versions recorded by white anthropologists.

In the past fifteen years, many tribes have begun to gather their stories more systematically, but the effort has just begun and is often aimed at educating the children, so that only children's books are produced. In elementary texts, the stories are usually purged of grosser elements. Even when an adult tribal member sets out to tell the old stories, the result sometimes seems less authentic than the old versions by ethnologists.

Now this is tricky business: we necessarily compare the story in front of us to some imagined standard of "authenticity" which may be inaccurate; we sometimes wind up endorsing a version passed on by whites and rejecting a tribal version; and certainly we must remember that the tribe "owns" its tradition and has the right to shape and modify and control it. But if the issue is accuracy to, say, an 1880 version of a story, then the tribal members and the whites may find themselves in the same boat, depending mainly on turn-of-the-century white writings that froze in print the Indian perceptions of that day. That is why people like Linderman are so important now. Though their work will necessarily contain some misperceptions, it may also preserve aspects of the oral tradition that have been lost to tribal memory.

Frank Linderman, then, is one of a number of men and women who from 1880 to 1930 provided an invaluable service in preserving the Native American past. And while he and his good friend Charlie Russell, and James Schultz, were in ways thoroughly European romantics, they were also excellent observers who tried to see the world through Indian eyes. Russell used to be regarded as a romancer, portrayer of the Wild West of movies and pulp fiction. Now, however, we have realized that his work is irreplaceable, and John Ewers, ethnographer of the Blackfeet, has a Russell print hanging behind his desk at the Smithsonian. Ewers says Russell's version of Blackfeet hunters returning home with meat may be the most accurate picture we have of a Blackfeet camp in the days of the buffalo. Schultz's unique views of traditional life, gained through a Blackfeet wife and his association with trader Joe Kipp from 1879 to 1884, have long been appreciated. (A biography of Schultz was published in 1986.) Recently Linderman's *Plenty-coups* (originally titled *American*) and *Pretty-shield* (originally *Red Mother*) have been brought back into print. Frederick van de Water's assessment of *Plenty-coups* in a 1931 letter to Linderman was prophetic: ". . . not only a great book . . . one of those volumes . . . too good for the present, that is due to be 'discovered' by someone long after you and I are dead."

Linderman was apparently a man of great integrity, and this integrity had several effects. It probably weaned him from politics, possibly from insurance, and certainly put him in the unusual position of being trusted by Indians: ". . . if my father came back and stood on one hill and I saw Frank Linderman on another hill I would not go to my father, I would go to Frank Linderman. You know I do not lie. This is the Truth" (Day Child). As a direct result of their trust in him from his first meeting with the Flathead Red Horn until his death, Indians came to Linderman for help, helped him, and finally offered to him and to him alone their life stories. It was not considered wise or good for a Crow or other plains tribesmen to speak of the dead, which Plenty-coups would have to do to recall the old days, nor did Indians often trust white men to tell their story with a straight tongue. But Plenty-coups sent for Linderman, who was renowned by 1930 as a sign talker and Indian sympathizer, and said to him:

> You are my friend, Sign-talker. I know your heart is good. I will tell you what you wish to know, and you may write it down. (4)

And when they had finished:

> I am glad I have told you these things, Sign-talker. You have felt my heart, and I have felt yours. I know you will tell only what I have said, that your writing will be straight like your tongue, and I sign your paper with my thumb, so that your people and mine will know I told you the things you have written down. (309)

Plenty-coups would speak only to a trusted friend, not to an anthropologist.

Linderman had a clarity of style in all his writings, and a fine and exact humility. His was a keen mind keenly aware of the limits of knowledge. After a lifetime of association with Indians, he wrote in the introduction to *Plenty-coups*:

> I am convinced that no white man has ever thoroughly known the Indian, and such a work as this must suffer because of the widely different views of life held by the two races, red and white. I have studied

85

the Indian for more than forty years, not coldly, but with sympathy; yet even now I do not feel that I know much about him. He has told me many times that I *do* know him—that I have "felt his heart," but whether this is so I am not certain. (vii)

His humility and integrity were important to his actions as well as to his words. Linderman not only got us *to* Plenty-coups; he then got *out* of the way. That is a remarkable achievement, and the greatest justification of Plenty-coups's trust in him. Consider Linderman's position in 1929–30. He was not a paid scholar or researcher or anthropologist, nor was he seeking such a position. He was very demoralized by the low sale of his writings for fifteen years; he had written one novel in 1922, would soon write another, and was well aware that novels, especially pulp novels, were the way to make money. Here was tremendous material dumped in his lap. He had tried running the Kalispell Hotel for two years and now was poor again at Goose Bay. Yet he never considered a selfish use of the Plenty-coups story; he carried Plenty-coups's message, and to a remarkable extent he stayed out of the book. His few appearances are graceful, sympathetic, and knowledgeable.

Of those romantic observers who came to see the West before it was gone, Linderman was one of the most astute, reliable, and helpful. He said in a letter of 1922: "It is hard for some of my friends to believe that I feel it a duty to, in some way, preserve the Old West, especially Montana, in printer's ink, and if I can accomplish a small part of that duty I shall die contented." I hope he realized, before he died in 1938, that he had done more than a small part of his duty. His service to whites and Indians will be remembered.

Plenty-coups

The old Crow Chief who sat beneath the cottonwoods on Arrow Creek had been a young man when all the momentous changes of the 1870s and '80s took place. He remembered raids on neighboring tribes before the whites came, and fighting against the Cheyenne and Sioux with General Custer. Most of all he remembered the disappearance of the buffalo. He "refused to speak of his life after the passing of the buffalo" ("You saw what happened to us when the buffalo went away"), and the tale he told of the old days is still amazing, at least to these white ears.

The tale is amazing partly because the plains Indians were so tough. At daybreak in January, the Moon of the Popping Trees, children would strip and jump into the ice-choked river to see who could retrieve the most peeled sticks. They seemed to have been oblivious to pain:

> "The scar on my chin?" He laughed, his deep chest giving power to his merriment. "Plain-bull was with me when I got it, and I was with him when his head was split open. . . . We were packing in buffalo meat on a horse not yet broken . . . [the horse] let me have both hind feet. They broke my jaw, so that after spitting out most of my teeth on the snow, I was obliged to tie it together to hold it up where it belonged. It would not stay any place and kept falling down. I had to drink soup for more than a moon, but excepting that scar and a place on my side where a bullet burned me, I have no marks on my body that I did not make myself. I have been lucky. My medicine is very strong." (115)

Oblivious, too, to death:

> Big-nose intended to count a double coup and jumped from his running horse beside the Pecunie to take his gun. As he sprang toward him the fellow fired, and Big Nose fell with his own thigh broken.
> They faced each other, each with a broken thigh, neither able to stand, Big Nose wholly unarmed because he had thrown away his gun when he jumped from his horse so that he might count a fair coup. I saw the Pecunie raise his knife. . . . (220)

And amazing because this toughness is mixed with such delicacy:

> All my life I have tried to learn as the Chickadee learns, by listening,— profiting by the mistakes of others, that I might help my people. (307)

Behind this strange mixture of blood and chickadees is a single tone, like a musical theme that keeps returning: love of the old ways. Plenty-coups would have been perfectly happy to continue without the benefits of European progress.

We may hear this with several reactions. First, Plenty-coups's opinion is nearly universal in the tales of Indians, so we must respect their love of the old days. We cannot simply talk of poverty, hunger, and cold and thus assuage our guilt. They say they were doing fine without us.

But on the other hand, we should not use their preference for the old days to imagine a primitivist paradise—stable, timeless, "natural" —before we came. As I mentioned in Chapter 1, the life that Plenty-coups loved had only evolved in the previous hundred years and was itself partly a product of white conquest and pressure.

The horse had been brought by the Spanish to Mexico and had escaped and multiplied northward into the plains by 1750. By then, English colonies on the East Coast were pushing tribes West with a domino effect, so that some Mississippi woodland tribes were bumped farther and farther out on the plains. Using the horses they found there, they soon developed a culture that even at the time of Lewis and Clark was evolving away from agriculture and villages and toward a more nomadic, buffalo-running society.

In addition, the smallpox brought by the whites to both coasts had been sweeping in waves of epidemics from tribe to tribe for hundreds of years, and we will never know what the original population of this country was. What we do know, as Lewis and Clark's journals attest, is that the West was not a stable paradise. The buffalo and tribal warfare culture which Plenty-coups knew and loved may well have suited his needs, but several of its ingredients—the horse, the gun, the relocation on the plains—were fairly recent. The disappearance of the buffalo was the nail in the coffin of a way of life already under tremendous stress, for a culture that already had adapted to many changes forced by white pressure from the East. The way of life continues to change. The culture survives.

Some have surmised that the tribal warfare itself, rather than being traditional, was the result of a culture under stress. Certainly the raids and counter-raids, the stealing of wives and children, the vicious cycles of revenge, seem to have been hard on the tribe no matter how much fun and honor the young warriors might have found in it. A contemporary feminist might say this was a testosterone culture run wild; that male hormones, instead of serving tribal defense and security, or conquest of new territory, had produced a self-defeating game of tragic proportions. A feminist might add that nuclear arsenals represent the same instincts hammered into technological form, stored, and likely to be equally self-destructive. Aggression does not always defend tribal interests.

It is fascinating that precisely this view seems to have been held by the Crow woman, Pretty-shield, contemporary of Plenty-coups, who in 1931 gave Linderman her story. Hers is one of the very few reports we have from a woman of the buffalo culture days. Chapter 14 is remarkable:

> When our enemies were not bothering *us*, our warriors were bothering *them*, so there was always fighting going on somewhere. We women sometimes tried to keep our men from going to war, but this was like talking to winter winds; and of course there was always some woman, sometimes many women, mourning for men who had been killed in war. These women had to be taken care of. Somebody had to kill meat for them. Their fathers or uncles or brothers did this until the women married again, which they did not always do, so that war made more work for everybody. . . . We women did not like war, and yet we could not help it, because our men loved war. . . . And then there were the orphans that war made. They had to be cared for by somebody. You see that when we women lost our men, we lost our own, and our children's, living. I am glad that war has gone forever. It was no good—*no good*!

Linderman adds, "Here her signs were most emphatic."

Amidst these changing circumstances, and in a culture that may have been temporarily destabilized, Plenty-coups and his people also knew a social stability that we can hardly imagine. Religion and politics, it seems, were so unquestioned that they hardly existed as concepts (if a concept implies an awareness of alternatives). Many have noted that Indians never struck their children, and many Indians were

shocked at the British tradition of "Spare the rod and spoil the child."
For whatever reason, Plenty-coups looked back on a childhood of
respect for authority that we Europeans might envy:

> This talking between our mothers, firing us with determination to dis-
> tinguish ourselves, made us wish we were men. It was always going on
> —this talking among our elders, both men and women—and we were
> ever listening. On the march, in the village, everywhere, there was
> praise in our ears for skill and daring. Our mothers talked before us of
> the deeds of other women's sons, and warriors told stories of the brav-
> ery and fortitude of other warriors until a listening boy would gladly
> die to have his name spoken by the chiefs in council. . . . My people
> were wise. . . . They never neglected the young or failed to keep be-
> fore them deeds done by illustrious men of the tribe. Our teachers were
> willing and thorough. They were our grandfathers, fathers, or uncles.
> All were quick to praise excellence without speaking a word that might
> break the spirit of a boy who might be less capable than others. The boy
> who failed at any lesson got only more lessons, more care, until he was
> as far as he could go. (8–9)

Was it like living within a high school team, surrounded by perfect
coaches? Of course that comparison seems belittling, since we are
taught that school teams are not the most important things in life. It
is also misleading because power and authority were so fluid among
adults of the tribe; there were societies with various functions, and
open democratic councils, and respected elders but no chief of state.
Like Linderman, we must conclude that we simply cannot know this
degree of respect for such a distributed yet powerful authority. And
then there is Pretty-shield's demurral.

Reading Plenty-coups, our heads spin from bloody tales, talks with
chickadees, and scenes so romantic they are straight out of James
Fenimore Cooper: "So we showed off to each other and had a great
time. I cannot tell you how beautiful the enemy looked, dressed in
bright colors and wearing wonderful war-bonnets of eagle feathers
that waved in the wind" (136).

Finally we are left with an old man who has lost almost everything. When young, he had gone on a vision quest to the top of Crazy
Mountain, across the ravine from what would very soon be the ranch

of Spike Van Cleve, who went to Harvard and wrote *A Day Late and a Dollar Short*. What could that world, coming so quickly, have to do with the young Crow warrior, fasting for two days on the bare summit? Finally an old man spirit-guide appeared on that summit and took Plenty-coups to the grove of cottonwoods "where we are sitting now," he said to Frank Linderman.

"Ho," said Plenty-coups, making the sign for "finished." "And here I am, an old man, sitting under this tree just where that old man sat seventy years ago when this was a different world." (75)

6
McNickle: Homing In

D'ARCY MCNICKLE WAS A MIXED-BLOOD SALISH INDIAN FROM ST. Ignatius on the Flathead reservation. He was born about 1904 and was abducted by whites, as were several of the characters in his novels, and taken to an Indian school in Chemewa, Oregon. He later attended the University of Montana in Missoula and Oxford University in England. He became an anthropologist and administrator. He lived for a time in New York, worked in the Bureau of Indian Affairs (BIA), and taught at the University of Saskatchewan. By the time of his death in 1977, McNickle had helped to found the Newberry Library in Chicago (foremost Native American library in the country) and the National Congress of American Indians. He had written four scholarly books, a biography of LaFarge, and three novels. One is for children; the other two are not, and are set in his homeland between St. Ignatius and Flathead Lake, between the summit of McDonald Peak and the Flathead River. Those few miles where McNickle had grown up confine the action of the books, but into those pages he poured his knowledge of a wide, wide world, Indian and white. He knew the old world of Plenty-coups through the stories of the elders, and he knew also the modern world of European power and law.

Both of his novels were first drafted in the thirties; *The Surrounded* was published right away, in 1936; *Wind from an Enemy Sky* was left in manuscript, and printed from his papers in 1978 after his death. In one chapter of *Wind*, the rich white liberal, Adam Pell, lunches with a U.S. Supreme Court justice at the Harvard Club in Boston. In the following chapter, old Two Sleeps, a Salish Indian, climbs up into the Mission Mountains for a vision quest, as worried for the future of his tribe as Adam Pell was for the future of the Constitution. Both chapters are handled perfectly. The conversation at the Harvard Club is vivid and exact; then the Mission Mountains and tribal problems unfold in the mind of Two Sleeps. No other author in the history of American letters could have written those two chapters back to back, getting the dialogue right; no other American author has had that kind of experience in both worlds and, therefore, that authority.

McNickle's two novels, in their handling of plot and in their general approach to Indian problems, prefigure the Native American novels which would follow. He was a seminal author, and in this chapter I would like to consider how his work raises crucial issues about Native American versus white literature and life, issues that take us through the major novels of the "Native American Renaissance" from the thirties right down to the present day.

We have already discussed some aspects of Native American versus European expectations in the nineteenth century. Europeans coming West were often fleeing civilization; as "primitivists" they looked at "nature" as the opposite of civilization, and therefore expected Indians to be uncivilized; Garcia's and Boone's conceptions of the "wild life" out West were specifically white, not Indian. Those observations are the tip of an iceberg. One of the most interesting stories of the American West, hardly told, is that here, European individualism came face to face with Third World tribalism. The resulting conflicts and misunderstandings continue to this day. Indian novels offer a unique perspective on this huge collision of cultures and values.

Homing

American whites keep leaving home: *Moby Dick, Portrait of a Lady, Huckleberry Finn, Sister Carrie, The Great Gatsby*—a considerable number of American "classics" tell of leaving home to find one's fate farther and farther away. To be sure, Ahab or Gatsby might have been better off staying put, and their narrators might finally be retreating homeward, but the story we tell our children is of Huck Finn lighting out for the territories. A wealth of white tradition lies behind these plots, beginning with four centuries of colonial expansion. The traditional European novel of a young man's personal growth became in America especially the story of a young man or woman leaving home for better opportunities in a newer land. In *Letters from an American Farmer*

(1782), Crèvecoeur defined Americans as a people who leave the old to take the new:

> *He* is an American, who, leaving behind all his ancient prejudices and manners, takes new ones from the mode of life he has embraced, the new government he obeys, and the new rank he holds.

The home we leave, to Crèvecoeur, is not only a place; it is a past, an "ancien regime," a set of values and parents, a way of government and life before the revolution.

Such "leaving" plots embody quite clearly the basic premise of success in our mobile society. The *individual* advances, sometimes at all cost, with little or no regard for family, society, past, or place. The individual is the ultimate reality; hence individual consciousness is the medium of knowledge, and "freedom," our primary value, is a matter of distance between one's self and the smoke from another's chimney. Isolation is the poison in this world of movement, and romantic love seems to be its primary antidote. Movement, isolation, change, personal and forbidden knowledge, fresh beginnings; these are the ingredients of the American Adam, the man who would start from scratch. *His* is the story we tell and always in our ears is Huck Finn's strange derision: "I been there before."

In marked contrast, most Native American novels are not about going out, diverging, expanding, but about zooming in, converging, contracting. The hero comes home. "Contracting" has negative overtones to us, "expanding" a positive ring. These are the cultural habits we are considering. In Native American novels, coming home, staying put, contracting, even what we might call "regressing" to a place, a past where one has been before, is not only the primary story, it is a primary mode of knowledge and a primary good.

Let us begin with the plots of some prominent Native American novels, and then see how these plots thicken. In McNickle's *The Surrounded* (1936), Archilde comes home from Portland, where he "can always get a job now any time" playing the fiddle in a "show house" (2), to the Salish and Kootenai ("Flathead") reservation. He has made it in the white world, and has come "to see my mother . . . in a few days I'm going again" (7). From the very beginning, however, family ties, cultural ties, ties to place, and growing ties to a decidedly "reservation" (versus assimilated) girl are spun like webs to bind him down. He does not leave and finally is crushed by the white man's law. It seems to be a "tar baby" plot; Archilde takes one lick and then another at his own backward people, and suddenly he is stuck. At first, being assimilated into a white world, he had expected to remain mobile, thinking of "wherever he might be in times to come. Yes, wherever he might be" (5). McNickle's repetition underscores the plot: whites leave, Indians come home.

Although whites would usually find in such a homing-as-failure plot either personal disaster or moral martyrdom, McNickle's point of view toward his home village of St. Ignatius is more complex. His novel does not present Archilde as simply sucked into a depressing situation, although he certainly is; the novel applauds his return to Indian roots. At first Archilde is "on the outside of their problems. He had grown away from them, and even when he succeeded in approaching them in sympathy, he remained an outsider—only a little better than a professor come to study their curious ways of life" (193). He has, in short, the charm of an anthropologist. When he stays, however, to gratify his mother's wish for a traditional feast and to help his Spanish father harvest the wheat, "It was a way of fulfilling the trust placed in him. He was just learning what that meant, that trust" (177). And as he watches his mother dress her grandson for the feast, he begins to appreciate the old ways, and to enter a different time:

> Watching his mother's experienced hands, he could guess how she had lived, what she had thought about in her childhood. A great deal had happened since those hands were young, but in making them work in this way, in the way she had been taught, it was a little bit as if the intervening happenings had never been. He watched the hands move and thought these things. For a moment, almost, he was not an outsider, so close did he feel to those ministering hands. (215–16)

We can hardly wish such beauty to be "outmoded," and although Archilde cannot save his mother or with any convenience apply her old "mode of life" to himself, the point of view of the novel offers profound respect for the past, for family and tradition, and more trou-blingly, asks us to admire Archilde's involvement on the reservation even as it leads to personal doom.

The plot of *The Surrounded* is typical. In McNickle's other novel of contemporary Indians, *Wind from an Enemy Sky*, a young boy on the Salish-Kootenai reservation is abducted by whites to a mission school (as happened to McNickle) and four years later returns, an outsider, to his very traditional grandfather and tribe. The plot hangs on the tribe's attempt to recover from white authorities a lost Feather Boy medicine bundle. In the course of the book, the young boy and the reader gain increasing respect for this futile effort to "bring back our medicine, our power" (18), a perfect example of an activity whites cannot easily appreciate. As in *The Surrounded*, action focuses in concentric circles from the outside world to the few miles between McDonald Peak and the Flathead River, and just as Archilde had recovered his traditional mother, so young Antoine is initiated by his conservative grandfather into the tribe. The traditional Indians, however, once more win the past only to lose the war.

Three other important Indian novels also tell of a wanderer in the white world coming home. In N. Scott Momaday's *House Made of Dawn* (1969), an Indian serviceman comes back to the reservation, drinks and kills, drifts in L.A. and finally returns to the pueblo to give his grandfather a traditional burial and participate in the annual healing race, which his grandfather had once run. In James Welch's *Winter in the Blood* (1974), an Indian who has quit his job in an Oregon hospi-tal returns to the ranch in northern Montana, to a desperate round of drunken bar-hopping that leads, finally, to discovering his grand-father, pulling out of his lethargy, and throwing the traditional tobacco pouch in his grandmother's grave. In Leslie Silko's *Ceremony* (1977), an Indian serviceman returns from Japan to the Laguna tribe in the Southwest, and slowly breaks from a pattern of drinking and mad-ness to participate in a healing ceremony guided by an old medicine man, a ceremony that begins with a quest for cattle and ends with an amended story and rain for the desert land.

In a sixth major Indian novel, Welch's *The Death of Jim Loney* (1979), an Indian on Montana's Highline refuses to leave—despite pressure and opportunity—his hopeless town and native land. As his circle spirals inward to one place, one past, he shrinks back into the darkest corner of all—suicide. In all these books, Indian "homing" is presented as the opposite of competitive individualism, which is white success:

> But Rocky was funny about those things. He was an A— student and all-state in football and track. He had to win; he said he was always going to win. So he listened to his teachers, and he listened to the coach. They were proud of him. They told him, "Nothing can stop you now except one thing: don't let the people at home hold you back." (*Ceremony*, 52)

First let us agree on the obvious: in these six novels, an Indian who has been away or could go away comes home and finally finds his identity by staying. In every case except Loney's, a traditional tribal elder who is treated by the novel with great respect precipitates the resolution of the plot. That elder is a relative—usually parent or grandparent—with whom the central character forms a new personal bond. In every case including Loney's, the ending sought by the character is significantly related to tribal past and place. These "homing" plots all present tribal past as a gravity field stronger than individual will.

In all these Native American novels, tribalism is respected even though it is inseparable from a kind of failure. Under examination, that "homing" to tribe is complex: tribalism is not just an *individual's* past, his "background." Tribe is not just lineage or kinship; home is not just a place. As Kenneth Lincoln observed in *Native American Renaissance*:

> Grounded Indian literature is tribal; its fulcrum is a sense of relatedness. To Indians, tribe means family, not just bloodlines, but extended family, clan, community, ceremonial exchanges with nature, and an animate regard for all creation as sensible and powerful. (8)

These novels suggest that "identity," for a Native American, is not a matter of finding "one's self," but of finding a "self" that is transpersonal. To be separated from that transpersonal time and space is to lose identity. These novels are important not only because they depict Indian individuals coming home while white individuals leave, but also because they suggest—variously and subtly and by degrees—a tribal rather than an individual definition of "being."

The tribal "being" has three components: society, past, and place. The "society" of the tribe is not just company; it is law. Catherine, Archilde's aging mother in *The Surrounded*, makes clear that what they have lost are the customs, rituals, and practices of law that bind people together into more than a population. In the central feast scene, the Indians lament the loss of dances, ceremonies, and practices banned by secular and religious authorities, just as conquered white Americans might lament the loss of courts, due process, and private ownership of land. The tone of the discussion is that under white rule "mere anarchy is loosed upon the world." *Wind from an Enemy Sky* is filled with discussions of white attempts to break Indian law:

> What kind of law is that? Did we have such a law? When a man hurt somebody in camp, we went to that man and asked him what he was going to do about it. If he did nothing, after we gave him a chance, we threw him away. He never came back. But only a mean man would refuse to do something for the family he hurt. That was a good law, and we still have it. We never threw it away. Who is this white man who comes here and tells us what the law is? Did he make the world? Does the sun come up just to look at him? (89)

Just as in American law, these tribal guarantees of rights within the nation are not necessarily extended to foreigners (other tribes). So in *Wind* the young Indian's murder of the white man tending the white dam is met by the chief with a shrug, the casual counterpart of colonial invasion: "The man up there was not one of us. He has people to mourn for him. Let his own people be troubled" (65).

In each of these novels, the character seeks a meaningful relation to a meaningful structure: he becomes a healthy man through accepted social ritual (*Ceremony, House*) and a self-respecting man through deeds traditional and necessary to his people (McNickle, and Welch's *Winter*). Self-realization is not accomplished in these novels by individual acts or by romance; that would be incomprehensible. Henry Jim in *Wind* tries assimilation, which means being a free individual, by farming his own land and living in his own frame house. By white standards he succeeds. He has a rooftop widow's walk overlooking the valley—the government had decided to showcase Henry Jim. But, says Henry Jim:

> "The government man said it would be a good thing. He wanted the Indians to see what it is like to have a nice house like that. In those days I had the foolish thought that a man stands by himself, that his kinsmen are no part of him. I did not go first to my uncles and my brothers and talk it over with them. . . . I didn't notice it at first, but one day I could see that I was alone. . . . Brothers, I was lonesome, sitting in my big house. I wanted to put my tepee up in the yard, so people would come to see me, but my son and his wife said it would be foolish, that people would only laugh. . . . Two days ago I told my son to put up this tepee; it is the old one from my father's time. 'Put up the tepee,' I said, 'the stiff-collars can stay away. I want to die in my own house.'"
>
> Every voice in the circle murmured. Antoine looked up, stealthily scanning each face, and he could feel what was there among them. It shamed them that they had stayed away and had been hard against this old man. It shamed them, and they were in grief. (117–18)

So the first assumption of Native American tribalism is that the individual is completed only in relation to others, that man is a political animal (lives through a relationship to a village-state), and the group which must complete his "being" is organized in some meaningful way. That meaning, not just land, is what has been lost:

> . . . now in old age she looked upon a chaotic world—so many things dead, so many words for which she knew no meaning. . . . How was it that when one day was like another there should be, at the end of many days, a world of confusion and dread and emptiness? (*Surrounded*, 22)

The second component of tribalism is its respect for the past. The tribe, which makes meaning possible, endures through time and appeals to the past for authority. Tribal reality is profoundly conservative; "progress" and "a fresh start" are not *native* to America:

Modeste was silent for a long time. Then he announced that he too . . . had turned back to that world which was there before the new things came. (*Surrounded*, 210)

Most of the western tribes shared a belief in a "distant past":

Back in time immemorial, things were different, the animals could talk to human beings and many magical things still happened. (*Ceremony*, 99)

The elders—Old Betonie in *Ceremony*, the grandfather in *House Made of Dawn*, Catherine in *The Surrounded*, Bull in *Wind from an Enemy Sky*, and Grandfather Yellow Calf, who talks to the deer in Welch's more skeptical *Winter in the Blood*—all are in touch with a tradition tracing from the distant past and all extend this connection to the young protagonists. Only Loney fails to find a connected ancestor, and only Loney fails.

On the other hand, whites, mobile in time as well as space, have left their own past behind. The liberal Indian agent in *Wind*, Rafferty, reflects on Henry Jim's request:

And he asks me to help bring back this old bundle, whatever it is—this old symbol. It's been gone twenty-five or thirty years, but he thinks the people should have it. Nobody in Marietta, Ohio, would make such a request—in Marietta, if it's like towns I know, they're trying to get away from the past. (36)

Most instructive is McNickle's white priest welcoming Indian children to a mission school:

You students, now, you listen to me. I want you to appreciate what we're doing for you. We're taking you out of that filth and ignorance, lice in your heads, all that, the way you lived before you came here. . . . Forget where you came from, what you were before; let all that go out of your minds and listen only to what your teachers tell you. (*Wind*, 106)

There is a scene in the movie *The Killing Fields*, after the Communists have taken over Cambodia, showing Communist education of the young. A child approaches the blackboard, crosses out the drawing of parents and erases the hand holding parent to child. The teacher approves and tells the children that the past is dead, the old ways are gone, and this is Year One. Americans, and Communists in Russia and China (all three are revolutionary societies), have often taken the same approach to education: erase the past and teach new values. In Communism, parents are replaced by the party and state; in America they are replaced by individualism: "free to be you and me."

Quite apart from the tyranny of educational brainwashing is the stupidity of the white demands from an Indian point of view. Indians were understandably startled at the political and religious disagreements among whites, and at their rapid and ill-considered change of all within their grasp. Whites often seemed powerful but not smart, or as Plenty-coups said, smart but not wise. In opposing the past, whites were opposing a fundamental reality and were likely to fail:

> "They're just like young bears, poking their noses into everything. Leave them alone and they'll go away."
> . . . Wait until a hard winter comes . . . they would go away and the world would be as it had been from the beginning, when Feather Boy visited the people and showed them how to live. (*Wind*, 131; 135)

Native Americans had excellent grounds for valuing the past, grounds that do not seem as impractical, quaint, or primitive as "faith" in Feather Boy. The source of respect for the past in Indian life and novels is respect for authority. Since Socrates and the growth of free inquiry and ingenious manipulation of the natural world, we have hardly known such stability. At least in the last 400 years, few Europeans have absorbed the respect for parents, elders, customs, and government, the belief in *the benevolence of power* that Plains Indians knew.

White culture, believing that power corrupts, naturally encourages dissent. A culture believing that power is benign, however, naturally respects its elders. We should not see the regressive plots of these novels as returns only to a "distant past" of a primitivist paradise, magic, and medicine bundles. Right down to the raising of young and the conduct of tribal councils, Native Americans successfully practiced a system which engenders respect for the immediate as well as distant past. That is, the past, too, is a part of tribal authority and culture and therefore part of identity. Each plot of these six novels hinges on the insufferability of individuality in time as well as space: the present, severed from the past, is meaningless, outcast, homeless. The connotations of "regression" are cultural; going back to a previous condition is not necessarily a romantic "escape" from an unbearable present of maturity and anxiety. Indeed, Native Americans said and still say that the white attempt "to get away from the past" is the escapist fantasy that will not succeed.

To white Americans, then, the individual is often the ultimate reality; therefore individual consciousness is the medium of knowledge, and our "freedom" can be hard to distinguish from isolation. In contrast, Native Americans value a "transpersonal self" and this transpersonal self composed of society, past, and place confers identity and defines "being." That an individual *exists* is not contested, and Native American life and novels present all the variety of personality expected in our species, but the individual alone has no *meaning*. "The modern age puts a distressing emphasis on personality," said T. S. Eliot, grousing about our culture's attempt to draw meaning from individual variation. In all six novels, the free individual without context is utterly lost, so it would be misleading to apply to him so hallowed an English term as "individual." No "free individual" who achieves white success in these six books is really admired, and certainly the free "mode of life" they have "chosen" is not preferred to tribal context. So to call Welch's narrator in Minough's bar or Loney at the football game an "individual," implying all the weight of dignity, promise, and law which is carried by that term in white culture, is misleading. In every one of these books the protagonist seeks an identity which he can find *only* in his society, past, and place; unlike whites he cannot find meaningful "being" alone. Individuality is not even the *scene* of success or failure; it is nothing.

In a similar way, "knowledge" is formed and validated tribally in Native American life and in these books, although of course the individual cortex does the thinking. Consider the vision quest, the most radically isolated "knowing" an Indian was encouraged to seek. Alone for days, fasting and punishing the body, the young man sought the hallucinatory dream or vision which would help him realize his identity by revealing his spirit helpers and special animal partners, and which also would supply information to the tribe. Quite apart from the obvious acculturation involved in a person going on a vision quest in the first place, the *interpretation* of the vision, that is, the conversion of phenomena to knowledge, was usually tribal. Plenty-coups, for instance, had his private dream but depended on the tribal council to determine what it meant.

Not only is knowledge usually sought, interpreted, and applied in social context in these books, but useful knowledge is also knowledge from the past. From Henry Jim's point of view:

> It was not just an old story intended for the passing of an afternoon. As he had announced, he had come to ask for something—and a white man, a government man, might not understand the importance of the thing he asked unless the story was carried back to the beginnings. Today talks in yesterday's voice, the old people said. The white man must hear yesterday's voice. (*Wind*, 28)

These plots are regressive because Native American knowledge is regressive; "I been there before" is a primary virtue. It does not seem too strong to say that in these books both meaningful "being" and meaningful "knowledge" are supra-individual, aspects of tribe.

The third component of tribalism inherent in these novels is place. In all six novels the protagonist ends *where* he began. Even in Welch's work, the most contemporarily realistic of the novels, the reservation is not just a place where people are stuck; it is *the* home. Curiously all six of these Native American novels (and those of Louise Erdrich) are from Inland West reservations and all six come from tribes not drastically displaced from their original territories or ecosystems.

Place is not only an aspect of these works; place may have made them possible.

In each book the specific details of that one place are necessary to the protagonist's growth and pride. In *Ceremony*, "All things seemed to converge" on the Enchanted Mesa: "The valley was enclosing this totality, like the mind holding all thoughts together in a single moment" (248–49). In *House Made of Dawn* that one particular road must be run, in McNickle the Mission Mountains must be the last stand, in Welch the gate where Mose was killed, the ditch where his father froze, and Loney's Little Rockies, on the reservation, must be the scenes of growth. Conversely, white disregard and disrespect for place is crucial to these books:

> . . . the cities, the tall buildings, the noise and the lights, the power of their weapons and machines. They were never the same after that: they had seen what the white people had made from the stolen land. (*Ceremony*, 177)

> These mountains, trees, streams, the earth and the grass, from which his people learned the language of respect—all of it would pass into the hands of strangers, who would dig it up, chop it down, burn it up. (*Wind*, 130–31)

McNickle and Fey, in their scholarly work *Indians and Other Americans*, identified the concept of individual, transferable title to the land as the "prime source of misunderstanding" (26) between whites and Indians. McNickle thought that Indians understood land payment as a gift and perhaps as a rental fee for land use, but that probably, even late in the nineteenth century out West, Indians could not conceive of private land ownership. The Cherokees by 1881 had learned and dissented: "the land itself is not a chattel" (27). McNickle and Fey eloquently state the difference between the white transmutation of land to money and the Native American view:

> Even today, when Indian tribes may go into court and sue the United States for inadequate compensation or no compensation for lands taken from them, they still are dealing in alien concepts. One cannot grow a

tree on a pile of money, or cause water to gush from it; one can only spend it, and then one is homeless. (28)

So all six novels depict Indians coming home and staying home, but "home" is not the "house" of white heaven as dreamed by Catherine in *The Surrounded*: ". . . everything they wanted, big houses all painted, fine garments . . . rings . . . gold," all out of sight of neighbors (209). Home to the Indian is a society: "Then I went to the Indian place and I could hear them singing. Their campfires burned and I could smell meat roasting" (209). In all of these novels the protagonist succeeds largely to the degree that he reintegrates into the tribe, and fails largely to the degree that he remains alone. Such aspirations toward tribal reintegration may be *treated* by a novelist sentimentally, or romantically, or as fantasy, but these aspirations are not *inherently* sentimental or romantic. Rather, they constitute a profound and articulate continuing critique of modern European culture, combined with a persistent refusal to let go of tribal identity, a refusal to regard the past as inferior, a refusal—no matter how futile—of even the *wish* to assimilate.

The exact point of contact, or conflict, or misunderstanding between the European individual and the Indian tribe is captured in Guthrie's *The Big Sky*. Remember the passage that opened this book, when Boone in 1842 has finally gained the long-sought object of his obsession, Teal Eye, and has settled down in her family's encampment on the banks of the Teton River west of present Choteau, within a few miles of Guthrie's home. Boone had always wanted to be an Indian, and now the mountain man from Kentucky sits in buckskin in the heart of redskin land:

> A man could sit and let time run on while he smoked or cut on a stick with nothing nagging him and the squaws going about their business . . . and feel his skin drink the sunshine in and watch the breeze skipping in the grass and see the moon like a bright horn in the sky by night. One day and another it was pretty much the same, and it was all good . . . off a little piece Heavy Runner lay in front of his lodge with his head in his squaw's lap. . . . In other lodges medicine men thumped on drums and shook buffalo-bladder rattles to drive the evil spirits out of the sick. They made a noise that a man got so used to that he hardly took notice of it. (257–58)

Boone "hardly took notice" of the sick rattles. In the previous two chapters, Boone had ridden into their camp seeking Teal Eye. First we were told by the interpreter that her father, "Heavy Otter dead. Big sickness." The sickness is small pox. Within pages we and Boone learn: "White man bring big medicine, big sickness. Kill Piegan. Piegan heart dead. . . . Goddam dead" (250). But Boone has only one thought: "Ask him about the squaw." The suspense of the scene hangs on whether Teal Eye is already married. Later, within minutes of Boone's post-coital streamside revery, Red Horn will be saying, "The white Piegan does not know. He did not see the Piegans when their lodges were many and their warriors strong. We are a few now, and we are weak and tired. . . . We are poor and sick and afraid" (262). Boone certainly *does* know that they are very sick, that Teal Eye has lost her father and many relatives, and that the tribe's "heart is dead . . . we are weak and tired." Red Horn sees the political result of disease and white encroachment: "We are weak. We cannot fight the Long Knives" (262). In the midst of this crushing tribal despair Boone not only finds perfect happiness (hardly noticing the sick rattles), but has the audacity to blend his personal contentment with historical revery:

> It was a good life, the Piegan's life was. There were buffalo hunts and sometimes skirmishes with the Crows . . . it was as if time ran into itself and then flowed over . . . so that yesterday and today were the same. . . . and it was all he could ask, just to be living like this, with his belly satisfied and himself free and his mind peaceful and in his lodge a woman to suit him. (258)

Apparently, Guthrie at this moment shares Boone's primitivism, thinking this sounds like a pretty good life. Never does Boone participate in rituals or councils, nor are they narrated. Never is Teal Eye's point of view offered—is she perfectly happy as her society and past unravel? What is the marital consequence of Boone's blindness to her grief? We only know, "What she cared about most was to please him." "Teal Eye never whined or scolded . . . just took him and did her work and was happy" (259–60). We are asked to share Boone's happiness, achieved through freedom from constraint. When the elders crowd Boone, asking him not to show white men the pass through the mountains, Boone stomps off and does it. Nobody tells *him* anything. "Strong Arm is a paleface," says Red Horn, unable to comprehend Boone's loneliness. "He will go back to his brothers. . . ." "No! . . . Damn if ever I go back . . ." (262).

Boone had gotten away from it all, away from a hated father (who, like Garcia's, physically threatened him), away from kin, race, towns, away even from the red brothers around him and possibly away from his wife. He is free, disconnected from society and past, with no respect for any authority but himself. He does love place, but it is not an Indian's place. In his view the sun is disconnected from any larger reality, the river disconnected, the present time disconnected —or rather all are connected only in the moment of an individual's sensation, the lone source of meaning.

To this day, the irony of Boone's streamside revery in the Black-feet camp, as he and apparently Guthrie think he has happily "gone native," has to be pointed out to white Montana students. But as we saw, the Indian students read it differently. Treasure Island. Boone is nowhere near Indian country; he is living in white heaven: in suburbia, on about as fine a piece of real estate as you could find, with a pretty wife and a full refrigerator and utterly alone. Garcia and Guthrie, while very knowledgeable about Native Americans, still had to believe that to live in nature is to be "wild and free," apart from civilization. Primitivism thus shapes the extreme "white plot": Boone wanders away from his kin and custom to an untouched para-dise. This plot *is* escapist, and casts the rogue male, lonely and vio-lent, as the culture hero of a mobile society. Although Huck needs a family, the lone gunslinger needs a town, and Boone needs a wife, the primitivist remains within his culture: the mobile individual is the sole source of value. Emerson's "Thou art unto thyself a law" is the exact opposite of Native American knowledge. In the homing plots of Native American novels, what can look to whites like individual re-gression to some secure Eden may be an enlargement of individuality to society, place, and past:

Archilde sat quietly and felt those people move in his blood. There in his mother's tepee he had found unaccountable security. It was all quite near, quite a part of him; it was his necessity, for the first time. (*The Surrounded*, 222)

The typical Indian plot, then, recoils from a white world in which the mobile Indian individual finds no meaning ("He had lost his place. He had been long ago at the center, had known where he was, had lost his way, had wandered . . ."—*House*, 96), and as if by instinct comes home:

As an adolescent sent off to school for the first time, he waited for the dead of winter to run away from Genoa, Nebraska, a government boarding school, and traveled almost a thousand miles, most of the time on foot, to reach home in the spring. He didn't like to talk about it, how he sheltered, what he ate. By the time he reappeared as part of the Little Elk population he was a grown man. (*Wind*, 80–81)

This "homing" cannot be judged by white standards of individuality; it must be read in tribal context. D'Arcy McNickle of St. Ignatius perceived all of this, and first captured it in a form that whites could read and understand. He is the father of the Native American literary renaissance that continues to this day.

7
Native Nature: Chickadee Jive

FOR MOST READERS, THE WORDS "NATURE IN NATIVE AMERICAN novels" evoke primitivist expectations of the sacred earth prior to the evils of civilization. First we have assumed, however, that the "natural" is the opposite of the "civilized." The famous "sacred reciprocity" of Indians and nature certainly exists, but the ways in which nature is "sacred" within Indian novels can be surprising. Sometimes that chickadee patter sounds like Black street jive.

In Native American novels, nature is urban. It is a bit perverse to put it that way, but as we shall see, the perversity has its truth.

The handling of nature is most interesting in the works of James Welch. In *Winter in the Blood*, one of the finest Native American novels yet written, nature is unpredictable and various. Indeed, just as there is no real category "Indian," but only various tribes, so in Welch there is no "nature," only various instances—of what? Consider the "function of nature" in this passage:

> Later, as we drove past the corral, I saw the wild-eyed cow and a small calf head between the poles. The cow was licking the head. A meadowlark sang from a post above them. The morning remained cool, the sun shining from an angle above the horse shed. Behind the sliding door of the shed, bats would be hanging from the cracks. (14)

The wild-eyed cow reminds us of his brother's death, while the bats hardly fit the "pastoralism" of nurturing and meadowlarks on a cool morning. Are bats benign symbols to Native Americans? Is the narrator revealing his dark mind, imagining evil behind the door of appearance? No and No. Cows and bats happen to be hanging around the barnyard; they are not abstracted to a homogeneous whole; they are not symbols. They "function" to reveal that the narrator respects what's there. A similarly disjunct and intriguing image occurs in Mc-Nickle's *Wind*:

> The students came from many miles away and from many tribes, all snatched up the way coyote pups are grabbed and stuffed into a sack while mother coyote sits on her haunches and licks her black nose. (107)

The passage presents coyote pups in a straightforward comparison to human children; naturally, when the coyote mother is introduced we expect a parallel to human mothers; then, as she "sits on her haunches and licks her black nose" we seek the meaning of that action *in human terms*. Are coyotes and Indian mothers whacked on the nose as children are snatched? No, coyote snatchers tell me, the pups can be taken without a blow. Is this chilling indifference? Not on the part of humans; in McNickle's novels, several children are taken and mothers vehemently protest. The parallelism simply breaks down; the mother coyote takes over the text, licking her nose for coyote reasons and thinking coyote thoughts. Nature is not a symbol, subordinate to the human need for understanding. Animals have their own rights in life and art.

> Mosquitoes swarmed in the evenings outside the kitchen window and redwing blackbirds hid in the ragged cattails of the irrigation ditches. (*Winter*, 104)

When Keats mentions the murmurous haunt of flies on a summer's eve, or Emily Dickinson tells of a great blue fly interposed between herself and the light, we scramble to figure out why. The remarks have an effect on us because we are accustomed to using nature, abstracting it, confining it to our purposes. In Welch's work, such interpretive reaction to each natural phenomenon would engender (and has engendered) silly misreadings. The natural world in Welch is strangely (to whites) various, objective, unsymbolic, as if it had not yet been taken over by the human mind. Indeed, the book as a whole, although it hardly seems a hymn to farming, is filled with landscape beautiful as well as harsh, and Welch himself says the book began as a kind of Highline pastoral:

At first I thought of even making it a travelogue. If you were a tourist coming along Highway 2 there on the Highline, all you might want to do is get through this country as fast as possible so you'd reach either the Rocky Mountains on one side, or, say, Minnesota on the other where the country gets green and lush again. I wanted to highjack a carload of those tourists and tell 'em, "O.K., here's what's here," and take 'em out on the hills to the south there and just look at all the little plants—you know, the little flowers that happen, the insects, the snakes, a coyote or maybe a herd of antelope. Then I wanted them to smell what an alfalfa field smells like, I wanted them to smell what a corral smells like at 5:30 or 6:00 in the morning when the dew is on the manure and a kind of sweet smell comes out. (*Dialogues with Northwest Writers*, 165)

What about the deer in *Winter in the Blood*? It is a bold move by Welch and an exciting moment in the novel when this most realistic and antisentimental of narrators walks into Yellow Calf's world. We have to wonder how the author will handle the scene, even as the skeptical narrator wonders how he will handle the old man's claims. The narrator begins by offering advice:

> "No man should live alone."
> "Who's alone? The deer come—in the evenings—they come to feed on the other side of the ditch. I can hear them. When they whistle, I whistle back."
> "And do they understand you?" I said this mockingly.
> His eyes were hidden in the darkness. "Mostly—I can understand most of them."
> "What do they talk about?"
> "It's difficult . . . About ordinary things, but some of them are hard to understand."
> "But do they talk about the weather?"

The narrator's pressing is ours; surely even deer that can talk are simple-minded, "primitive." The old man's answer is wonderful:

> "No, no, not that. They leave that to men." He sucked on his lips. "No, they seem to talk mostly about . . ."—he searched the room with a peculiar alertness—"well, about the days gone by. They talk a lot about that. They are not happy."

"Not happy? But surely to a deer one year is as good as the next. How do you mean?"

"Things change—things have changed. They are not happy."

"Ah, a matter of seasons! When their bellies are full, they remember when the feed was not so good—and when they are cold, they remember . . ."

"No!" The sharpness of his own voice startled him. "I mean, it goes deeper than that. They are not happy with the way things are. They know what a bad time it is. They can tell by the moon when the world is cockeyed." (67–68)

The narrator has tried mockery, humor, and the assumption that animals are simple, but at every point he is foiled. Leave the silly reductions to men, he is told; deer are more sophisticated.

The scene is cleverly constructed. The narrator has been quickly drawn into a discussion of what the deer say and why, and old Yellow Calf observes, "You don't believe the deer," as if their talking were assumed and only the content could be questioned. The narrator tries to duck the issue of his own belief, and suggests that the deer could be wrong. Yellow Calf says "no matter":

"Even the deer can't change anything. They only see the signs." (69)

"Even . . . only." The sly old fellow has pulled ahead at every turn, and the final verb of the chapter bows gracefully in his direction:

I started to wave from the top of the bridge. Yellow Calf was facing off toward the river, listening to two magpies argue. (70)

"Argue." The narrator has entered the old man's world, and will soon discover that Yellow Calf is his grandfather.

We have finally come to sacred ground, to an Indian listening to animals, to Grandfather, to the language and mind of nature—and the deer grumble like philosophers in a Paris cafe.

Native American nature is urban. The *connotation* to us of "urban," suggesting a dense complex of human variety, is closer to Native American "nature" than is our word "natural." The woods, birds, animals, and humans are all "downtown," meaning at the *center* of action and power, in complex and unpredictable and various relationships. The *way* they interact resembles Black street jive, not Walt Disney idylls of pastoral escape. Welch's Raven in *Fools Crow* could play the lead in "The Little Shop of Horrors." You never know who you'll meet on the street. Pretty-shield tells of her training:

> "One day in the moon when leaves are on the ground [November] I was walking with my grandmother near some bushes that were full of chickadees," Pretty-shield continued. "They had been stealing fat from meat that was on the racks in the village, and because they were full they were all laughing. I thought it would be fun to see them all fly, and tossed a dry buffalo-chip into the bushes. I was a very little girl, too little to know any better, and yet my grandmother told me that I had done wrong. She took me into her arms, and walking to another bush, where the frightened chickadees had stopped, she said: 'This little girl is my granddaughter. She will never again throw anything at you. Forgive her, little ones. She did not know any better.' Then she sat down with me in her lap, and told me that long before this she had lost a close friend because the woman had turned the chickadees against her."
> (*Pretty-shield*, 154–55)

The reasons for the similarities of "urban" and "natural" in Native American literature are not difficult to unravel. Europeans have long assumed a serious split between man and nature, and since 1800 they have often preferred nature to man's works. When European whites have imagined a beautiful union of "man and nature," they have assumed the union would look not like the "human" world but like the "natural" world; therefore they perceived the Indians as living in a "primitive" union of man and nature that was the antithesis of civilization. However, respecting civilization as they knew it, Native Americans experienced the union of man and nature as "human," "civilized." Thus, the variety of personality, motivation, purpose, politics, and conversation familiar to human civilization is found throughout Indian nature. "Mother Earth" is not wild. Nature is part of tribe. That is why its characteristics are "urban," and that is why Welch's deer talk like philosophers in a Paris cafe.

The deer are human-like beings at the center of the civilized world. That sentence, of course, reflects white concerns. From the Indian point of view, the deer are simply beings, as are humans, in the world, all of which is centered and civilized. Nature is "home," then, to Native Americans in a way exactly opposite to its function for Boone. Nature is not a secure seclusion one has escaped to, but is the tipi walls expanded, with more and more people chatting around the fire. Nature is filled with events, gods, spirits, chickadees, and deer acting as men. Nature is "house": "There was a house made of dawn. It was made of pollen and of rain, and the land was very old and everlasting" (*House*, 7).

What gives this system divinity is the same combination of authority, distant past, and brotherhood that unites the tribe; the Indians' "sacred reciprocity" with nature does not derive its sacredness from a transaction with an awesomely distant or alien natural world. One's meaningful identity includes society, past, place, and all the natural inhabitants of that place.

Such incorporation of nature into the body of tribe has two major and apparently (to whites) antithetical consequences in these Native American novels. First is the grand attention to place, the *macro* sacredness of earth that has been noted by whites because it can be hammered to fit primitivist expectations. Second is the apparent fragmentation of the natural world into a huge cast of individual, civilized *micro* characters: cows, bats, mosquitoes, blackbirds, coyotes, magpies act in their individual, peculiar ways. *Reality*, to be sure, is still tribal, located in the larger system, but the paradoxical effect of this "micro" brotherhood is to stress the individuality of fellow inhabitants. In *Loney*, when they have driven to the Mission Canyon for a precious moment in the place where Loney will die, Rhea sees a deer "through the rear window. It was a large deer, without antlers. It stood broadside, its head turned directly toward the car. Rhea watched it flick its right ear, then lift a hind hoof to scratch it" (15). The deer's casual individuality helps make the moment sacred, as Rhea says, "the best secret ever."

In a brilliant passage in *The Surrounded*, McNickle deliberately juxtaposed the "micro" sacredness of nature to the symbolic perception of nature preferred by whites. Archilde is at a mission school, and one afternoon a cloud "by curious coincidence . . . assumed the form of a cross—in the reflection of the setting sun, a flaming cross."

> The prefect was the first to observe the curiosity and it put him into a sort of ecstasy. . . .
> "The Sign! The Sign!" he shouted. His face was flushed and his eyes gave off flashing lights—Archilde did not forget them.
> "The Sign! Kneel and pray!"
> The boys knelt and prayed, some of them frightened and on the point of crying. They knew what the Sign signified. . . . The Second Coming of Christ, when the world was to perish in flames!

The cloud, of course, melts away, but curiously Archilde does not need this empirical proof to reject Christianity's symbolic use of nature:

> It was not the disappearance of the threatening symbol which freed him from the priest's dark mood, but something else. At the very instant that the cross seemed to burn most brightly, a bird flew across it. . . . It flew past and returned several times before finally disappearing—and what seized Archilde's imagination was the bird's unconcernedness. It recognized no "Sign." His spirit lightened. He felt himself fly with the bird. (101–3)

What a marvelous scene: Archilde trusts the bird to know if its world, *their* world, is coming to an end. Just as Yellow Calf trusted the deer to have seen true signs, Archilde trusts the bird not to have seen false ones. The bird, like the ear-scratching deer, reassures him through its "unconcernedness" and he feels a symbiosis with this individual, sentient brother in the sky. He is saved not by a "strange" symbol, but by the "familiarity"—the family status—of what *is*. Therefore he rejects the fiery Christian apocalypse prescribed for this evil earth, estranged from divinity, in favor of immediate brotherhood in a divine familial system.

Possibly because he works by the nuance of poetic image and avoids historical generalization, Welch makes the most use of that Native American world made up of thousands of unique characters interacting in a wealth of detail. In such a world, reconsider Indian

history. Whites were advancing not only on Indians, but on the chickadees listening, the bird unconcerned, the deer scratching. White willingness to wage environmental war was shocking to the Indians, as
Pretty-shield said:

> . . . kill *all* the buffalo. Even the Lakota, bad as their hearts were for us,
> would not do such a thing . . . yet the white man did this, even when
> he did not want the meat. (250)

Killing a *man* who could kill you was understandable and honorable;
killing our brothers was a senseless attack on the system that makes
meaning possible.

From the Native American point of view, then, whites waged war
not only on individual Indians, on tribes, and on the macrocosmic
sacred earth, but also on the microcosmic individuals of the tribe
spread across the plains and through the woods. The history of *that*
war is one aspect of Welch's recent historical novel, *Fools Crow*.

> . . . he pulled his musket from its tanned hide covering. . . . Then he
> heard the raven call to him. He was sitting on a branch. . . . "You do not
> need your weapon, young man. There is nothing here to harm you."
>
> White Man's Dog felt his eyes widen and his heart begin to beat like a
> drum in his throat. Raven laughed the throaty laugh of an old man. "It
> surprises you that I speak the language of the two-leggeds . . . I speak
> many languages . . . I even deign to speak once in a while with the swift
> silver people who live in the water—but they are dumb and lead lives
> without interest. I myself am very wise." (56)

Raven has been sent by Sun to help White Man's Dog direct his
bullet toward a white intruder; he fulfills that role with the personal
arrogance of Raven alone. We are brought into a world that is both
one, and myriad.

These Native American novels, then, embody tribalism in their
plots and in their handling of nature as part of the family. From
McNickle's pioneering work to the recent books of James Welch,
Native American novelists have told their stories in a Native way.

8

Welch's Winters and Bloods

JAMES WELCH WAS BORN IN BROWNING, MONTANA, IN 1940, OF Blackfeet, Gros Ventre, and European descent. His family moved now and then away from a family farm, and he graduated from high school in Minneapolis in 1958. He attended college at Northern Montana in Havre, transferred, and received a B.A. in liberal arts from the University of Montana in Missoula in 1965. Then he entered the university's Master of Fine Arts program as a graduate poet.

Welch began writing poetry under Richard Hugo, already in 1965 a well-known poet and director of the creative writing program. Hugo told of having Welch in a poetry writing class. Welch handed in a poem called "In My First Hard Springtime," which began:

> Those red men you offended were my brothers.
> Town drinkers, Buckles Pipe, Star Boy,
> Billy Fox, were blood to bison. Albert Heavy Runner
> was never civic. You are white and common.

Hugo said that when he came to "Albert Heavy Runner was never civic" he knew he had nothing to teach this young man except to tell him to keep writing.

Keep writing he did, under the tutelage of Hugo and Madeline DeFrees at the university. His book of poems, *Riding the Earthboy 40,* appeared in 1971 from Harper and Row. In 1974 Harper published his first novel, *Winter in the Blood,* and in 1979 his second, *The Death of Jim Loney,* both set on the Highline among contemporary Indians. His third novel, *Fools Crow,* came out from Viking Penguin in 1986.

Winter in the Blood is told in the first person by a nameless Native American narrator who has just returned home. His girlfriend has run off, and he sets out from his mother's ranch to find her. He doesn't find much except trouble in the bars of Malta, Dodson, Harlem, or Havre, and we learn that he has lost more: a father and brother, at least.

In the second half of the novel, after the narrator's cruel slapping of a woman he hardly knows has made him disgusted with his own distance from everyone and everything, the young man's numbing indifference begins to crack. Discovery of his grandfather, respect for his grandmother, and plans for his own future seem to suggest new resolve. Maybe.

Welch's first two novels pose the same question: Has the hero/ narrator improved his lot? Is there *any* redemption or success in this Highline world of poverty, distance, and booze? The questions are doubly interesting because they raise issues of white versus Native American values, and they also raise regional issues: How do people react to Malta, Montana? How does our own life experience—urban or country, rich or poor—affect our reading? Montanans, I find, read these novels quite differently than New Yorkers do. The difference is in perception of kinds and degrees of success.

In McNickle's *The Surrounded*, Archilde seems a failure as he is led away in handcuffs for killing the sheriff, while the white Indian agent shouts what sounds like a hostile review of *The Death of Jim Loney*: "You had everything, every chance, and this is the best you could do with it! A man gets pretty tired of you and all your kind!" (*Surrounded*, 296) Yet for all the apparent failure, *The Surrounded*, as we have seen, maintains the momentum of a Plains Indian success story: Archilde returns, fighting, to the tribe. Simultaneously, by white standards, he is going to the usual fates imposed by Europe on his kind: hell and jail. Loney and the narrator in *Winter in the Blood* certainly suffer failure; do they also, like Archilde, achieve some kind of success? Welch himself believes that *The Death of Jim Loney* and *Winter in the Blood* have positive endings (*Dialogues*, 176), but for whites especially, the achievements are hard to perceive. Kenneth Lincoln, writing with considerable awareness of Indian points of view, finds *Loney* "almost too real" (168).

In this chapter, I want first to consider *Winter in the Blood* and *The Death of Jim Loney*, which present similar and precise challenges to white and Indian readers alike. Then I will consider Welch's very different novel, set in 1869–70, *Fools Crow*.

Winter in the Blood

When Welch published *Winter in the Blood* in 1974, he was hailed for his spare prose and social realism, and compared to Hemingway. He had published one book of poems, and to have his first novel reviewed on the front page of the *New York Times Book Review* was an honor. His style was certainly in Hemingway's no-nonsense, realistic tradition, although Welch added the poetic image that gives depth to simple sentences: ". . . the paring knife grew heavy in the old lady's eyes." Paragraphs and chapters in *Winter* often end with echoing images that stop the reader and force reflection: the knife was heavy in her eyes; pheasants are "like old men . . . full of twists." The effect is anti-narrative, begging us not to read on but to stop and think about what we have just read. Welch's surrealism, too, especially in the bar scenes, is anti-narrative, taking the reader out of the story by exploding it, forcing us to search for connections among the shards.

Realism, surrealism, and the shock of poetic image may describe Welch's technique, but his voice never shares the decadence and erudition of Hemingway and other writers of the twenties. His voice is always sincere, closer to Vittorini's *In Sicily*, as translated by Wilfred David (and introduced by Hemingway), which Welch knew and admired. Vittorini used realistic prose to tell of coming home to his native subculture, Sicily, strange to most readers and half-strange to himself, and of finding there no easy location of his own needs. That is the voice of *Winter in the Blood*.

The sincerity of *Winter in the Blood* made it an important book from the very first paragraph, because it presented the elements of the old "western" in a totally new voice. Imagine walking into a New York editor's office and saying, "I have a novel here with horses, Indians, a log cabin, and tumbleweeds." (This, by the way, is *not* how publishing works.) The editor would imagine a "western" novel as it has been defined by Hollywood and the popular press; that is, he would imagine the West as it has been invented, packaged, and sold to eastern and European audiences to satisfy their fantasies of adventure and escape. William Eastlake told Bill Kittredge not to let a publisher put a picture of a horse on any novel he might publish. "The people who buy it will think it's some goddamned shoot-up." Eastlake and Wright Morris are two of the few who have fought for real westerns. Imagine, then, if you were expecting Zane Grey, Louis L'Amour, and Hollywood, how different Welch's first paragraph would seem. The narrator is not an adventurer or visitor in the exciting West; he is taking a leak. The scene is not new, but old. The horses, Indians, log cabin, and tumbleweeds are not exotic subjects, they are simply the context of someone's life:

> In the tall weeds of the borrow pit, I took a leak and watched the sorrel mare, her colt beside her, walk through burnt grass to the shady side of the log-and-mud cabin. It was called the Earthboy place, although no one by that name (or any other) had lived in it for twenty years. The roof had fallen in and the mud between the logs had fallen out in chunks, leaving a bare gray skeleton, home only to mice and insects. Tumble-weeds, stark as bone, rocked in a hot wind against the west wall. On the hill behind the cabin, a rectangle of barbed wire held the graves of all the Earthboys, except for a daughter who had married a man from Lodgepole. She could be anywhere, but the Earthboys were gone.

Most surprising, perhaps, is the lyric tone. A great deal has been accomplished in that paragraph, mainly through style. Welch's editors did not like the character taking a leak in the first sentence, but he stuck with his version because he wanted it clear that this brilliant and sensitive narrator could be the Indian we see pissing in the pit along Highway 2 between Dodson and Malta. So that little bit of social realism is thrown at us right at the start. Yet *inside* his head, nothing is common, all is delicacy and, in the rhymes and rhythms, all is song: "roof had fallen *in* . . . mud . . . had fallen *out* in chunks. . . . Tumbleweeds, stark as bone, rocked in a hot wind against the west wall." And the final line quietly situates the book, and the character —perhaps also family, tribe, race—in a land of loss: "the Earthboys were gone."

In that paragraph, Montana literature suddenly speaks about contemporary life in a beautiful, delicate, rhythmic yet realistic voice. There is no catering to cowboy fantasies and, for that matter, no attempt to refute them. Here is pure attention, by some speaker who is clearly sensitive and articulate, to living, in Montana, near Malta. We know his life will be taken seriously. We know it will be from *his* point of view. This is how art is made.

What does the character (never named) in *Winter* find when he comes home to his mother's ranch? A most interesting debate occurred in Havre in January 1986, when a room full of people from Montana and the Highline, many white, many Native American, discussed *Winter in the Blood*. Those present included Bill Thackeray, the very able and knowledgeable professor of English at Northern Montana, and Minerva Allen, a poet herself as well as Native American administrator, and a great many Montana writers in addition to Welch.

The debate followed roughly the pattern I have noticed in the classroom and in the national criticism on this book. Apart from the few who resent the hard realism, those from Montana, especially those from the Highline and especially Native Americans, tend to see a positive ending to an accurate, often tragic, and at times funny book. Those from the East, especially professional critics and New Yorkers, tend to be overwhelmed by the bleakness of the people and land, and they find the book depressing.

This pattern is interesting partly because it shows how the cultural experience of readers will affect their reading. If you are depressed enough by no rain and miles of sagebrush dotted with trailers, you may not notice the narrator swinging around to respect for his grandmother. I find my Montana students, especially those from the Highline, better readers of this book than most East Coast critics, who are so distracted by setting they misread character.

Our relation to land makes a difference. When James Welch's book of poems was accepted in New York he was flown back East, and found himself at the Catskill Mountains country house of a famous editor. The Catskills are low and lush; Montana readers have to picture broad-leaved trees and dark forests reaching to the tops of rolling hills, and a green lawn, greener than anything between the Mississippi and the Cascades, sloping down from a spacious white house. The New York editor and Welch sit in white lawn chairs, sipping gin and tonic and watching shadows spread through the sheltered valley below. "Your poems are good," says the New Yorker, "but they have too much wind and bones."

That was it, says Welch. At the words "wind and bones" he could see the Highline, his home, and he knew that the editor had no notion of that world, none at all, and probably thought wind was a literary device, a symbol, a part of his technique. Welch decided that he could never have too much wind and bones in his work. And I have found, teaching Montana books to in-state and out-of-state readers, that something harsh and distant, some rough equivalent to wind and bones, is comfortable to Montanans or at least very familiar, yet distracting to those from climes with more green: trees and cash.

Although readers from more lush environments often find *Winter in the Blood* bleak, there is no denying the positive aspects to its end. The narrator of *Winter* has found his grandfather, learned his grandmother's history, reconciled himself to his brother's death, and in the final sentence, he alone in his family has honored his past by throwing the pouch on grandmother's grave. His distance is now more like Yellow Calf's, serene in a cockeyed world, surrounded by graves of those gone. Those are strong upturns in the Indian "homing" plot.

The narrator also improves his "white" plot, the story of himself as a free individual. His futile but whole-hearted attempt to drag the cow out of the mud—an unprecedented action adventure ("the rope against my thigh felt right")—his new confidence in his knowledge, his resolve to buy Agnes "a couple of crémes de menthe, maybe offer to marry her on the spot," coupled with his returns to tradition suggest an existential hero: he can't really *change* anything in his absurd universe; the past may be dead and Agnes worthless, but he is creating the slightest new dignity, confidence, and meaning within himself, spinning it out of his guts as well as his past. In *Winter in the Blood*, the white existential plot, the Indian homing plot, and the first-person poetic brilliance coincide. In case there's any doubt about an upturn, in the Epilogue the narrator, who throughout the book has said that there are no fish in the river, observes: "The air was heavy with yesterday's rain. It would probably be good for fishing" (175). Montanans know that cinches it.

Winter in the Blood has an immense effect on Montana students. The absolute rightness of the towns, the bars, the characters, and conversation amazes them; for many from the Highline it is like looking into a mirror for the first time, finding a world you were only *in*, out *there*. Indians find their lives treated without condescension or romance; whites find a mirror of place, plus an entry into the Indian world. Meanwhile, the sensitivity of the style provides its counterpoint to the sordid events. Some students respond with fine writing and a dry Welchian irony of their own:

> From Tank Hill, the dipping twin strands of year-round Christmas lights along Cut Bank's Main Street looked like the Golden Gate bridge.
>
> That's what we always said, anyway, as we parked on raw winter nights near the looming oil tanks, popping Great Falls Selects and taking in the sights. To the west was the winking airport beacon; to the south, the frost-haloed yardlights of a few farms; below us, the pale and scattered lights of town; behind, the oil tanks; and to the north, blackness and Canada.
>
> For awhile, we'd feel high, wild and powerful—suspended and full of ourselves in the sub-zero emptiness. Then the car would shudder hard in the wind, and blasts of sand-dry snow would skitter across the hood. We'd toss out our empty cans and hear them clatter frantically across the frozen ground as we roared back to the safety of town. We drove slowly down Main, and the swaying Christmas lights didn't look like anything at all.

For Dee McNamer from Cut Bank, writing on Welch in 1982, bleakness was not a distraction; it was home. As she said, the Highline produces two responses: "a sense of exhilaration and freedom, and an undercurrent of horror." She knew how to look for signs of life in that desert, and has gone on to write fine fiction of her own (and ironically enough, in *The New Yorker*, several pieces in "The Talk of the Town").

While *Winter in the Blood* allowed Montanans and others accustomed to hard minimums to glimpse, at least, a hopeful homing in, Welch's second book, *The Death of Jim Loney*, seemed unrelievedly bleak. In *Loney* white values are more severely rejected, the third-person narration hides Loney's mind, and the "homing" plot is harder to find. *Loney* offers an even more severe test of pessimistic/optimistic reactions. Whereas *Winter* tends to divide Montanans and easterners, *Loney* tends to divide Indians and whites, or perhaps, tends to divide every reader within him or herself. Because it raises the toughest issues, and has not received as much attention as *Winter in the Blood*, I would like to review *Loney* in the light of what I've been saying about Indian novels and the cultural expectations of readers.

The Death of Jim Loney

Jim Loney's friends believe he should get out of Harlem, Montana. He should try "leaving behind all his ancient prejudices and manners," as Crèvecoeur had advised. He is bright, has performed well in school, and seems to lack only the motivation to do something with himself. Rhea, his white lover from Texas, like Garcia from the Rio Grande and Boone from Kentucky, has come to the Montana plains for "a complete break with my past" (86). She next wants to go to Seattle: "Don't ask me why I chose Seattle. I guess it just seems a place to escape to" (87). Rhea wants Jim Loney to escape with her.

Ironically, Rhea is in competition with another escape artist, Loney's beautiful and upwardly mobile sister, Kate, who works for the government in Washington, D.C. Kate, though Indian, also offers Loney the white way of novelty, mobility, and meaning through individual experience and possession of things. Leave, she says, and "you would have things worthwhile . . . beautiful country, a city, the North, the South, the ocean . . . You need that. You need things to be different, things that would arouse your curiosity, give you some purpose" (76). Kate has chosen to change her Indian life through white knowledge, "learning as a kind of salvation, a way to get up and out of being what they were" (90).

Kate and Rhea are very attractive characters. Unlike Silko, Momaday, and McNickle, Welch does not bring "the enemy" onstage in these two novels; he avoids didactic or dogmatic overtones, and the oppression represented by white culture appears in the gaps between images, between possibilities, between plots. Even the stupid white sheriff, Painter, is treated quite sympathetically, as is the successful ranch-owning Indian, Pretty Weasel, who quit his basketball scholarship at Wyoming to come home in "automatic response, the way a sheepdog returns to camp in the evening" (81).

Neither the white world nor white success seems odious in this book. On the other hand, Harlem, Loney's hometown, is not the end of the world—"but you can see it from there." Traditional Indian culture is less evident here than in any other novel we've considered. Loney's Indian mother is dead; his white father and Kate are his only kin; he lives off the reservation, in town. The reader easily joins Kate and Rhea and most critics in urging him to leave, to find "purpose" in "things" that are "different."

You can see that the book is almost playing into the hands of white prejudice against Indians. Here is a character who indeed seems lazy, useless, irresponsible, especially since he's bright and could do better. There is no attractive traditional culture and there are no family ties holding him down; he is miserably depressed; why doesn't he leave and make something of himself?

Twice in the book Loney analyzes himself. In each case, he draws much of his vocabulary and values, his conscious knowledge, from the white world, but then like a sheepdog he keeps trotting back to family, past, and place as the source of identity:

> "I can't leave," he said, and he almost knew why. He thought of his earlier attempts to create a past, a background, an ancestry—something that would tell him who he was . . . He had always admired Kate's ability to live in the present, but he had also wondered at her lack of need to understand her past. Maybe she had the right idea; maybe it was the present that mattered, only the present. (88)

Loney returns to thoughts of his surrogate mother for a year, Aunt "S," hardly known, now dead, the only real family he has had.

A few chapters later Rhea asks, "What is it that troubles you?" Loney visibly tiptoes the line between individual psychology and tribal consciousness: "I don't even know myself. It has to do with the past . . . I know it has to do with my mother and father . . . an aunt I lived with . . . who she really was and how she died." Then he suddenly tells Rhea of the extraordinary white bird that appears "when I'm awake, but late at night when I'm tired—or drunk . . . Sometimes I think it is a vision sent by my mother's people. I must interpret it, but I don't know how."

The question of whether he will go to Seattle suddenly becomes, quite clearly, a choice between two cultures, two plots. Whites leave, Indians stay home. Rhea says:

"Did it ever occur to you that if you left you would leave these . . . visions behind? You might become so involved with a new life that your past would fade away—that bird would fade away for good."
"I don't know that I want that to happen." (105–6)

From the white point of view, the change of interests offered by a life of wandering might lay to rest Loney's troubling hallucination. From the Native American point of view, his vision-knowledge is inextricably tied to past and place, although he lacks the tribe ("my mother's people") to interpret it. That knowledge would be entirely lost if he moved away. The scene ends as Rhea and Loney discuss his geographical place. The mixed-blood Loney has the ambivalent responses we might expect from someone representing both races:

"This is your country, isn't it? It means a great deal to you." . . .
"I've never understood it. Once in a while I look around and I see things familiar and I think I will die here. It's my country then. Other times I want to leave, to see other things, to meet people, to die elsewhere."

Genetic determinism is troubling to liberals; reading these books, however, one sometimes wonders if the mixed-blood has two knowledges in his bones.

The Death of Jim Loney cannot be read without Native American context. The most obvious example occurs right away:

He walked and he realized that he was seeing things strangely, and he remembered that it had been that way at the football game. It was as though he were exhausted and drowsy, but his head was clear. He was aware of things around him—the shadowy trees, the glistening sidewalk, the dark cat that moved into the dark. (4)

In the white world, we trace this "altered state" backward to tough drinking and forward to trouble. Anyone familiar with Plains Indians, however, will recognize a possible vision-quest state of mind, which would suddenly make Loney the doctor instead of the patient. Sure enough, seven chapters later, the bird appears in the book for the first time: "And again, as he had that night after the football game, he saw things strangely, yet clearly. . . . he saw the smoke ring go out away from his face and he saw the bird in flight. . . . It came every night now" (20).

Loney did not "seek" the state of mind or the bird, as far as he knows. Indeed, that is his situation throughout the novel: he thinks white, would not mind being white, but he seems to have Indian-ness visited upon him. He is the reluctant victim of a vision without quest, of vague yearnings for family, past, and place that halfway yield to white interpretation—this individual has a problem, "he will not allow himself to be found" (34), and "it had everything to do with himself" (134)—and halfway yield to tribal analysis: Loney needs to come home.

There are a number of tribal aspects to Loney's tale. The bird vision is dramatically important although never explained, never interpreted. We are offered an Indian with a spirit-helper as helpless as he. Throughout the book Loney yearns for family, with dreams of a mother long dead, aching memories of one Christmas with the kind "aunt," the tracking of a worthless father at last brought to bay in his trailer. Loney's inability to find an adequate father or elder stands in marked contrast to the other Native American novels and seems indivisible from his downfall. Ike is an anti-grandfather, the perfect opposite of elders Betonie, Bull, and Yellow Calf in other novels. And he is white.

Beyond the bird and the family themes and Loney's obvious ties to place in the novel are some tribal fringes which become surprisingly central. Loney's sleeping dreams are prophetic. When Ike says, "You might need this" and hands Loney the shotgun with "a familiar grin"

(149), we and Loney remember Ike's identical words as he grinned and handed him a shotgun in a dream months before (24).

Not only does the book introduce dream knowledge, but several narrative intrusions or outside views of Loney are decidedly "blood" in point of view. Most exquisite is the ancient Indian grandmother at the airport, welcoming home her soldier grandson whom "she had lost" to new experiences abroad in the white world:

> And it filled her with sadness, for she knew that what he had gained would never make up for what he had lost. She had seen the other boys come home. And she stared past her soldier at Loney's wolfish face and she thought, That's one of them. (58)

She knows that half of Loney has left for the white world, and cannot come home again. Loney himself "never felt Indian":

> Indians were people like the Cross Guns, the Old Chiefs—Amos After Buffalo. They lived an Indian way, at least tried. When Loney thought of Indians, he thought of the reservation families, all living under one roof, the old ones passing down the wisdom of their years, of their family's years, of their tribe's years, and the young ones soaking up their history, their places in their history, with a wisdom that went beyond age.
>
> He remembered when the Cross Guns family used to come to town . . . old Emil Cross Guns . . . sitting in the back seat . . . Loney recalled going up to the window and touching his hand. . . . Now he [Pretty Weasel's father] was old, but in a white man way, thrown away. Not like Emil Cross Guns.
>
> Loney thought this and he grew sad . . . for himself. He had no family and he wasn't Indian or white. He remembered the day he and Rhea had driven out to the Little Rockies. She had said he was lucky to have two sets of ancestors. In truth he had none. (102)

Loney's connection to this distant past is Amos After Buffalo, the little boy who helps him chip his frozen dog out of the ice and is upset that the dog is not buried. Amos is from Hays on the reservation, "way out there" (54), and when Loney is ready to die ("It's my country then") he chooses to do it in Mission Canyon of the Little Rockies, just past Hays and the mission school. As he walks through Hays in the dark, his thoughts are of Amos and the real Indians: "Amos After Buffalo will grow up, thought Loney, and he will discover that Thanksgiving is not meant for him . . . and it will hurt him . . . and he will grow hard and bitter" (166). Then, in a parallel to the deer conversation in *Winter*, Loney suddenly and quite seriously addresses the strange dog trailing him through town, and for a moment he has indeed leapt back into the tribe's distant past, when animals and men worried together over things like proper burials, a pouch on the grave: " 'You tell Amos that Jim Loney passed through town while he was dreaming. . . . Give him dreams. Tell him you saw me carrying a dog and that I was taking that dog to a higher ground. He will know.' . . . The dog was gone" (167).

Amos had said, "Do you know where I live?" (54) Now, in Hays, Loney knows. Loney's own confidence and command, and the truth of his dreams throughout the novel, lead us to assume that the dog is off to deliver the message, but Welch's spare style and disjunct images almost hide, or rather force us to consider, to supply our own rhetoric for, the immense distance between the bars and trailers of Harlem and this dog-dream-messenger. Loney then walks to his death thinking of his past which "brought me here," thinking of the old Indians in the canyon, "the warriors, the women who had picked chokecherries" (168), and finally of the mother who "had given up her son to be free" (175). But freedom hasn't worked for either the mother or the son who "would not allow himself to be found." The only thing left is not Boone's heaven of suburban isolation, or Catherine's tribal heaven of singing around the fire, but Welch's half-breed heaven, Highline grace: "But there had to be another place where people bought each other drinks and talked quietly about their pasts, their mistakes . . . like everything was beginning again" (175).

What is this novel about? Welch considers the end positive because Loney has tried to understand his past, and because he has taken control of his life by orchestrating his death. But that existential plot is hard to affirm in Loney. Loney's decisiveness is almost gratuitously self-destructive. The white existential plot offers only the tiniest shred of affirmation: he accepts responsibility for accidental murder (arguably with unconscious intent, for Pretty Weasel has threatened him with intimacy, good memories, and success). When he shoots Pretty Weasel, as poet Linda Weasel Head has remarked, "he sees death for what it is—a release from the realities that he cannot comprehend." He then stages his own unnecessary execution. Many isolated events serve this weak white plot: shooting Pretty Weasel, shooting at his father, setting up the policeman's shot all are acts of an indecisive loner in submission to his own arbitrary yet self-willed fate. From that white point of view, he is indeed a sad case.

But the refusal to leave his place, the mourning of lost ancestors, the bird vision, the prophetic dreams, the violence, and the scenes with Amos After Buffalo all create another pattern, a pattern of proud Native American resistance to assimilation: this is *our* disaster, and I will make my stand on *our* ground in honor of my ancestry and ancestral knowledge. Like Old Bull in *Wind*, Loney has "received" the bullet from the Indian upholding white law, and "This is what you wanted, he thought." Loney's individuality, his "existence," and most of his conscious knowledge in the white sense may be isolated, but his dreams and desires and finally his resolution are not. Those aspects of Loney constitute a loyalty to a tribe and a tribalism he never individually knew.

The tension between the white and Indian plots *is* the tension in *Loney*. In Welch's work, the individual psychic drama is a kind of melody played against the pedal bass of tribal past. Much more than *Winter*, *Loney* forces us to hear the counterpoint of these competing strains. *Loney* takes us realistically to the blurred edge of consciousness of a Highline Indian who knows there *must* be something good in his people, past, and place, but who doesn't even know why he knows that. The book dares us to see Loney's final homing as not at all the perversion it seems to be, however much, like Kate and Rhea, we still want Loney to leave. In *Loney* more than in any other Native American novel, the reader is placed squarely in the mixed-blood's situation, unable to choose between a white realism that seems to offer at best lonely success or intelligent despair, and an Indian pride in tradition that must seem a dream. For the reader as well as the mixed-blood, the white and Indian plots are not good and bad opposites but simultaneous, inescapable forces—centrifugal and centripetal—

that can leave one so stuck in orbit that even Loney's decisiveness—one jump back toward the center—becomes a quantum leap.

The mixed-blood's situation is not comfortable. Like most readers, I found *Loney* at first a most uncomfortable book. So did Anatole Broyard in *The New York Times* (Nov. 28, 1979), who sounded like a peeved Indian agent: "Is he threatening us with his unhappiness? Why do so many of our serious novels have to be read like unpaid bills?" That, of course, is exactly the point. From the Indian point of view, this entire nation is an unpaid bill. Broyard's ignorance of the subject matter (he thinks Rhea improbable) and his distaste for guilt are beside the point; the novel doesn't even try to recover those vast debts, nor does it directly threaten us. The limbo itself makes Broyard whine, life without individualism *plus* life without tribe, the impression Kenneth Lincoln had of a " 'breed's' novel, neither Indian nor white" (*Native American Renaissance*, 168).

However, the novel is *both* Indian and white, and things *do* matter: Loney's various refusals have their large and mysterious (and very accurate) aspects; the *reason* for his refusals may not be so much existential as tribal, and that matters a great deal. Tribalism gives dignity and honor to Loney's choice. Loney's refusal to leave constitutes a resistance to the ruling white mythology of success through individual advancement. Those who would have Loney leave, or rather that part of every one of us which would have Loney leave, are requesting another Indian biography depicting success through capitulation. Such a happy "comedy," as Arnold Krupat points out, would serve the status quo, the "moral norm" of the ruling class (*Smoothing*, 270). That is exactly why Dan Cushman's comedy, *Stay Away Joe*, is disturbing to me: while sympathetically and hilariously presenting Indian failure, it does so by complacently serving the white point of view. That makes the novel most readable, unfortunately, to whites and Indians alike.

All these Native American novels, and other recent ones such as Louise Erdrich's brilliant *Love Medicine*, *Beet Queen*, and *Tracks*, present American individuals, who are Indian, seeking to transfer energy to a tribal context. Loney dies two deaths: his white suicide is certainly a perverted assertion of individuality, yet his loyalty to Amos, the dog, his past, and place is a transfer of energy to tribe. Thus his bird vision is a liberation of self, a reconnection to tribal past. Loney dies watching his past, "the beating wings of a dark bird as it climbed to a distant place."

The homing plot of *Loney* marries white failure to Indian pride, and if that marriage is "almost too real," it is not the fault of Welch. These novelists are not offering Indian answers, but reflecting continued respect for tribal identity while realistically depicting the disadvantages of nonassimilation. The challenge to whites is to appreciate how these novels present a single, eloquent argument against dereservation and assimilation, and for the necessity of working out an identity in relation to one's past. These are neither formula nor protest novels. Welch had not read McNickle before writing these two books.

He had read McNickle and much more, however, before writing his third novel, *Fools Crow*. And that novel is so different it must be treated separately.

Fools Crow

Fools Crow could have fought against Plenty-coups. He is renamed (from White Man's Dog) after fooling the Crow Indians during a raid on their camp in the fall of 1868. In this very unusual novel, we are thrown into the Indian's world before the buffalo went away. We do not learn a white man's date until page 284. In the first paragraph, as White Man's Dog watches "Cold Maker gather his forces," we have no idea whether we are watching a hostile Indian with his soldiers, or the wind, or winter coming on.

It is winter. It may occur to you that White Man's Dog knows which it is, so we are not *exactly* in his world. Yet to say "winter" instead of "Cold Maker" would change whatever is happening into an abstraction of the white man's calendar, instead of presenting a personal force who appears that day, perhaps to stay, perhaps not, and whose cold commands will enter the plot. So also the beaver is called "wood-biter," changing the emphasis from our description of appearance (beaver from Old Teutonic and Aryan "brown") to the Indian description of behavior: a character who bites wood, not a thing which is brown.

This book, in other words, was impossible to write. We *cannot* enter an alien world in a comfortable manner. Should Welch render conversation in modern Blackfeet English, slang English, high English? There is no diction that can simultaneously be easy, yet shock us with difference. Welch chose a standard, slightly formal English (approximating Indian formalism) mixed with contemporary slang, and then elected to use Indian names and Indian concepts, and to ask the reader to get used to them. The result is an opportunity for us to come closer to the buffalo-culture Indian world than in any other novel to date.

The action takes us right away into a dramatic epic. A horse-stealing raid on the Crows, a visit to the fort, tribal warfare, and ever-present rumors of white encroachment all build a sense of a way of life active, dangerous, and threatened. An epic novel was a radical departure from Welch's previous work. The huge cast of characters, the sweep of events and the documentation of an entire culture—these seem more like McNickle's concerns.

The historical epic deprived Welch of some favorite tools, his "eye" and "ear" for realistic detail: the bar conversations, Lame Bull's stumbling eulogy, a small-town sheriff, Loney digging a dead dog out of the frozen mud with the broken blade of a pocketknife. Those absolutely "right" touches simply cannot be done in historical novels, or in novels about cultures in which we have not lived. Even if the author did "get it right," what reader could know dead certain that he had? So in the historical novel, author and reader cannot share the infinite details of daily living. Therefore, realistic fidelity to tiny nuances of speech and action, which is one of Welch's strengths, does not come into play.

For an author who had avoided abstractions, dogmas, and generalizations in his previous work, and whose talent lay in clear, precise image and realistic nuance, this novel was a challenge and a risk. He attempted it partly, I think, because he believed that it was important for the Blackfeet, that it was important for them to know how they had once lived and how they had come to their present life.

That sounds like a moral purpose, and it is, which also explains the general tone of this novel. The pride and certainty of a traditional culture fill the book; here are the ancestors Loney and the narrator of *Winter* had longed to find. That *spirit* of a people overwhelms even the historical disasters recounted, so that what might have been Welch's bleakest work, ending in the greatest massacre in Blackfeet and perhaps American history, becomes instead his most positive work, singing the praises of tradition, of dedication to one's community, of hope itself. When Fools Crow is shown the future by Feather Woman, the tone is positive: "Much will be lost. . . . But they will know the way it was." And she advises, "There is much good you can do for your people" (359). In spite of calamitous events, Fools Crow remains courageous, without being naive or ignorant. His uncrushed spirit also lifts the book, paradoxically, from its thoroughly local and tribal setting. One feels that these are the choices all people under siege might face, that even under the worst circumstances one could choose belief over despair.

Welch succeeds in bringing us to those imagined old days, but we should not use the novel simply for vicarious historical experience. Some very interesting literary and cultural issues are embedded in the narrative.

The characters in *Fools Crow* are not treated, at the surface level, in as subtle or complex a manner as those in Welch's earlier novels. Although vivid and believable, they seem to stand before us as givens, as people already formed, understandable and understood, almost archetypal. Indeed, a hostile reader could see in Fools Crow and Fast Horse the Good Indian and Bad Indian of mythology (as presented in Berkhofer and Billington). White Man's Dog is a loser at first, we are told. He will change, we know. Fast Horse looks like trouble. Indeed, he is. Whereas the main characters in *Winter* and *Loney* are essentially elusive and mysterious, and figuring them out *is* the project of the book, in *Fools Crow* the characters are intelligible entities and action is the primary concern.

In *Fools Crow*, answers to psychological questions are sometimes given quite directly: ". . . there was a steadiness, a calmness in White Man's Dog that Yellow Kidney liked. These were rare qualities in a young man on his first adventure. He can be trusted, thought Yellow Kidney. He will do well" (21). And we trust Yellow Kidney; the boy will do well. This is not a point-of-view novel. Is the novel psychologically naive, or on horse raids are people's qualities obvious? The second proposition comes closer to the truth, and I want to discuss the way in which the portraits in *Fools Crow* appear two-dimensional, like modern paintings saying "Here I am, what you see is what you get." And why, like Picasso's portraits, they are intended to be that way.

I said the book was an impossible task, and the handling of character is a fascinating aspect of that impossibility. Modern American fiction is largely psychological fiction. Character and motivation are the primary concerns in most *serious* novels and short stories; stories of pure action, from detectives to cowboys to "Rambo," are considered less important. But the traditional Indians did not share our concern with psychology, while to them behavior and event were terribly important. To push the novel too far toward analysis of an isolated personality or motivation would itself doom any attempt to recapture a tribal past.

Our European interest in psychological fiction is relatively recent. Samuel Taylor Coleridge and other romantics, around 1800, first gave currency in English to words such as "psychology" and "consciousness" as we understand them, and our overriding concern with "personality" is a twentieth-century obsession, not always healthy. When we teach our students to read *Hamlet* as a character study, we are partly projecting modern concerns back onto Shakespeare's text. Once *Gulliver's Travels* (1726) was read as a straightforward satire of humankind; only in this century did we find Gulliver himself an untrustworthy narrator. Most cultural historians feel that the collapse of European empire and the demise of traditional Christianity in the last hundred years, that is, the decline of benevolent authority which I have mentioned, forced us to put more emphasis on the individual and therefore on character and personality as the final truths in a world without shared values. Subjectivity of perception, private consciousness, individual psychology: when the state, religion, and culture have lost credibility, the buck stops there.

White Man's Dog/Fools Crow did not live in our world. Whether a man acted rightly or wrongly mattered a great deal to him, but he trusted his tribe and religion and tradition to define right and wrong action, and he would have been much less interested than we are in *why* he acted as he did. Fools Crow's father is very well presented in the novel; he is deeply concerned for his sons' characters and actions, but he does not have any interest in making moral judgments on their desires. Their consciousness or unconsciousness, if you will, is not a subject of contemplation. What matters is how they have acted and whether they can bear with dignity and honor the consequences of their actions. It may occur to readers that just in having guaranteed *consequences* of actions, their culture differs from ours. We seem to live in a world in which you might get away with anything; that's not true in a small town (band) of eighty people, living a traditional life.

What happens to "psychological" issues? Consider White Man's Dog's dreams. Early in the novel, he covets his father's third wife, a young, beautiful, unhappy girl his father had taken in more as waif than as lover. This is big trouble. Psychologically, the two are drawn together, they are always physically close, glances between them feed the flames. Only the taboo remains. For White Man's Dog to act or decide not to act is a crucial moment, and would be for any adolescent in his first requited love.

How is the decision handled, by the character and by the novel? Their love is consummated in a dream, a dream that both share although Wolverine, spirit-helper to White Man's Dog, graciously obscures his recall. The sharing of the dream and of a certain stone which survives the dream becomes complex; he knows that she knows . . . and having shared a dream, they are able to purge their lust. That is, the dream becomes a form of externalization and communication that replaces, or displaces, or is their culture's analogue to individual psychology. Within the dream, she says:

> "Do you desire me?"
> "I can't say. It is not proper."
> "Why not? This is the place of dreams. Here, we may desire each other. But not in that other world, for there you are my husband's son."
> (119)

At this moment, dreaming seems to function for them as it does in European theory, allowing expression of hidden desires. But when they have the same dream—not only of desire, but of place, action, conversation, and when Wolverine enters both dreams and manipulates them, and when the talisman stone survives, we are moving away from the individual unconscious to something else entirely.

Anthropologist Karl Kroeber has spoken of Indian dreaming displacing energy from individual to tribe; consider Fools Crow's last and longest dream, his vision quest to Feather Woman. This is also, to us, a critical psychological moment. Fools Crow will look ahead, and react with courage or despair. But *he* does not look; he is *shown* by Feather Woman. And *she tells him* how to react. Is Feather Woman part of his psyche or part of his tradition?

Dreaming in this novel is exactly the opposite of dreaming in Freud. Instead of taking us deeper into psyche and individual variation, it takes us out of private psyche and into a public world. So in Indian terms, the dreams *are* psychological subtlety, but they occur at the level of tribe. Psychological conflicts are externalized and conceived in relation to tradition. That is why the portraits can seem two-dimensional, while the situation is not. From the Native American point of view, Wolverine is not a figment of White Man's Dog's imagination; rather, White Man's Dog's psyche is expanded to include Wolverine. A discussion of character, then, would have to account for Wolverine and his motivation, Feather Woman and her experience . . . and not just as "dreams" in the Freudian sense of individual inventions, but as aspects of tribal present and past.

It is not surprising that Native American tales tend to take Coyote's or Raven's characters for granted, and then tell stories of action —action and moral consequences, not escapist adventure tales. So we cannot simply say the characterization in *Fools Crow* does not exhibit the tensions, complexities, ironies we have come to expect in advanced literature, including Welch's own previous work; we have to say that the arena of psychological action is expanded in this novel to include dream, myth, tribe. And then we have to say that this book does *not* seem "modern" in the European sense, exactly because the characters, with conflict displaced and purged, seem to stand before us whole, confident, complete. The only "modern" character, Fast Horse, torn by anxiety, guilt, and angst, is driven out of the tribe. *His* story, we could say, Welch told in his first two novels; this one is entirely different. This story is about a culture where people felt whole with themselves, whole with their past, whole with power. Whether it did them one bit of good is answered in the book: yes.

Once again, writing a novel about a culture you cannot directly know is a strange situation. Say a Missoula freshman who has never left Montana wants to set a story in Beirut. From his research and reading he may learn much; he may know the names of all the factions, the streets, the political issues; but he cannot know what *that* street of shops smells like to an Arab boy from a village in the south. And he can only guess at character and motivation. This is in ways a no-win predicament because on the one hand we must assume that human beings in other cultures are like us, and on the other hand we must assume that they are not. In the case of *Fools Crow*, that past can only be recaptured by guesswork. "This book may be the closest we will ever come in literature to an understanding of what life was like for a Western Indian before the cataclysms of the last century." That is from Dee Brown, author of *Bury My Heart at Wounded Knee*.

There are many uses of books, many reasons to read. One venerable reason is to learn of other people and places, to see life through their eyes. It is a remarkable experience, to be drawn into a story of a culture so different from one's own. We begin to see and feel how Boone, Garcia, and Nannie looked from the other side. It is also strange to go back to the original disasters and find one of our most positive books. The critic Frank Kermode said that ghost stories, good ones, are about how the past haunts the present. Welch's first two books were ghost stories, haunted by tribal memories and loss. But in *Fools Crow* the dead ancestor doesn't haunt, he returns to life, fleshed out, and he encourages—which means, to give heart. Fools Crow is the ancestor of the Indian lawyer in Welch's latest novel.

This concludes our section on Native American authors, who have been writing clearly and effectively about experiences which began "when the buffalo went away" and "the hearts of my people fell to the ground," experiences which continue today in the proud and often tragic homings of these books. True art, as Dreiser said, speaks plainly. As an Eskimo contemporary of Dreiser's said to Knut Rasmussen:

> Our narratives deal with the experiences of man, and these experiences are not always pleasant or pretty. But it is not proper to change our stories to make them more acceptable to our ears, that is if we wish to tell the truth. Words must be the echo of what has happened and cannot be made to conform to the mood and taste of the listener.

Part III
Making Certain It Goes On

Think of those big trout, Bud, fifty years
back and more and no limit then, no game regulations
and no sonic booms cracking the dam
or the dam tender's house, mortar and stone.
How those big rainbows danced
on their tails. How fishermen believed skies
full of willing women. This land spreads big
as the big sky and there's plenty of room
for the dead, for enemies who died and dead friends.
I know what poets I'd bury here and everyone's
a king. I'd ring the reservoir with their stones
and all night their spirits would dance over
the waters. All day trout would dance on our leaders.
We imagine a man in the dam tender's house
stationed there decades ago and forgotten,
beginning to crack like the house. If he came
to us asking the year we'd say "welcome,"
we'd say we too forget the President's name.
Here the hard wind blows all hurt away:
the maimed bison moaning at the bottom
of the jump, Indians starving that year
no bison were seen, the sadness of children
and the sadness of none. We would be
hard as that wind. We're lucky enough to cast down it
and just as we guess the high white jet trail
a major run, say Chicago-Seattle, your bobber
moves some right slightly wrong way and we know
no matter how faint that nibble seems
it could be fifty years old, something real big.
Still no limit, Bud. No limit that counts.
                                        —Richard Hugo, "Pishkun Reservoir"
                                        (for Bud Guthrie)

9
Hugo's Poetry

We spend our lives remembering what we love, to be sure who we are.

POETS SHOULD "TAKE A BRIEF LOOK AT SOMETHING MOST PEOPLE ignore," said Dick Hugo, and he must have said that partly because he felt ignored, or worthy of being ignored, not as a poet but as a man. Left with his grandparents at the age of one, sent to live with friends in Seattle at eleven and again at eighteen, he spent much of his poetic career locating and describing the dispossessed within his poetry and heart: "What endures is what we have neglected." His own autobiographical essays in *The Triggering Town* and *The Real West Marginal Way* tell us much about his background. But he wrote poetry not so much to win his way into *our* hearts as to take into *his* own heart the other orphans on the block. Old men, old cars, bums, derelict towns, abandoned ranches—his poetry welcomed people and places born of human love, then left behind.

He looked at things "most people ignore," not out of intellectual curiosity, not to seek the obscure, but out of a deeply felt need, the need of orphaned people, towns, rivers, fish to find a home:

> I thought that if I could look the world square in the eye in the poem . . .
> that somehow I would be able to survive, and that I would be worthy
> of love, of affection, of owning a home.

The basic subject matter of Hugo's poetry—locating the dispossessed—was personal enough, obsessive enough to deserve a passionate style, which is what he began to develop under Theodore Roethke's guidance at the University of Washington in 1947. Roethke was transmitting the "singing" tradition of William Butler Yeats, the rich iambic melodies and internal rhymes of impassioned verse ("We were the last Romantics," said Yeats. Wrong. Elegiac self-centeredness will never die). Roethke's personality as well as his stylistic tradition suited the bearish and boorish young Hugo: Roethke was a large, uncontrolled man, a role model for the vulgar and ungainly. He was no upright Boston Brahmin, no slender Parisian aesthete, but a big mess of a man who could write.

> He was kind of an outrageous man, and had all kinds of problems, and I was an outrageous young man, and I realized one day that as silly as this man sometimes appeared, he was able to create beautiful things. And it occurred to me that maybe there was a chance for me, too . . . maybe I can salvage something out of this absurd creature I am.

Hugo's early work created the identity he needed, the voice of an urban orphan at camp: intense, street-wise on the riverbank, never far from a bar. Although he insisted this identity was deceptive, that he was always "a softy," the intensity must have been right, for he reinforced this tough stance with a style denser than Roethke's. He packed lines with strong stresses and relentless energy, a pressure essentially urban and, like sixties Black verse, reflecting the constant movement and overlapping riffs of jazz:

> I'm a poet of density. That is to say at least in my first two books, my syllables are all strongly accented. I achieve this through elisions, a very thick line, a heavy line. I do this through syntactical shifts. . . . the first auditory art I heard that had any value were the big swing bands on the radio: Benny Goodman, Bob Crosby, and later Artie Shaw. This swing music is where I developed the idea of getting something else going before the thing died out. Just as one series of riffs was coming to an end, something else would start.

Such fast and toughened poetry was a distinct advantage for Hugo as a young western writer. By beginning with extreme density and tight control, he was able to flirt more openly with sentimentality and regional subjects. He had paid his dues, had commanded respect for technique, and that allowed him—as form often does—a more personal voice and a more personal subject. He could take more chances, especially the chances of carving closer and closer to the bone of feeling and place:

> Bill Kittredge, my colleague . . . said once if you're not risking sentimentality you're not in the ballpark, and that struck me as a very wise statement.

> I had been interested in Bill Stafford's work, in how close he was able to take a poem to the line of sentimentality without falling over it.

With one book published (*A Run of Jacks*, 1961) and another on the way (*Death of the Kapowsin Tavern*, 1965), Hugo went to Italy in 1963 (and again in 1967) to return to old war haunts, and he believed that the Italian openness helped him break out of his tough-guy stance into more vulnerable poems. The resulting book (*Good Luck in Cracked Italian*, 1969) "took the stamp of regionalist off my back for good" (*Trout*, p. 208). In the Italian poems the lines are less dense and the personal voice is more open, but it's still Hugo: all environment is pressure and those nearly crushed draw his eye.

In one of the poems, "Centuries Near Spinazzola," he refers to a curious incident from the war, curious not because as a young airman, lost in a field, he had refused cigarettes to a mother and children, but because he felt so bad about it afterwards: "I think that it's one of the real mistakes I ever made" (*Trout*, p. 217). Only the rich don't give to the poor; Hugo must have been shocked to realize that in that incident he'd been on the other side, the side of power, of the crushers, and that he had instantly been corrupted into behaving like *them*. He never forgot the scene, and to the end of his life he was embarrassed by power or responsibility. There is no tradition of working-class poetry in English; if there were, Hugo, curiously, would be at its country core.

In 1964, Hugo came back from Italy to a job at the University of Montana. He cruised his new domain, looking for the monuments of neglect that "triggered" many of his best poems, and simultaneously loving and hating the vast landscape that was replacing the ocean as his central image of emptiness, of the pressure of nihilism that surrounds each continent, ranch or home: "the remote ugly west where the space between people, like the enormous, empty land, soars finally into void."

His personal life (including a divorce and failed love and feelings of inadequacy in the role of teacher), his drinking, his despair made his early years in Montana some of his worst. However, his bitter self-neglect found in the Montana landscape and ghost towns a hall of mirrors, and with the freer line and voice he had explored in the Italian poems he was ready to write one of the best single books of his career, *The Lady in Kicking Horse Reservoir* (1973). Through some alchemy his poetic resourcefulness and confidence had increased even as he sank, and when he quit drinking in 1971 "then all of a sudden I burst loose." By 1973 he knew who he was, he knew how to write, his personal life was straightening out with his marriage to Ripley Schemm, and he had begun a nine-year "hot streak."

The Northwest had always had more than its share of abandonments waiting for Hugo's pen, and consequently his poetry, although *intensely* personal, was never *merely* personal. His own sense of abandonment dovetailed with the region's history of disaster: the crushing of the Indians, the fur trade boom and bust (1825–45), the mining boom and bust (1860–1900), the homestead boom and bust (1909–19; 66 percent failed), the oil and lumber booms and busts (to the present), the water boom and bust (in full swing now). Following his creed ("a brief look at something most people ignore") Hugo cared not for those building each boom, but for those left behind when the boom had passed:

> Cracks in eight log buildings, counting sheds
> and outhouse, widen and a ghost peeks out.
> Nothing, tree or mountain, weakens wind
> coming for the throat. Even wind must work
> when land gets old. The rotting wagon tongue
> makes fun of girls who begged to go to town.
> Broken brakerods dangle in the dirt.
>
> Alternatives were madness or a calloused moon.
> Wood they carved the plowblade from

turned stone as nameless gray. Indifferent flies
left dung intact. One boy had to leave
when horses pounded night, and miles away
a neighbor's daughter puked. Mother's cry
to dinner changed to caw in later years.

("Montana Ranch Abandoned")

Because dispossession, abandonment, and abuse are an integral part of western history, Dick Hugo was a social and political poet, a western poet not just in his landscape and subject but in having the point of view of the abandoned, of the guy on the bottom: "In my land only the ignored endure, / the wolverine, nameless streams the state / forgot to dam . . ." ("Sailing from Naples"). The regionality of his stance, and his historical-political context, tend to be overlooked by eastern critics (including excellent ones: Martz, Vendler, Pritchard, Howard), while western students see it at once.

The fringe colonies of Europe have always resented the centers of power. England used the New England colonies for lucrative trade and opposed trans-Allegheny settlement, fearing that the colonists would break loose. They did. Jefferson feared that the trans-Mississippi settlers would break loose from Washington's power, and he sent Lewis and Clark to Montana in 1805 partly to keep the West in the nation. He succeeded. Montana has been colonized, exploited, and abandoned by the East several times, and this economic and political colonialism has its counterpart in culture: like all dominated and dispossessed peoples, westerners often feel culturally inferior to the center of power. Twain feared his own ignorance and his disposition to boorish alcoholism exactly as Hugo did, and also feared, as did Hugo, that western degradation was his only asset. In "Second Chances" the bottle says to Hugo: "Come back, baby. You'll find/a million poems deep in your destitute soul." The West is full of false facades and crumbling "Opera Houses" proclaiming our fears: we are not grand.

So to be "Northwest" and especially to be Montanan is partly to feel intimidated by the rich and powerful back East. Hugo's voice of personal degradation captures the political and social reality of a region's degradation. Hugo ponders all this as he eats in a tower restaurant high over the Yale campus:

> Top Of The Park, Hillis. Top of the World.
>   . . . I am out of wisdom,
> eating French toast cooked the year
> Yale was founded, too timid to complain,
> too far from home to trust my manners.
> I'm sure I'm being observed
> and my act is not clean. Western paranoia.
> John Wayne. Three centuries short
> of history. One of stability. Way ahead
> in weather and rustic charm you can't trust.
> With Yale below in gold light, I feel
> I should have read Milton, ought to be
> in the know about something, some key remark
> Dryden made about Donne. Not concerned
> with the way we talk to old cars,
> pat their hoods and murmur "sweet hero."
> Two hundred thousand miles and only
> five changes of oil and one valve grind. . . .
> Out west, survival is enough. . . .
>
>   ("Overlooking Yale")

We should not too long stress the negative. Dispossession and despair are Hugo's material—the given—not his product, what he gives. Above, for instance, there's a delightful victory over Yale as Hugo uses the ruse of intellectual and class inferiority to tug on our American heartstrings. Like Huck Finn he lacks book knowledge, but his commonsense phrases ("in the know") happen to be perfect and he has a sound and generous, if road-weary heart—"old hero," we murmur, and pat his vast Buick of a hood.

If the disenfranchised, the exploited, and abandoned find a way to remain, if they endure (Faulkner's word for the victory of southern blacks), it is often by means of strength of character, pride. By some such formula the adolescent toughness of Hugo's first two books (sometimes a Humphrey Bogart toughness, as he said, but sometimes more like an orphaned Jimmy Dean) grew in the seventies into a

stronger, more mature voice ("now I'm in my Leslie Howard period"),
a voice for a region's and a species' will to endure:

> I imagine them resting a moment, then grim with resolve
> starting down to the sea to get the next stone,
> and one woman thought strange but obeyed,
> urging them on and muttering hard at the sky
> a word we've lost. It sounded like "shape." It meant "world."
> ("The Standing Stones of Callanish")

Learning through suffering is a formula for art at least as old as
Aeschylus, and it lies behind the classic western plot. Easterners—
Europe, really—come west expecting paradise, opportunity, a fresh
start. Then the work begins and the winter comes and the market
prices fall and soon one is, as Nannie Alderson put it, "pioneering in
earnest." The process is one of illusion, disillusionment, endurance. It
was vividly observed by Moses Austin in a Kentucky diary of 1796; his
paragraph could stand at the head of western and Montana literature:

> Ask these Pilgrims what they expect when they git to Kentucky the
> Answer is Land. . . . can any thing be more Absurd than the Conduct of
> man, here is hundreds Travelling hundreds of Miles, they Know not for
> what Nor Whither, except its to Kentucky, passing land almost as good
> . . . but it will not do its not Kentucky its not the Promised Land its not
> the goodly inherateance the Land of Milk and Honey. and when arrived
> at this Heaven in Idea what do they find? a goodly land I will allow but
> to them forbidden Land. exhausted and worn down with distress and
> disappointment they are at last Obliged to become hewers of wood and
> Drawers of water. (*The Frontier Mind*, 26)

The condition of hewing wood and drawing water is not necessarily
bad, but it isn't paradise. The note of endurance, the seed of pride, is
there. So at the end of many poems of western disillusionment, Hugo
sounds a similar note of vitality:

Fort Benton

This was the last name west on charts.
West of here the world turned that indefinite white

of blank paper and settlers faded one at a time alone.
What had been promised in Saint Louis proved
little more than battering weather and resolve.

    . . . This is the town to leave
for the void and come back to needing a home.
It may be the aged river or the brick hotel
on the bank, heavy as water, or the ritual
that shouldn't be hard to start: the whole town out
shouting "come back" at the breaks one day a year.

In the context of western history, Hugo's sense of dispossession
was in another way elevated from the personal to the political: not
only was his dispossession regional, but his resistance to it, his resentment, was the voice of a region: the people in Fort Benton *shout
at* the Missouri breaks; they do not speak with them. Hugo was never
"regionalist," if that term refers to someone who pictures a region as
delightfully "out of it" or "unusual" or "colorful," someone who indeed values that region's distance from power. Pastoral, sentimental,
and local-color authors do just that; they enjoy a region's "dispossession." Hugo resented it. He never wished to escape society, money,
or control. His impotence he hated; it was a region's impotence, his
rage their rage:

The principal supporting business now
is rage. Hatred of the various grays
the mountain sends, hatred of the mill,
The Silver Bill repeal, the best liked girls
who leave each year for Butte.

                              ("Degrees of Gray in Philipsburg")

The primary prayer of his work is not for escape but for real towns, a
real economy, real power—a home. *Then* one can go fishing.

Many pastoralists from Virgil to Dillard had money enough to retire
from the court to the country by choice. Hugo sometimes indulged
self-pity and self-hate and welcomed degradation, but it was always
a *degradation* that he *suffered*, never a privileged escape. In all his work
you won't find a pleasant bar. Necessary maybe to the dispossessed,

or in the Kapowsin tavern, a disgraced sanctuary, but not pleasant.
Forget the ferns:

> Home. Home. I knew it entering.
> Green cheap plaster and the stores
> across the street toward the river
> failed. One Indian depressed
> on Thunderbird. Another buying
> Thunderbird to go.

("The Only Bar in Dixon")

This is serious drinking beside the beautiful Flathead River, beside
the beautiful buffalo range, near the towering Mission Mountains—
the land does not redeem. The ranches are serious, the sage flats and
wind and winter are serious, the rivers yearn—"the Flathead goes
home north northwest"—for the sea. These countryside poems are
the cry of a region for something better, not the whine of the privileged to get away. Hugo did not write of things *other* than power, he
wrote of the *absence* of power. And absence implies presence: the parents, the rich, the militarily superior, the nation that has discarded this
waste. If Hugo lacked the grace of an aristocrat in handling power and
responsibility, he also resented, on behalf of most people on earth,
being denied the chance to acquire such grace.

Montana's colonized status and consequent resentment of power
is a part of our literary as well as historical heritage. When hearing
of all the interesting writers in this region, people often ask "Why
Montana?" "Why Missoula?" No one knows the answer. In a *New
York Times* article Max Crawford said it's a cheap place to live. Perhaps
Butte and its highly politicized, urban background helped raise the
level of consciousness all over the state; perhaps it's just the fishing.
But what we do know is that Montana's writing tradition began with
H. G. Merriam, and he came here mad as hell at the establishment to
the east.

Way to the east. Oxford, England. *The* establishment. Merriam
grew up in Denver and went from the University of Wyoming to Oxford in 1904, with the very first class of Rhodes Scholars. Imagine
how intimidating Oxford must have been in 1904 to a young man,

and a poor man, from the West. At that time, there was nothing like the current craze for western style, the look of the Marlboro man, the fashionable jeans and boots in Paris. Although he admired his education there, Merriam was made to feel like a hick. He disliked the British nobility, and when he returned to the West he was ready to tell people to write about their own culture, not to imitate British literature. He came to UM in 1919 and founded the second creative writing program in the country at Missoula. In 1921 he founded *The Frontier*, a journal for stories, poems, and, later, reminiscences (not even *pretending* to be "art"). From the time of his arrival, he preached regional literature: write about your own experiences, write in a style and dialect that suit your material, describe life as you know it. The bottom line of such advice is simple: *your* life matters. The rich don't own meaning, and they don't own art.

Students who took his classes and advice at UM include A. B. Guthrie, Jr., Dorothy Johnson, Dan Cushman, and many others. His successor as head of creative writing was Walter Van Tilburg Clark, who wrote *The Oxbow Incident*, one of the first "westerns" to redefine the genre. A few years later, Dick Hugo arrived. So when Hugo convinced Jim Welch, in 1968, that Malta, Harlem, Havre, and the reservation could supply the material of great novels, that he should write about his own background, Hugo was following a tradition dating to at least 1919. That tradition has for sixty years been encouraging Montana authors to write not about the West the East needs, but the West the West knows. And from the time Merriam arrived, that tradition has had a relation to power, class, money. That's why Hugo's dispossessions, and his willingness to write about them, are not just personal; they are a region's voice.

Hugo did not wish to be part of an elite; he would have been happy if everyone had enjoyed his work. But poetry is not easy. His distance from the very audience he identified with sometimes pained Hugo, and his down-and-out poems are not always well received in the communities they so unprogressively describe.

This creates a challenge for the teacher as well as the poet. I have had men on both sides of me reciting lines from "The Only Bar in Dixon," in that bar. Then they told me to tell Hugo to keep his butt out. He and Jim Welch and J. D. Reed had written three poems on that bar after a fishing-drinking trip up the Flathead, and all three poems appeared together, under the same title, in *The New Yorker*. The boys in the bar had been quoting mainly Welch's poem; Hugo was incredulous and hurt. He hadn't meant any harm. Saying the redheaded bartender was "yours for a word" was just a way of making a poem; hell, they didn't know her at all (she, the owner, has since forgiven the poets). "Besides," he said, "I called it home!" ("Home. I knew it entering. / Green cheap plaster . . ."). His poem had other compliments as well:

> This is home because some people
> go to Perma and come back
> from Perma saying Perma
> is no fun.

What could you say? Well, Dick, they can't read poetry worth a damn. Or, maybe they don't want to live in your home. He was really hurt when the poems separated him from the people he wished to join, who he believed he *was*.

In the case of that poem, *The New Yorker* proved a difficult audience too. In one line, Hugo had written "The Flathead goes home north northwest" (it flows into the Clark's Fork, then northwest to the Columbia, and then to the Pacific). *The New Yorker* fact editor evidently misread his map, and had the gall to inform the local fisherman that the Flathead flows north north*east*. Hugo's reply: "Perhaps that's why it looks so spectacular climbing the divide."

Sometimes, however, local readers see much more clearly than professors what is going on in these poems, and that always delighted Dick. I have had very interesting days teaching "Degrees of Gray in Philipsburg" in Philipsburg. Or "Hot Springs" in Hot Springs. That poem begins:

> You arrived arthritic for the cure,
> therapeutic qualities of water
> and the therapeutic air. Twenty-five
> years later you limp out of bars . . .

Just as I was about to begin a Chautauqua lecture by reading those lines to a packed Hot Springs hall, an old man, maybe eighty, appeared in the back and slowly made his way forward to a seat in the front row ten feet away. He put his cane between his legs and looked up with red eyes and a toothless grin. "Oh God," I thought, "I can't do this poem." But I had no other bright ideas, so in I plunged. When I got to the lines, "You have a choice of abandoned homes to sleep in," he laughed his toothless laugh. A few others tittered. Then:

> You have ached taking your aches up the hill.
> Another battery of tests. Terrible probe
> of word and needle. Always the fatal word—
> when we get old we crumble.

He laughed again, and the hall joined in. Other lines became unaccountably hilarious—"If some day a cure's announced, for instance/ the hot springs work"—and finally his laughter taught me how to read the affirmation at the poem's end:

> They kept no record
> of your suffering, wouldn't know you
> if you returned, without your cane, your grin.

He just kept smiling. *He* was the audience Hugo wrote for; he was the audience Hugo loved.

Curiously, the Indians of Montana must have helped Hugo write a more positive poetry; in ways they may have forced his maturation. More visible than around Seattle, less assimilated into the dominant culture, the Montana Indians usurped Hugo's position of down and out. His claim to sympathy was challenged by a group, a nation more dispossessed and taking it just as hard:

> These Indians explain away their hair
> between despair and beer. Two pass out
> unnoticed on the floor. One answers to a cop
> for children left five hours in a car.
> Whatever I came here for, engagement

with the real, tomorrow's trip to Babb,
the first words spoken "white man"
split my tongue. I buy a round of beer
no phonier than my money is wrong.

("A Night at the Napi in Browning")

Hugo again finds himself uncomfortably cast in the role of the powerful, with money and a "real" life, and as when in Italy he refused the
woman cigarettes, he fears he will be phony and wrong. He would
rather be the underdog at Yale. His worst fear is that as a person of
responsibility he will speak with forked tongue, and in this poem I'm
afraid he does, for his attempt to shift attention from the Indians' dispossession to his own white guilt, his attempt to sink lower than they,
makes a weak end.

And I, a Mercury outside, a credit card,
a job, a faded face—what should I do?
Go off shaggy to the mountains,
a spot remote enough to stay unloved
and die in flowers, stinking like a bear?

Although the lines are well written, his petulant, willed exile from love
and his imagined death (with us, of course, tearful at his poetic grave)
should not be claiming our attention. The Indians have usurped our
sympathy, and here is Hugo's guilt crowding them out.

I suspect the Indians must have helped change Hugo's stance because
in those years, 1964–73, from arrival in Montana to *The Lady in Kicking Horse Reservoir*, as he was becoming less pitiable, more positive in
voice, more resilient, and ready for marriage and owning a home, at
the very same time the Indians were kicking him upstairs, forcing him
into the role of a man with something to lose. He responded to new
circumstances with new positivism, wrung at some cost from the old
negations.

The formula of salvation through suffering and humility, for instance, which in the Napi poem takes a sentimental turn toward self-
pity and suicide, in many poems of the period takes a turn toward a

humility that is as cosmic as personal. The same themes (Indian dis-possession, white guilt, and how to respond to both) in "Bear Paw," the scene—still an extraordinary site—of Chief Joseph's final military defeat and moral victory, lead to a fine end in which whites and Indi-ans are brought together, the one nation in noble defeat, the other in bad need of it:

> The wind is 95. It still pours from the east
> like armies and it drains each day of hope.
> From any point on the surrounding rim,
> below, the teepees burn. The wind
> is infantile and cruel. It cries "give in" "give in"
> and Looking Glass is dying on the hill.
> Pale grass shudders. Cattails beg and bow. . . .

> . . . Marked stakes tell you
> where they fell. Learn what you can. The wind
> takes all you learn away to reservation graves.

> If close enough to struggle, to take blood
> on your hands, you turn your weeping face
> into the senile wind. Looking Glass is dead
> and will not die. The hawk that circles overhead
> is starved for carrion. One more historian
> is on the way, his cloud on the horizon.
> Five years from now the wind will be 100,
> full of Joseph's words and dusting plaques.
> Pray hard to weather, that lone surviving god,
> that in some sudden wisdom we surrender.

This poem goes several lines beyond the weeping face at the Napi in Browning. It goes beyond egocentric self-destruction to chastisement —which presumes a superior force. What we and the Indians surren-der to is wind pouring like armies, before which Indians literally fade into the grass while we pray for salvation by acknowledging weather, "that lone surviving god."

Hugo's winds, weathers, and landscapes are a considerable part of his poetry. Rarely backgrounds or scenes, his landscapes are more usually characters, and like characters they can play many roles and have an active relation to the speaker: "Pray hard to weather." The land always excited Hugo; in the union of himself and landscape the poet was conceived:

> . . . after I got out of the service, when I was sitting on a Seattle bus— it was at 16th SW and Holden Street—I was thinking about what *east* meant to me, that is to say, there were four hills east, if you walked from our house. For about a mile you would walk over four hills, and we called them by numbers: First Hill, Second Hill, Third Hill, and Fourth Hill. And then on the top of the Fourth Hill it opened up into the big Duwamish River Valley, and I was thinking about taking an imaginary journey, somehow, over these four hills, going east from the house, and somehow that this would go on forever. [I knew that the entire nation . . . lay on the other side of those mountains, there it was, a whole nation, and that here I was in the west.—Author's tape] And I don't know how this led to sudden knowledge. I never said, "You're going to be a poet," but I remember at that moment it suddenly came across my mind that I would spend all my life writing poems. (*Trout*, 207)

The huge space that was the continent became, in many early poems, the space that was the sea. Hugo needed that space in his poetry or just beyond, a void out of which we carve our homes and bars. When he came to Montana that sea became "Open Country":

> It is much like ocean the way it opens
> and rolls. Cows dot the slow climb of a field
> like salmon trawls dot swells, and here or there
> ducks climb on no definite heading.
> . . . .
> And you come back here
> where land has ways of going on
> and the shadow of a cloud
> crawls like a freighter, no port in mind,
> no captain, and the charts dead wrong.

The "lone surviving god" of land and weather to which we pray is not always diabolic, pouring like armies from the east. When the void is genuinely other, out there, like Stafford's sea it saves us from self-centeredness, it offers an alien grace. As often as not, however, that void overlaps the human world, penetrates the psyche and is penetrated, giving birth to images of despair:

> Decaying shacks, abandoned ranches, desolation,
> endless spaces, plains, mountains, ghost towns:
> it's ready-made for my sensibilities.

In that list the landscape and the psyche are overlapped, as in "Point No Point":

> Even in July, from this point north
> the sea is rough. Today the wind is treason
> tearing at our flag and kicking that commercial
> trawl around. We and salmon are beached
> or driven down.

Hugo's vast outer spaces are usually in tension with a dense inner space and a dense poetics, so that far from being a place to relax, that "big sky" (when merged with the psyche) is humming with the wall-to-wall pressure that throughout his work seems essentially urban, driving, banging, strained:

> space that drives into expanse,
> boredom banging in your face,
> the horizon stiff with strain.
>
> ("Ocean on Monday")

Within such a horizon we all are driven to makeshift bars, and thus Hugo's own orphaned search for home is lifted above the personal not only by the regionality of the themes and by the universality of the psyche, but also by the universality of a landscape or cosmos which forces us to shelter. Sometimes his environments seem like a deep sea pressure, and the only thing that can save us is something equally strong within pressing back:

> Believe the couple who have finished their picnic
> and make wet love in the grass, the wise tiny creatures

cheering them on. Believe in milestones, the day
you left home forever and the cold open way
a world wouldn't let you come in. Believe you
and I are that couple. Believe you and I sing tiny
and wise and could if we had to eat stone and go on.

("Glen Uig")

That last line—"could if we had to eat stone and go on," now carved
on his tombstone—is the heart of Hugo, for beyond the issues of content, style, or historical context is the voice. Dick Hugo was a presence.
He had a booming laugh, an outrageous Falstaffian vitality, and in his
poems a tender toughness "as bear-blunt and shufflingly endearing"
as the man. He was master of a strong, affirmative style, a compas-
sionate voice that had to be heard. He never played around. He was
never interested in the perfect image poem, the little jewel of virtu-
osity that no one needs. Like many older poets—Yeats, Stevens, Penn
Warren—he was beginning (in *31 Letters and 13 Dreams*, *White Center*,
and *The Right Madness on Skye*) to use more conversational, accessible
lines that don't pressure us with the poet's poetics so much as with
his need to make us believe. "Please hear me," these poems say, not
"Be amazed." Alas, Hugo died far short of the age, seventy, when
those other poets were entering their final and most graceful phases.

Because of that booming voice, that resilient energy, humor, and
heart, Hugo's poetry is essentially positive and American. He speaks
of the past in order to come to the present, of despair in order to
come to hope, of dispossession in order to come home. The voice is
straightforward—he *does* "look the world square in the eye"—and his
nuances of technique tend to make the voice stronger, not more complex: as the poet Dave Smith (one of Hugo's best critics) said, in style
Hugo was "a meat and potatoes man." That's what he wanted to be.
That's what he was sure he was.

The power of Hugo's voice was never more clear than at his memorial service in Missoula, when Hugo's presence—for it was that—gave
voice to the people. In an hour of great eloquence and riotous taste-
fulness, the most eloquent, most tasteful, and most hilarious were
old friends farthest from the university: John Mitchell from Seattle

and Jennie Herndon of the old Milltown Union Bar, Laundromat and Cafe. Their talks have been reprinted in *CutBank* 20, the Hugo Memorial issue. Something in Hugo and his poetry gave them supreme confidence in their speech, and if poetry is "the mind in the act of finding what will suffice," as Wallace Stevens said, they became poets that day.

10

Doig's House of Sky

IF YOU THINK BACK OVER THE AUTHORS WE'VE DISCUSSED—
Guthrie, Garcia, Alderson, Plenty-coups, McNickle, Welch, Hugo—
and if you know Montana, you might be struck with how much of
ordinary life is missing. The ordinary Montana life of small towns,
bars, family, women. Even ranching has barely appeared in Alderson
and Welch, and the towns in Hugo are just glimpsed. Welch's bars are
seen through the most depressed of narrators. What is missing in our
discussion, so far, is the twentieth-century agrarian life that replaced
the early pull-up-stakes, boom-and-bust frontier. Montana, growing
slowly for sixty years, has a population that stays put doing the same
things and liking it. After the busted homesteaders left in 1920, and
until the recent mining collapses in Butte and Anaconda, Montana
has been a remarkably steady-state universe. This is the opposite of
the frontier, and indeed one could argue that my own background in
a New York suburb where I never knew my neighbors and expected
always to leave, to find success somewhere far away, was more of a
"frontier" background than the agrarian life of most Montanans since
1920.

This became funny and obvious one day in class when a young
man in the back, a skeptical, lumberjack-shirted Montanan and an
excellent student, blew up at my reading of *The Big Sky*. "Who are
you to come out here and tell us . . . ?" he was saying. "My great-
great-grandfather came out from Boston homesteading in . . . ," etc.,
etc. And I heard myself saying (shouting?) in immediate response (we
were both laughing), "That's exactly the kind of blue-blood snobbery
he left Boston to get away from—who cares who your parents are? I
pulled up stakes and came West and now I'm stealing Montana literature from under your nose just like your great-grand-whatever took

land from the Indians while you sit on your butt talking pedigree. Who's the real pioneer? Who's the son-of-a-bitch from the East?"

We all laughed, and then the truth began to sink in. Montana *has* changed. Most of America, for fifty years, has been *more* mobile, more unstable, more unpredictable and opportunistic than Montana. So while our *myths* and self-images and, in some ways, Montana character, derive from that wide open nineteenth-century frontier, our twentieth-century reality is small-town stable. Ivan Doig captures the reality of twentieth-century Montana life: extended family, strong women, ranching, bars, small towns. *This House of Sky* is a true reminiscence about Doig's childhood, his father Charlie, and agrarian Montana.

There have been some good ranching memoirs and documents: Nannie Alderson, C. M. Russell, Teddy Blue Abbott, Walt Coburn's *Story of the Circle C Ranch*, Granville Stuart, Spike Van Cleve. *The Last Best Place* has some wonderful short pieces, such as those by L. A. Huffman and Orland Esval. More recently, Mary Blew's stories in *Lambing Out*, Teresa Jordan's *Cowgirls*, and Ralph Beer's novel *The Blind Corral* show Montana ranching from the point of view of those who know. But I was stunned when I read, in 1978, the opening page of *This House of Sky* in the *New York Times Book Review*:

Soon before daybreak on my sixth birthday, my mother's breathing wheezed more raggedly than ever, then quieted. And then stopped.

The remembering begins out of that new silence. Through the time since, I reach back along my father's tellings and around the urgings which would have me face about and forget, to feel into these oldest shadows for the first sudden edge of it all.

It starts, early in the mountain summer, far back among the high spilling slopes of the Bridger Range of southwestern Montana. The single sound is hidden water—the south fork of Sixteenmile Creek diving down its willow-masked gulch. The stream flees north through this secret and peopleless land until, under the fir-dark flanks of Hatfield Mountain, a bow of meadow makes the riffled water curl wide to the west. At this interruption, a low rumple of the mountain knolls itself up watchfully, and atop it, like a sentry box over the frontier between the sly creek and the prodding meadow, perches our single-room herding cabin.

The style, tense and dynamic with strong verbs and nouns made into verbs, was dramatically imaginative and anti-"western," following the lead not of John Wayne but of William Faulkner. Here was a child of homesteading and sheep ranching, a tight Scotsman at that, who poured heart and soul into a highly rhetorical, wordy, risk-taking prose. Like Welch's prose, Doig's declared that a Montanan could speak any way he or she pleased, that "western" writing did not have to be silence, one-liners, and grunts. Doig grafted this passionate rhetoric onto the terse reticence of his Scots-Montana father, and the result is a wonderful combination of halt and flow, ornament and pith:

> "I guess ye'd have to say that spell was none too easy for me, either." A tiny plopping sound of surprise, made by clucking his tongue against the roof of his mouth, might come from my father when he suddenly remembered something, or felt a quick regret of some sort. This time, the soft salute meant both those things. "Godamighty, Ivan, I did miss your mother." (16)

After *This House of Sky*, Doig wrote two novels immersed in the history of the Northwest coast, *Winter Brothers* and *The Sea Runners* (Doig lives in Seattle). Then he returned to the Montana scene with *English Creek* (1984) and *Dancing at the Rascal Fair* (1987). These two books are, respectively, the middle and the first in a planned trilogy about a Scots family that immigrates to Montana, their three generations intertwined with sheep-ranching and the Forest Service. The third book, now in progress, will come up to the 1989 Montana Centennial.

Doig's use of the Forest Service is interesting partly because it realistically reminds us of the omnipresence of government and government land in Montana, even though our literature, like our myths, has overlooked that issue. One of my favorite scenes in *Dancing at the Rascal Fair*, to my mind Doig's best book since *This House of Sky*, is when the ranchers along the Front Range north of Choteau are suddenly faced by a man from the brand new Forest Service telling them he will now control grazing rights on land they've used at will. The homesteaders, of course, forget that *they* received government land, and that a national forest, and control of it by the government, is not a new or radical principle. The clash of frontier individualism and government control is dramatic and believable. Research is one of Doig's strong suits. Trained as a historian and practiced as a journalist, careful and thorough by (Scots?) habit, his facts and situations and dialect can be trusted. These books are valuable and responsible fictions of the agrarian frontier.

The frontier that Doig presents is the second frontier, the homesteading boom after Nannie Alderson's mercantile dreams of the 1880s. A trickle of settle-down homesteaders in the eighties and nineties became a world-famous flood after 1909, with 250 hopeful homesteaders, for instance, getting off one train at Havre one evening in 1910. This agrarian boom of families wishing to start a new life filled the plains from 1909 until 1919, when several years of increasing drought followed by a vicious winter sent over half of them packing. Doig mentions this period in *This House of Sky* as his father's background, and covers it year by year in *Dancing at the Rascal Fair*. Just as Nannie presents so clearly the mercantile West of the first cattle boom, Doig captures the agrarian West of this century.

But these books are more than documents. If I had to put a finger on a consistent tone in Doig's Montana work, I would point to childhood: how it seems from a distance, how it looks to us later, the kind of right nostalgia we hold for that particular past which is our own. Doig loves to remember. His characters love to remember. All three of his Montana narrators—Doig, Jick, Angus—are sensitive, verbal remembrancers, entranced with the past, held by its magic.

Doig's is a personal, not a historical nostalgia. His history is realistic. The romantic glow of these books comes from a suffused desire, everyone's desire, to recapture a state of childhood which long predates Montana's entrance to the union. So the notion that "once this was a simpler world" is in Doig, too, but in *This House of Sky* it seems wrapped up with the personal loss of a mother at age six, and curiously wed to a most unsimple reality: a single-parent father, his terrible second marriage and divorce, a strange truce of father and grandmother for the child's sake. Doig's early life was a mess. Yet looking back, at least, he loved it. Doig's Montana is a world torn by the loss of security and homestead, seen through a curious combination of exacting realism and the soft-focus lens of a child's need for, and perhaps therefore creation of, paradise. Certainly that is true of *This House of Sky*.

This House of Sky

Most Montana and Inland West books are dominated by three elements: land, something between endurance and despair, and aloneness. *This House of Sky* has plenty of the first two—the subtitle is "Landscapes of a Western Mind," and the lesson is endurance—but the lone rogue male of nineteenth-century myth is finally gone. Everywhere is family, tied up in a web of style that mirrors the intricacy and mystery of relationship. And relations lie at the heart of this book.

The style is dazzling for the first eleven pages, perhaps partly because the writer, like every first-book author and especially one trained as historian and journalist, needed to prove to himself and everyone else that he could write. I think he proved it pretty well. Then the book settles down to stories of and hymns to his father, Charlie Doig. Charlie's dry, wry Scots wit becomes the anchor for Ivan's love of language, and the rhetoric of the book circles from Faulkner in toward Charlie: "Scotchmen and coyotes was the only ones that could live in the basin, and pretty damn soon the coyotes starved out" (24).

The family, as Doig says, "went about life as if it was some private concoction they had just thought up," which is the devil's truth. Ivan's mother dies in the first sentence, when Ivan is six; the family homestead is lost after the winter of 1919–20; Charlie becomes a hired man, usually foreman, around the valley; by page seventy Charlie has married his cook, and the following three disastrous years are erased from family memory and albums. After that debacle, desperately raising his son alone, Charlie forms an uneasy alliance with the maternal grandmother who had never liked him. That alliance grows into the family that the boy had always needed, and Bessie Ringer, the grandmother, becomes one of the strongest portraits of frontier women we have in print. This ideal family, one should remember, comes by way of two deaths, a divorce, and failure on the homestead.

As I say, the child's nostalgia in Doig's tone is mixed with plenty of historical realism. This book gives us every reason to believe that the frontier was hard on families. Things broke up, until the ones tough enough were left.

As the story is told, memorable portraits emerge: White Sulphur Springs, local bars from a child's point of view, school and Mrs. Tidyman (the Valier teacher who could spot a born reader), Bessie, and a father canonized in the eyes of his son.

Charlie Doig provides a classic western center for the narrative, or at least his son chooses to give him a classic western interpretation. Legendary horseman, small but tough with his fists, impervious to pain, honest, succinct, ironic, Charlie strides across the silver screen of the child's memory.

This book is an eloquent, moving reminiscence, a wonderful blend of documentary accuracy and imaginative prose. Because it is a memoir and not a novel, we take it pretty much at face value. Like Nannie's memoir, it encourages several questions, and some of the most interesting questions are raised not by my students at the university, but by the older Montanans who have attended discussions of this book around the state. In a federally funded program called "Let's Talk About It," *This House of Sky* was one of several books examined in meetings at local libraries in Montana. I was the speaker and discussion leader in the western part of the state, and Mary Blew, when she was Dean at Northern Montana College in Havre, traveled through central Montana discussing the book.

I was especially interested in Mary Blew's report. She grew up on a ranch in the Judith Mountains near Lewistown. She was discussing the book near Doig's old stomping grounds, where his work is immensely popular.

Several interesting observations concerned the child's point of view and the innocence of Montanans, as depicted in the book. First is the child's relation to his father. It seems entirely likely that women were in many ways more influential for Ivan than men, including his father. His first-grade teacher and, later, Mrs. Tidyman discovered and nurtured his literary talent; Charlie would have had him herd sheep. When Ivan decides that the Montana life is not for him, he is in essence rejecting his father's life and taking the course advocated and made possible by several women. But the book does not present it that way. Similarly, strong as Charlie is, he is hardly stronger than Bessie, and while the book does every loving justice to Bessie's character, Charlie remains the object of the boy's obsession.

You can see the proposition: Ivan's young life took place in a matriarchal world, while his myths and obsessions were patriarchal. Perhaps there was no way for him to remain a "western man" and admit that while he idolized Charlie's macho life, the women were offering him what he really needed. So their leadership and roles as models for the boy are necessarily, unconsciously slighted. On the one hand, Ivan felt he should grow up to be like his father, and that desire pervades the book. On the other hand, he was not like his father and did not want to be, and that plot—enmeshed with women—remains half hidden. Do we see here the faintest echo of a nineteenth-century sexism which held that men do rough and ready and outdoor things, while literature and language and art and culture are the province of women? Some Montana women have told me that they see, with some pain, similar distances grow between themselves and their sons. The western myth remains a male myth (and a simplified version of male at that), while this book offers ample evidence of a reality more complex.

The second issue raised by the book is the innocence and nostalgia woven into the child's point of view. For instance, in the bad marriage of Charlie and Ruth, Ruth is blamed. The child takes the side of the natural parent, and remembers it that way. The author Doig chooses to remain within the perceptions of the child Doig. A critical and disinterested portrait of Charlie is not going to be part of the book; this landscape of a western mind, while full of irony, remains thoroughly romantic. That sharp blend of irony and beauty seems particularly Scots romantic.

The only way in which these considerations negatively affect the book is near the end, when Doig leaves Montana to go "back East" to Evanston, to college. Because what he is rejecting is not squarely faced, and the class-conflict undercurrents at college are not clear in his mind, the eastern scenes are weaker than the western. What does he need that Montana, and his father's life, cannot offer? What is the relation of those needs to home? The final tone is a bittersweet pull, not entirely clarified, between adoration and rejection. Mary Blew has said that the story of "leaving Montana," the subtext of so many books, remains to be written.

The son's point of view supplies the love that is the heartbeat of the book. Doig admits often that his memoir will commit every crime of the heart in futile pursuit of an impossible goal:

> Memory is a kind of homesickness, and like homesickness, it falls short of the actualities on almost every count. . . . I wait for the language of memory to come onto the exact tones of how the three of us, across our three generations and our separations of personality, became something-both-more-and-less-than-a-family and different from anything sheathed in any of the other phrases of kinship. (239)

Doig's is the tribute every father might wish, and for that matter the tribute a state or a way of life might wish. The memories are eloquent, accurate, and warmhearted, sketching a Montana never before captured in print. The scene is social, not shoot-em-up, in a real Montana bar:

> Only now do I understand how starved my father was for that listening and gossip from Pete McCabe. Nowhere else, never in the silences of the life we led most of the time on the ranch, could he hear the valley news which touched our own situation, and in a tone of voice which counted him special. Nowhere else, either, did Dad's past as a ranchman glow alive as it did in the Stockman. Just then in its history, White Sulphur was seeing the last of a generation of aging sheepherders and cowboys and other ranch hands. Several of them, I remember, had nicknames of a style which would pass when they did: Diamond Tony, who had a baffling Middle European name and an odd, chomping accent to go with it; Mulligan John, called so for the meal which had become a habit with him in the aloneness of sheep camps; George Washington Hopkins, the little Missourian who insisted he was from Texas, and insisted too on being called simply Hoppy; a dressy little foreigner who had been dubbed Bowtie Frenchy; other immigrant herders who rated only Swede, Bohunk, Dutchy; towering Long John and silent Deaf John. Maybe half a hundred of these men, gray and gimpy and familyless,

making their rounds downtown, coming out for a few hours to escape living with themselves. Any time after dusk, you began to find them in the saloons in pairs or threes, sitting hunched toward one another, nodding their heads wise as parsons as they reheard one another's stories, remembering them before they were spoken. "Just waitin' for the marble farm," Pete McCabe said of them with sorrow, for he enjoyed the old gaffers and would set them up a free beer now and again, "you know they'd like to have one and don't have the money for it and I never lost anything doing it for 'em." Dad had worked with most of these men, on the Dogie or elsewhere, and their company seemed to warm him from the cold agony he had been through. (59–60)

Like so many Montana books, this one is about recovering a lost past. But it is the past of Jeffersonian pastoralism, warm and generous, full of family and town, not the past of easy opportunity or cowboy romance. The landscape of this western mind is equal parts tough times, nostalgia, and love.

This House of Sky was very popular, and runner-up for the National Book Award, at the end of a decade interested in *Roots*. Certainly part of the book's appeal is Doig's attempt to remember and understand his roots. But the book is also about the boy who went away, who turned from ranching and Montana to become a professional writer on the West Coast. To simplify a bit, this book includes both plots: the white American leaving home for a better life as a free individual, and at the same time a person trying to locate himself within the tribe. Indeed, some of the book's appeal comes from just that tension; if it was so grand, why didn't he stay? On the other hand, how refreshing to hear the honest truth: life on the land isn't for everyone. Only 7 percent of the people *in Montana* are in agriculture. So this book writes itself into the crack between nostalgia for our rural roots, and the success story of the mobile individual who got out. The story is in both plots essentially American, and neither we nor Doig really know what to do with our own rejections of parents and ways of life which we genuinely admire. Change seems to ride us, willy-nilly, its own forward way. A fine presentation of just these issues can be found in Bill Kittredge's essays, *Owning It All* (1987).

Near the end of his book, Doig wrestles with these dilemmas. I said

This House of Sky has a moral. What did Ivan get from his background that he could carry to Seattle, and beyond? He answers, I believe, on behalf of most Montanans:

> . . . my father stayed in the moments of my days steadily now, even as his body dwindled from me. All of his way of life that I had sought escape from—the grindstone routine of ranching, the existence at the mercy of mauling weather, the endless starting-over from one calamity or another—was passing with him, and while I still wanted my distance from such a gauntlet, I found that I did not want my knowing of it to go from me. The perseverance to have lasted nearly seventy years amid such cold prospects was what heritage Dad had for me; I had begun to see that it counted for much. (294)

I believe Doig's instincts here are morally and culturally right on the mark. It is not necessarily sentimental or nostalgic to look back on tougher times as producing some fine traits; yet who would choose tougher times? As I mentioned in the first two chapters while considering Boone's equation of ease and happiness, we humans may well be an animal that doesn't show its finest colors in luxury. So Doig writes, honestly and almost bewilderedly, about the situation the nation finds itself in: any fool must choose the easier life (by some definitions) when it is offered, yet the American character we admire sometimes seems to have been made of sterner stuff, in tougher times. Whether *that* is an historical illusion I leave to others; I'm not so sure it isn't true. The book ends with a way of life passing, a way Ivan rejected yet wishes to eulogize. He can only hope to have his father's guts. I think he does.

11

Maclean's River

"IN OUR FAMILY, THERE WAS NO CLEAR LINE BETWEEN RELIGION and fly fishing." So the most beautifully written of Montana stories opens.

> We lived at the junction of two great trout rivers in western Montana, and our father was a Presbyterian minister and a fly fisherman who tied his own flies and taught others. He told us about Christ's disciples being fishermen, and we were left to assume, as my brother and I did, that all first-class fishermen on the Sea of Galilee were fly fishermen and that John, the favorite, was a dry-fly fisherman. (1)

Only a hundred pages long, *A River Runs Through It* is set in Montana in the 1920s and is very close to autobiographical truth. The narrator tells of his preacher father and of his brother, a great fly fisherman whose life was sliding downhill "and, in the end," the narrator says right away, "I could not help him" (6). So Maclean weaves together two strands to make this tale: a hymn to his brother's fishing and the story of a family's futile attempt to help one of its own.

It may be surprising, but quite a few hackles are raised by this story of fly fishing, art, and family love. Montana Scots are cocksure enough anyway, and this one is a preacher's son as well as a distinguished English professor at the University of Chicago. Consequently, a lot of things in this book are very clear, and a lot of definite claims are made. The voice is strong, and personal, and people react.

Only two of the Montana books we're discussing cause real fights in class: Alderson and Maclean. A minority, often of very good students, dislikes *A River Runs Through It* intensely. In Nannie Alderson's case, it comes down to character: woman or wimp. The arguments over *A River Runs Through It* also center on character, not that of the brother-hero but of the narrator. Is this a brilliant book by a self-righteous old bastard of a narrator, or a book graced by charity as well as brains? Since this first-person tale is ambitiously religious and moral, and directly concerned with whether or not we can be our brother's keeper, the questions are appropriate.

These problems raise interesting issues about Montana culture—after all, Maclean formally offers a frontier theology—but we can set aside the big issues for the end of this chapter. First let's see what's going on in this dense little nugget of a story, not easily assayed.

The Book

Norman Maclean was born in 1902, a year after Guthrie, and this story shares the profound primitivism common to their generation. God is in nature, the devil is in town. The blacksheep brother, Paul, is judged "beautiful" by the preacher father and the narrator on the basis of his fishing, that is, on the basis of his being one with the natural world, however sordid his life might be in Helena. We remember Doig's rancher—"If I moved to town I'd either be a preacher or a drunk"—and the saying, "You can't judge a man by what he does in town." The tendency of the frontier is antisocial. One fine paper in the Montana Writers course was from Ralph Beer, who ranches and writes (*The Blind Corral* was his first novel) near Helena. The paper, on Maclean's preference for country over town, began:

I have lived most of thirty years on a fourth generation family cattle ranch which still is not completely fenced. Through this ranch runs Jackson Creek—narrow, but long enough to keep the ranches along its length isolated from one another. Only when winter closes the common road do we become close neighbors. We feed our stock, take turns plowing snow, and sit in one another's kitchens drinking coffee, talking births, scours, feed grain prices, and spring. Perhaps because the road is closed, sooner or later our talk will turn to town, and in that talk I find we share a general dislike for the place. We are not, it is certain, the friendly and hospitable Westerners the Chamber of Commerce makes us out to be. We often distrust those with whom we do business in Helena or Butte. We are wary of strangers and dislike men wearing suits who have soft hands. The ranchers along my creek share a common distrust of those who make their living with the Law or teach in the local schools, while we take our living from the ground. When I was seven years old I knew about whores. I also knew that like the men who bought our cattle and took our checks, they wore fine clothes, had soft hands, and lived in town.

It's all there, really, the virgin land versus the whoring town. Boone, Maclean, Beer: this river runs deep and, as we shall see, is the main channel of Maclean's religion.

The book is also primitivist in the way it looks back to a lost past; it is one of our most elegant, witty, moving, unashamed songs to Montana before the fall: "What a beautiful world it was once. At least a river of it was. And it was almost mine and my family's and just a few others who wouldn't steal beer."

But this lament for a lost brother and a lost past is *not* primitive in consciousness. The style is controlled, reflective, eminently aware. Like Welch, Hugo, Doig, and other contemporary Montana writers, Maclean clearly believes that only the full limits of human speech can reflect the lives of an intelligent populace. And also like other writers, he strikes compromises between his graceful private speech and western one-liners. His style is full of complex subordinations and private musings, punctuated by tough-guy, no-nonsense Montana lines: "I won't fish with him. He comes from the West Coast and he fishes with worms" (9).

The book's style is actually in the tradition of piscatory prose. Since at least Isaac Walton's *The Compleat Angler* in 1653, which Professor Maclean mentions in passing on page 5, through Henry David Thoreau and many others, fishing has often seemed the perfect combination of action and reflection, and thus a philosophical literature has grown up around the sport.

But that's not all; Maclean's preacher father and his Presbyterian teachings figure prominently in the book's theology. Maclean quite properly breaks western myths by reminding us of all the highly educated, literate people—not only preachers—who came to the frontier, and thus this turn-of-the-century Missoula household grew up with an education which puts ours to shame. Every morning the boy would write, and rewrite, for his father. His education shows, and Maclean chooses to let it show.

So we have in front of us a book conceived and written in the most sophisticated manner, on the most primitivist of topics—innocent nature against the evil town, way back in our lost past—and as behooves a professor and a Scot, Maclean tackles the issues head on. How may western man be saved? That's the question the book asks. By nature and by fishing, of course. No surprise. But exactly why and how can fishing save a fallen angel like Paul? The book proposes a formal theology for salvation across the wide Missouri, a salvation pretty close to what a lot of Montanans have in their hearts, and that is part of the book's power. Not to mention accuracy.

Brother Paul is the spiritual hero, and he is surprisingly close to some of the oldest mythic ideals of standard "westerns." He is tight-lipped and two-fisted, a man of action and, in the novella, of few words. A newspaper reporter in Helena, he sees the tough side and plays poker with the tough boys. The intellectual narrator does the talking; Paul just lives badly, and fishes well.

When he fishes, he becomes a spiritual being, one with his rod and the river. This is also a stock western tradition, from James Fenimore Cooper to the present: the Mute Mystic. Take this rough man of action, this anti-intellectual, hard-drinking good old boy and put him in the woods and presto! He's God's own. "You can't judge a man by what he does in town."

What does our hero, this rough, mute mystic *know*? Maclean does not leave us hanging. The gospel according to Paul's brother (disciple of martyred Paul) is that grace is achieved by nature plus art. That is, you need a river, and you need to learn how to cast.

Maclean makes this religion charming, funny, and believable. The ingredients begin with a father whose Presbyterian soul is remarkably sensual.

> . . . he never asked us more than the first question in the catechism, "What is the chief end of man?" And we answered together so one of us could carry on if the other forgot, "Man's chief end is to glorify God,

and to enjoy Him forever." This always seemed to satisfy him, as indeed such a beautiful answer should have, and besides he was anxious to be on the hills where he could restore his soul and be filled again to overflowing for the evening sermon. . . . Unlike many Presbyterians, he often used the word "beautiful." (1–2)

From this Dionysian and Presbyterian father springs Maclean's western religion, itself a blend of Emersonian ecstasy and, as his father says, "Marine-style" discipline.

Two things are beautiful: God (implying, of course, God's woods and rivers), and man *if* he works at it. Enter fly fishing. The father "believed that man by nature was a mess and had fallen from an original state of grace . . . only by picking up God's rhythms were we able to regain power and beauty" (2). God's rhythms are innate in fly fishing. "It is an art that is performed on a four-count rhythm between ten and two o'clock," says their father, indicating the arm positions of two and ten o'clock in front and behind, and buttoning his casting glove. Casting is subtle, difficult, and comes only with practice. This is a Protestant ethic religion; Montanans admire skill and don't shirk work. To Maclean's father, "all good things—trout as well as eternal salvation—come by grace and grace comes by art and art does not come easy" (4).

Grace, beauty, salvation—participation in God's plan—are all possible. They are earned by disciplined work which allows one to take on God's rhythm, and to practice it in God's space. Paul is the master fisherman. Standing in the Blackfoot river, which to this day can make you believe you have religion or have stupidly ignored it, Paul enters the realm of grace. At that moment, his existence has simply nothing to do with the rest of his life.

How many Montanans *really* believe that if they were standing before their God, the moments *He* would count as religious, the moments *He* would look to for signs of grace, come on those few frosty mornings a year as they hunt, or fish, holding still for a second of disciplined awareness in the midst of sacred space. And all the rest of their lives, no matter how important in other ways, would drop away: love of wife, family, good works in the community, support of neighbors and friends . . . Only in those wild and natural moments, many feel, are they absolutely real, only then have they stripped down to some pure level of being, only then are they part of divinity; indeed, though only Emerson has dared to say it, only then are they divine. Maclean has captured this sensibility, with beauty and intelligence. It is a real part of our culture, especially of what is often called "redneck" culture. This feeling is real. This feeling is American. This feeling is religious. Maclean does it justice.

Such an earned ecstasy comes with side effects which sound familiar. In practice, it has been largely a man's religion, in its essence it is private, and by common agreement it renders irrelevent towns and man's laws. Here, then, is a common link between Emerson in 1840, the lone male of western movie fame, and right-wing survivalist fanatics in Idaho in 1988. What all of these except Emerson lack, Maclean adds as the final condition of grace: God's spirit precedes all. The point is important, and governs the end of the book.

A problem common to many experiential religions is the emphasis they place on the individual. Since most (all?) religions are trying to assert, and to make contact with, something *beyond* the individual, a paradox arises. You must do this alone, yet more than aloneness is revealed. The leap from an individual means to a cosmic end, a leap which excuses individualism as an intermediate stage, was a problem with Emerson's doctrine and Maclean squarely faces the issue. Is Paul pleasing himself in the beautiful river, or is the river as well as Paul a slice of something bigger? And if so, just what is this ultimate, Godlike entity and our relation to it?

The argument appears first on page 95. The father has finished fishing, and when the narrator approaches him on the river bank, he has put aside his book.

> "What have you been reading?" I asked. "A book," he said. . . . "A good book."
>
> Then he told me, "In the part I was reading it says the Word was in the beginning, and that's right. I used to think water was first, but if you listen carefully you will hear that the words are underneath the water." (95)

His good book is of course *The* Good Book, and he has been reading the first chapter of John: "In the beginning was the Word, and the Word was with God, and the Word was God." Most translations since the King James (1611) don't dare mess with this beautiful and crucial passage. The New English Bible from Oxford keeps the same sense: "When all things began, the Word already was. The Word dwelt with God, and what God was, the Word was."

The New Testament Greek translated here as "word" is "logos," which means not only word but by extension language, and something like the principle of order itself, of which, to the Greeks, language was the most dramatic example. Hence they also used "logos" to mean reason, or orderly process (the Greek word survives in our "logic"). In Sophocles' *Oedipus the King*, when Oedipus becomes angry and distraught, Creon says, "If you will only use your 'logos' with me," which could be plausibly translated, "If you will only be reasonable," or, "If you will only speak in complete sentences." Although conventional Christians sometimes interpret the "logos" in John as Christ, I see no reason why it should not mean order itself. In the beginning was the principle of order, pure order, beautiful order, the promise of a design shining and articulate and complete within itself, and order was with God and order was God. In the transcript of his National Public Radio interview Maclean agrees, for he says that he and his father were "deeply concerned about the design of things," and that design is "the logos, the word" in their conversation on the river bank.

This spiritual category comes *in the beginning*. The preacher-father then admits, "I used to think water was first, but . . . the words are underneath the water." That is, he used to think that creation preceded logos, but now he agrees with John; he knows that logos came first. The narrator, however, is still a heretic. In particular, he is a naturalist, deriving meaning from creation, not from spirit-logos, and he replies, ". . . you are a preacher . . . ask Paul, he will tell you that the words are formed out of water."

> "No," my father said, "you are not listening carefully. The water runs over the words. Paul will tell you the same thing." (96)

The narrator is not listening to the river, his father claims, and further-more, Saint Paul would agree: spirit (word, logos, design) precedes creation (water).

Let's make sure these crucial distinctions are clear. Either the universe is a chaos of natural phenomena, out of which we wring meaning, or it is itself meaningful, based on a design, a logos, which preceded material creation. The narrator, and Freud, and most science since 1860 chooses the first option. Either the material world constitutes meaning, or humans imagine, invent, find meaning by reacting to material creation; the logos is our invention. Either way, "the words are formed out of water." Spirit is a way of listening to the Blackfoot. No, the father says, if you listen well, you will hear the spirit in and behind the Blackfoot; order preceded the river. Spiritual meaning is not something we get out of creation; it made creation possible. Each party to the debate, the narrator and his father, thinks Paul is on his side.

If the father is right, Paul is not just escaping evil civilization to have a nice experience in nature; he and his casting rhythm are part of creation, and part also of the logos, the meaningful order, that made creation possible. He and the river, then, are running over the same bed, responding to the same law, the word which is God.

The father is proved right at the end of the story, when the narrator gracefully converts from the natural to the spiritual, to the religion which will guarantee that Paul, now dead, has been saved. The lovely final paragraphs of the story grant that the words—of God and family—lie under the river:

> Of course, now I am too old to be much of a fisherman, and now of course I usually fish the big waters alone, although some friends think I shouldn't. Like many fly fishermen in western Montana where the summer days are almost Arctic in length, I often do not start fishing until the cool of the evening. Then in the Arctic half-light of the canyon, all existence fades to a being with my soul and memories and the sounds of the Big Blackfoot River and a four-count rhythm and the hope that a fish will rise.
>
> Eventually, all things merge into one, and a river runs through it. The river was cut by the world's great flood and runs over rocks from the

basement of time. On some of the rocks are timeless raindrops. Under the rocks are the words, and some of the words are theirs.

I am haunted by waters.

The Trouble

First a very bright student, Mary Kay Kriley, thought the narrator was a tyrannical snot and a sexist in dealing with all the women, not just the whore Rawhide and his brother's Indian girlfriend. Certainly the handling of those two is disturbing, and the entire family of males, father and two sons, has an imperious streak.

Well. And I think the narrator is a son-of-a-bitch on page 22, when a perfectly nice couple is admiring his brother's fishing, and she asks, "You're going to wait, aren't you, until he comes to shore so you can see his big fish?" The narrator has been studying the spiritual-cosmic dimension of the casting line's loops and water drops: "No," I answered, "I'd rather remember the molecules." Like Maclean, I am a professor, but I have never found it necessary to say "molecules" to someone along the river, especially to a woman "in men's bib overalls," whose "motherly breasts bulged out of the bib." What he means is that he perceives the spiritual level, and she can only understand the physical. Put this together with the other portraits of women, who are either beloved stay-at-homes (albeit tough ones) or sluts, and you get the idea that fly fishing leads to an all-male heaven. Well, as Huck Finn said, choose heaven for climate and hell for society.

These are minor points compared to the issue of brother against brother. We cannot review here all the scenes and complex evidence, but there is some reasonable doubt whether the two brothers are at love or war. Beyond the sibling rivalry and the stones thrown in each other's fishing pools, and even the narrator's clear observation that ne'er-do-well Paul is his mother's favorite, are the failed attempts at communication. Brother Paul resents offers of money; but then little else is offered, and we are asked to accept that between these reticent western men, conversation is no use. Do we believe that? Does the narrator? Certainly the book seems written partly to allay guilt; if Paul is canonized, the narrator's failure to save him is irrelevent.

It is an interesting issue that has sparked some first-rate readings by students, although I for one accept Maclean's psychology. Once certain habits of pride and silence are established, well-intentioned attempts to communicate simply may not work, while kind action—"Let's go fishing"—may speak volumes. On the other hand, plenty of realistic detail suggesting family tension is in the text, and we have to sort out for ourselves the comparative triumphs, or illusions, of family love. Lewis Moseley, a graduate student in Religious Studies in 1987, launched a very interesting investigation into the dark possibilities of the book. Here are some excerpts from his paper for Montana Writers:

> In this story all things do *not* come together. In a house full of men and rods and rifles the wife and mother faces her great problems silently and alone in her bedroom (102). All those fish are never cooked and eaten. In this world catching your limit is not followed by a feast; it is rather the signal to knock off and start the serious drinking. . . .
>
> To briefly document the alcoholism: drinking in the morning (10,11), drinking on the job (7,10), denial of hangover (34), denial that drinking beer is drinking (56), the testimony of the desk sergeant, "He's drinking too much" (23), being sued for assault and destruction of property (23), the existence of "Black Scots" in father's family, whom uncle's father doesn't speak about (27). This is far from a complete list. . . .
>
> This father ". . . always felt shy when compelled to praise one of his family . . ." (101). Compelled! He never seems to tire of being the task-master and teacher to his own family. . . .
>
> Paul may be a type of the mute western American man and his case is desperate. He is unable to put "LO" and "VE" together when he sees them tatooed on the cheeks of old Rawhide's ass but he does have a sharp eye for what's left in the whiskey bottle that Neal and the whore have been drinking from. We do Paul a disservice and share the blindness of his father and brother if we picture him as drawing some sort of nourishment and strength from fishing which in fact he is not receiving. The fishing trips give Paul a respite from his demons but not extended healing. There is ample evidence that the role of master fisherman increases Paul's isolation, comes between him and others. "He tried to put his arm around my shoulders but his fish basket with big tails sticking out of it came between us and made it difficult" (47). "He was a master of an art. He did not want any big brother advice or money or help, and in the end, I could not help him" (6).
>
> This last is a most interesting statement. The real reason Paul doesn't

want any advice or help is that he is an alcoholic who doesn't want to change. "I like the trouble," he says (58). Yet the narrator's concept that a man who has mastery in an art is somehow unapproachable, that he may use his forte as a fortress for his ego and remain impregnable to the comment of others, is consistent with a picture of isolated male egos having external relations with, or should I say against one another. All this leaves Paul just where he is, playing the family role of master fisherman and drunk, and leaves the relationship between the two brothers unchanged. . . .

I see Paul's troubles, the drinking and whoring, as foredoomed attempts to find a place for himself, to unite himself to something in the world apart from the "close, loving, family." The futility of these means is as great as that of the father's "faith that his son had died fighting" (104). A black sheep sent as a sacrifice into the world of bastards. The hand, a source of Paul's art and isolation, shattered in his death.

For me if there is saving grace in Paul's life it is not that he caught all those fish but rather that for his mother he was the only man in the world who leaned back and laughed when he held her in his arms.

Bill Kittredge, in a conversation about this chapter and *A River Runs Through It* (he wrote the first screenplay version of the book), thought there was something I did *not* say, and his dislike of the student's remarks quoted above clarified it for him. What's missing here, he said, and in *A River Runs Through It*, is the case for Paul. There is a western tradition of retreat and withdrawal that is not simply primitivist or escapist or alcoholic or Boone-stupid, but a valid protest, a real refusal, an abandonment of the ship of fools. That was the part of Hugo that would just go away, Kittredge said, and that often was right. The problem in *A River Runs Through It* is that the narrator doesn't really admire or understand this part of Paul, so he invents a fly-fishing religion that covers a distrust of Paul's misanthropic life. Kittredge therefore found himself agreeing with my analysis of the narrator's story, yet objecting to the student's attack on Paul.

Out of these varied reactions to the story and the cranky, imperious tone of both the father and the narrator, and from the obvious merits of the book, we may draw some conclusions. First, the book consists of a tension between an individual's fishing religion and a family's love. The fishing and the love *are* an opposition as well as a paradox.

In spite of Maclean's lovely attempts to join father and two sons in fly fishing tradition, and to make that tradition the focus of all that is "beautiful," Paul, when fishing, is isolated, as Moseley says, and the various fishing trips, which substitute for other kinds of interaction, do not help him at all. To encourage Paul to think that what he does on the river is important while what he does in town does not matter is quite possibly to contribute to his downfall.

The ideas we discussed in Guthrie have come home to roost. Paul's rejection of society is a rejection also of his social self. In making him a saint of fishing, the family is also contributing to his doom. As we have seen, to despise society is to relinquish control over it. Indeed, the narrator likes to apply Presbyterian predestination to psychological problems, thus absolving the family of control and guilt. Paul's daily life is like our western strip towns; if no one believes divinity can reside in town, no one will attempt to rectify communal life. Gas stations and burger joints? Hey, that's town. Debts, poker, whores, and booze? Hey, that's Paul in town. What can you do? That is why Paul's river religion, and love of Paul, can be seen as oppositions.

These family tensions are hard to perceive because the style of the book is so forceful and beautiful, and is firmly allied with Paul's primitivist religion. A world of beauty, harmony—of logos—glistens on the sentences like sweat. But the forces of disintegration are there, pulling against the unity so eloquently asserted by Maclean. And *that* is perhaps the book's real virtue. It is saved from pastoral sentimentality by that tension. The narrator's prickliness is a sign of his will; he is *imposing* divinity on this story, and the imposing requires some force, some will to believe, which gives the book enormous energy. This is a vision of family love, posed against a story of family abandonment and guilt. This book *needs* religion, the father *needs* to say of Paul, "He was beautiful," and the narrator *needs* to find words beneath the water and the rock. Otherwise the loss, and the guilt, would be too great.

And this brings our inquiry into Montana writing up to date. That natural world of America is still our world—"Montana is what America was"—and our authors have now found their own voices, their own eloquent voices, for considering and reconsidering what that enormous land and weather, those belittling mountains and ennobling rivers, mean.

Where do we go from here? Where we will go, as I hope to have implied throughout this book, is largely dependent on our awareness of where we have been. And since I would like to conclude with a few guesses about where we might be going, I will in the last chapter go all the way back to the very beginning, to the first serious western, *The Prairie*, 1827, by James Fenimore Cooper. Believe it or not, Cooper points the way.

12

Cooper: Then and Now

Les Osages, descendus hier à l'hôtel de la Terrasse, rue de Rivoli, n'ont point encore quitté leur appartement; ils ont paru à diverses reprises à leur balcon dans la matinée, et les curieux, qui étaient en assez grand nombre sur la terrasse, en face de leur hôtel, ont pu les voir fort distinctement.

—*Moniteur Universel* (Paris),
August 15, 1827

I WANT TO TAKE YOU BACK TO PARIS IN 1827. "THE OSAGE INDI-ans, newly arrived at the Terrace hotel, . . . have not left their apartment but have been clearly seen, on their balcony, by many curious people in the street below." What follows, the French being French, is a long account of their native costumes, and touching descriptions of their delight in street musicians beneath their balcony, as well as their concern for an old beggar beside the carriage road from Le Havre.

The Osage were straight from the prairies, but they were not the first plains Indians to visit Paris. According to one local pamphlet of 1827 (*Six Indiens Rouges*), the great-grandfather of one of the Osage Indians had visited Louis XIV (died 1715) and had returned to the Missouri to report to his tribe. Louis Philippe in exile had spent time on the Missouri, and knew and admired several plains Indians. The Indians on the balcony had certainly heard stories of Paris from elders in their tribe, and now they had come down the Missouri to New Orleans, by boat to Le Havre, and by carriage to Paris. Like other delegations, they would be well received and well inspected. The painter George Catlin brought fourteen "Ioways" to Paris in 1845; the newspaper *Constitutionnel* reported:

Today, at two oclock, they [the Indians] were taken to the Tuileries [Palace] in a four horse coach. After having been presented to the King and the Royal Family, these savages ["sauvages"] went to the Institute where members of the Academy of Sciences were able to examine them in the library.

Paris was excited by these visits; while the Osage were in town in 1827 three pamphlets were marketed and newspapers covered their every move. Only one, the *Courrier Français*, professed boredom, saying that the Indians were the sensation of the season, no doubt, but could not match up to the visit, the year before, of the African giraffe.

The papers and pamphlets tried their best to tell Parisians all about Indians and the American West. In *Six Indiens Rouges* you might be interested to learn, for instance, that the Osage of the lower Missouri go "northwest" in winter to eat "oysters, birds, and crocodiles." Which birds? We are told that their country (think Kansas) is rich in pigeons and parakeets. And that even their women climb the highest trees.

The American Revolution was fifty, the French Revolution thirty-five years old. Jefferson, who had spent many young years in Paris, was still alive, and the Frenchman Lafayette was again visiting Louisiana, writing descriptive letters back to French journals. To those men, one thing the Indians stood for was freedom, and in the pamphlets we find the characteristics of primitivism which we noted in the first two chapters. French and Americans projected their own new and hard-won liberty, their growing distrust of civilization, and their new political maxims onto Indians:

> This attachment to their native soil is extreme among them. It is a passion matched only by their ardent love of independence and liberty, qualities so precious that they would not exchange the least part of them for the benefits of civilization. Their favorite maxim is, "One can do anything one wishes unless it harms others."

Liberty is seen as the opposite of civilization, and defined as license— one can do anything one wishes—qualified only by John Stuart Mill's "unless it harms others." Obviously, Indian tribalism is overlooked.

Into this romance of Indians as free men of the noble forest stepped James Fenimore Cooper. He sailed from New York with his wife, two daughters, two trunks, a dog, and forty or so manuscript pages of what would be the first western, *The Prairie*. He arrived in Paris July 22, 1826, and finished the book by April 1827. All of his previous wilderness novels, famous in France, had been set in eastern woodlands; the Cooper Indians had been forest Indians. But this book, which he and many others thought his best, was set out West, where he had never been. He had hardly crossed the Hudson, never had been near the Mississippi, and the geography between Colorado and Montana was virtually unknown. His best map showed the distance between present Denver (Platte headwaters) and present Montana (Missouri headwaters) as about one fourth of the truth. The prairies in between have a single feature, "The Black Hills," which are shown stretching from Colorado to North Dakota, and the region is called "The Great Desert."

What did he write in Paris? He wrote, I think, a true book, which offered a vision of the West that can serve us well today. How, we may ask in amazement, did that happen?

It happened because the West scared Cooper. He had, by luck, new and accurate sources at his disposal. He began the book in New York with Lewis and Clark's journals (Biddle edition, 1814) open before him. He stole liberally, then apparently left that book behind and took with him Edwin James's new narrative of Major Stephen Long's expedition to the Colorado Rockies (to Long's Peak and present Denver, 1819–20). James was both the trip's chronicler and its botanist. His *Account of an Expedition from Pittsburgh to the Rocky Mountains*, issued by Cooper's publisher Carey and Lea in 1823, was only two years old when Cooper began *The Prairie*. Cooper was a new journalist of his time, rushing to write a novel out of the latest and most accurate documents from the West. He left his copy of James with the Duchesse de Broglie in France.

The West described by James was barren. Think how barren it must have seemed in Paris, as Cooper sat reading at his desk in the rue St. Maur (now rue Abbe Gregoire) on the Left Bank, surrounded by street sounds and smells and an opulence and elegance unknown in still-rural America. "I go to Soirees where Princesses and Duchesses are more plenty than hogs in the streets of New York," he wrote in a letter home. His wife, Susan, described dinner parties with Tallyrand,

Lafayette, with the King and the Dauphine (daughter of Louis XVI and the murdered Marie Antoinette): "the Dauphine . . . in white, blazing with jewelry, the coronet for her head and belt for her waist, was covered with diamonds . . . she wore feathers, in her hair . . . her train, which was six or seven yards in length, was borne by her Pages." Cooper must have read James's descriptions of "The Great Desert" with the distance that has always drawn Europe to our West. Cooper saw the prairie more clearly from Paris: bare and wild, the opposite of glittering civilization, one focus of a crowded Europe's dreams.

But Cooper's West is neither dream nor escape; it is hard times. Edwin James, the botanist whose journal Cooper appropriated, had a pretty clear response to the West. His party in 1819 took the Missouri up to the Platte (which enters from central Nebraska), wintered with the Pawnees, then in 1820 went west by horse to the Rockies at Long's Peak:

In regard to this extensive section of country, I do not hesitate in giving the opinion, that it is almost wholly unfit for cultivation, and of course uninhabitable by a people depending upon agriculture for their subsistence. Although tracts of fertile land considerably extensive are occasionally to be met with, yet the scarcity of wood and water, almost uniformly prevalent, will prove an insuperable obstacle in the way of settling the country. This objection rests not only against the section immediately under consideration, but applies with equal propriety to a much larger portion of the country.

—Major Stephen Long

We have little apprehension of giving too unfavorable an account of this portion of the country. Though the soil is in some places fertile, the want of timber, of navigable streams, and of water for the necessities of life, render it an unfit residence for any but a nomad population. The traveller who shall at any times have traversed its desolate sands, will, we think, join us in the wish that this region may for ever remain the unmolested haunt of the native hunter, the bison, and the jackall [coyote].

—Edwin James
(both quoted by Thwaites, Vol. 14, p. 20)

Their pessimistic response to the West, which did much to create the "desert" myth that forty years later would be reversed to a "garden" myth, was based on a very practical ingredient: water. Lewis and Clark's journals had been different. Ascending the Missouri, Lewis and Clark had praised the country the entire way except for a day of badlands near the Missouri breaks. Lewis and Clark kept declaring "excellent position for a town" (Sept. 15, 1804), and described "the wide plains watered by the Missouri and the Yellowstone . . . animated by vast herds of buffalo, deer, elk and antelope . . . fertile and well timbered" (April 26, 1805). They had made it clear to their commander, Thomas Jefferson, that the country was fit for immediate and prosperous settlement.

James, however, sang a different tune. Why? The sand hills of Nebraska, the worst country they traversed, are no worse than parts of Montana. The answer is that Lewis and Clark went by water, staring every day into that bottomland of cottonwoods, dense brush, wildrose, plum, and willow that is a totally different ecology from the dry prairies beyond. But the Stephen Long party, with Edwin James, left the river to travel overland by horse. Away from the water, they saw a different and increasingly frightening West: "a broad plain, unvaried by any object" (June 15, 1820); "an undulating plain . . . presenting the aspect of hopeless and irreclaimable sterility" (June 18); "vast unbroken plain . . . one hundred fifty miles . . . tiresome to the eye, and fatiguing to the spirit" (June 19); "This barren and ungenial district appeared, at this time, to be filled with greater numbers of animals than its meagre production are able to support . . . intense reflection of light and heat . . . the fatigue and suffering of our journey" (June 24); "an aspect of more unvaried sterility" (June 29).

For the Long party, it was not a good month. As he sat in their apartment above a girls' finishing school in Paris, Cooper must have turned those pages with wide eyes. And open mind.

The book he wrote had nothing to do with the western myths that would come into vogue by the Civil War, and which still shape our popular opinion: the myths of the West as a virgin land, a place for a fresh start, a strong, enduring, inviolable land. James and Cooper, writing before the myths were established and therefore sounding like contemporary revisionists, spoke of an old West, in decline, none too good to start with, and fragile. Furthermore, white incursions were likely to be disastrous.

Remember that James was a botanist. He had observed that the prairie seemed "filled with greater numbers of animals than its meagre production are able to support." In James's journal, Cooper had read of the settler on the Missouri who claimed to have killed in one year seventy deer and fifty bears. Later, James reflected on the buffalo's reputation for running away from the white man's scent: "We are aware that another cause may be found for this than the frightful scent of the white man, which is, the impolitic exterminating war that he wages against all unsubdued animals within his reach" (June 26, 1820).

The ecological sensitivity of the botanist had a considerable effect on Cooper. Not everyone in 1820 had a frontier mentality. James's remarkable statement reminds one of the Jesuit priest Nicolas Point and his disgust, as he drifted down the Missouri in 1847, at his own men shooting animals along the river bank for fun. It was not a matter of depletion for Point, but of moral hatred of greed and waste.

In reading the journals of Lewis and Clark and of James at the same time, Cooper would have been acutely aware of the rapidity of white settlement on the lower Missouri. He was looking at entries describing the same towns, the same river junctions, the same islands, fifteen years apart (1804 and 1819) on the Missouri below the Platte. The unstoppable tide of white settlement was rising. Place after place that had been beyond civilization in 1804, was covered by 1819. Just a few examples:

LEWIS AND CLARK:	JAMES:
June 1, 1804 (At the mouth of the Osage, well beyond the last settlement): "a high commanding position, whence we enjoyed a delightful prospect of the country."	*July 6, 1819* (At the mouth of the Osage): "a town has been 'located', and the lots lately disposed of at St. Louis . . . from fifty to one hundred and eighty dollars each."

June 5, 1804: "Cedar Island on the north, so called from the abundance of the tree of that name."

July 6, 1819: "Cedar Island . . . has furnished much cedar timber for the settlements below; but its supply is now nearly exhausted."

In writing *The Prairie*, Cooper shared Paris's *interest* in the Indians and the plains, but his point of view was being shaped by *facts* that had nothing to do with the romanticism in full bloom around him. In James, he read of a dry and fragile land, barely able to support its animals, facing a flood of white immigrants, many of them none too careful about the land or its inhabitants. Cooper developed a distrust of European progress that was not based on romantic and primitivist myths.

That distrust became the core of his book. The story is set in 1805, as Lewis and Clark are ascending the Missouri. The expedition is mentioned three times in the novel, and the meaning of Lewis's expedition, the meaning of whites coming to the West, is Cooper's subject. In their first meeting, the Pawnee hero Hard-Heart asks the old trapper about the white men (Lewis and Clark) ascending the Big River, and the very first words by the first Indians in the novel cut to the heart of the matter:

Have the pale-faces eaten their own buffaloes, and taken the skin from all their own beavers . . . that they come to count how many are left among the Pawnees? (42)

. . . The earth is very large . . . why can the children of my father never find room on it? (45)

Population expansion and resource depletion are central to our first western.

In the first big scene of the novel, the Bush sons, new to the prairie, settle in to camp at the only grove of trees in many miles. Wielding axes with a "sort of contempt," they "stripped a small but suitable spot of its burden of forest as effectually, and almost as promptly, as if a whirlwind had passed" (13). Cooper had read in James of Daniel Boone's comment: "I think it time to remove when I can no longer fell a tree for fuel, so that its top will lie within a few yards of the door of my cabin." (Boone died, in Franklin, shortly before James came through.) Cooper had also read in James of the expedition's practice of felling trees in prairie groves to feed their animals leaves for the night. This frontier tradition of a quick axe, and moving on, Cooper applies to the West as he read of it in James, and he sees trouble. So few trees, so many white men coming . . . seventy deer and fifty bear in a year. Careless exploitation, and a land of limits, lead to the climax of the opening scene, which contains several of the more remarkable passages in early American literature.

The old trapper, who has been long on the prairies and knows the fragility of the land, has watched the newcomers make camp. He shakes his head at "the desolation of the scene around him," at the "vacant spot in the heavens" where trees had stood, and he mutters about "man's wish, and pride, and waste, and sinfulness! He tames the beast of the field to feed his idle wants; and having robbed the brutes of the natural food, he teaches them to strip the 'arth of its trees to quiet their hunger" (89–90).

He is sitting with Ishmael Bush and sons around the campfire when he delivers his vision of the entire continent stripped, every tree cut down:

> Look around you, men; what will the Yankee choppers say, when they have cut their path from the eastern to the western waters, and find that a hand, which can lay the earth bare at a blow, has been here and swept the country, in very mockery of their wickedness. They will turn on their tracks like a fox that doubles, and then the rank smell of their own footsteps will show them the madness of their waste. (81)

The "hand" is God's hand; He has already swept the West bare, to mock the actions of men who will sweep the entire continent bare from the eastern to the western waters. And *then* they will see what they have done, turning on their tracks like a fox that doubles back, and realizing too late "the madness of their waste." Neither Emerson nor Thoreau nor Whitman nor Burroughs nor John Muir (his West was California) had imagined, even by 1900, the total destruction of the continent, every tree cut down. Cooper did because the West scared him, because he stopped taking the earth for granted.

Whether James and Cooper were overreacting to the West as a symbol of limits we have yet to know; irrigation solves nothing until we know how the water table and leached salts look after a few centuries; we're not yet sure what the loss of native grasses is doing to the soil; then there are the worldwide issues such as acid rain, the ozone layer, and oil for the tractors. Certainly it is questionable whether we are producing more protein, in a stable pattern, than the Columbia salmon runs and bison once supplied. We are still in the first hundred years—the first fifty with man-made chemicals—of our experiments in progress on the prairie.

Neither romantic, spiritual, nor moral, Cooper's fear of European progress was based on the bareness and fragility of desert land as James described it. This practical fear is inspired by the low-rainfall, high plains Inland West. In Cooper's first manuscript draft (now at Yale's Beinecke Library), the passage has "bare" twice: "a hand, that can lay the 'arth bare at a blow, has been here and swept the country bare." And the final sentence refers to "the madness *and folly* of their waste," tying the passage solidly to the old trapper's summary of the West's function in intellectual history: "I often think the Lord has placed this barren belt of prairie behind the States, to warn men to what their folly may yet bring the land!" (19) Barren land, "bare . . . bare," leads to fear, fear to humility, humility to a valuing of natural resources and to a practical distrust of the "folly" of unlimited progress. The Lord made the West as a warning.

That is the West we know. It is the West of Powell, Stegner, the later Guthrie, Hugo, Welch, Doig. It is a land of limits that encourages humility, realism, and endurance, a land which shakes out the dreamers and those who expect too much too easy. The West is not California.

Half of Cooper's book, especially the handling of the stock romantic pair of Middleton and Inez, is drivel; much is overwritten and long. But the best parts are wonderful, and often surprising. Cooper's West is not new but old; the James expedition had been fascinated by the Indian mounds outside of St. Louis, and in the age of archeology (the pyramids of Egypt, the Rosetta stone), everyone thought that an analogous ancient and grand civilization might have existed out West. Cooper further knew, from Lewis and Clark, how hard the smallpox had already hit the Indians. The result was a tragic vision of a West that had seen better days, and in which the Indians, who *do* know limits and have humility, are doomed. Lewis and Clark, Cooper realized, were visiting an old world, not a virgin land. That is an important point for American identity, for if the land was not virgin, we were not innocent.

Cooper's sources describe a West of violent and rapid change: windstorms, rain, baking sun, flocks of birds, and driving snow seem to spring from nowhere. But to the European mind, perhaps nothing was more dramatic than the coming and going of the buffalo. The finest image of a fickle West comes in James's journal, at the confluence of the north and south forks of the Platte:

> Immediately upon surmounting this undulation we saw before us . . . immense herds of bisons, grazing . . . obscuring, with the density of their numbers, the verdant plain; to the right and left, as far as the eye was permitted to rove, the crowd seemed hardly to diminish . . . at least ten thousand here burst on our sight in the instant . . . bulls . . . pawing the earth, and rolling . . . action . . . playfulness . . . real or affected combats . . . to and from watering places. On the distant bluffs, individuals were constantly disappearing, whilst others were presenting themselves to our view. . . . We retired to our evening fare, highly gratified with the novel spectacle we had witnessed, and with the most sanguine expectations of the future.
>
> In the morning we again sought the living picture but upon all the plain which last evening was so teeming with noble animals, not one remained.

In all of Europe and eastern America there was nothing like that spectacle: the vast space, the wild vitality, the suddenness of the coming and the going: Long's party saw the desert in the act of desertion. James hints at the effect such changes can have on one's point of view: like the old trapper, one abandons "sanguine expectations of the future."

The trapper himself is the oddest of western heroes. Though supposedly a man of action, he does almost nothing throughout the book except lean on his rifle and shake his head. He has a "look of emaciation, if not of suffering . . . an appearance of induration." Like an old oak, to which he is compared, he simply stands for much of the book and simply falls at the end. He has come "into these plains to escape the sound of the axe," but he knows he will be caught. He has learned what Nannie Alderson learned from the Cheyenne Little Wolf, "a quiet resignation to the inevitableness of things."

He is not John Wayne or Clint Eastwood, and indeed the trapper's passivity leads to some hilarious scenes that seem closer to Mel Brooks. The trapper has given up killing in self-defense, refusing "to add an hour to a life that has already stretched beyond four-score years." Crossing a river in a skin boat with his scientist friend, Dr. Obed Bat, and hotly pursued by murderous Sioux, "more than once the trapper had raised his rifle only to lower it," until amidst the war-cries the trapper says, "Do you greatly value life, friend Doctor?" The trapper then proposes to tell the Pawnee Hard-Heart, who is laboriously towing the boat just ahead of the Sioux, "to make the best of his way, and leave us to the mercy of the Tetons." At the Doctor's immediate and panic-stricken response, the trapper offers a soliloquy on the theme, "Lord, what a thing is fear!"

At other times they are saved from a stampeding buffalo herd or from Indians not by the trapper's action, but by the braying of the doctor's ass. In a delightful paragraph, Cooper sums up this western hero of action and inaction:

> . . . he stood musing on the course he should now adopt, with the sin-gular mixture of decision and resignation that proceeded from his habits and his humility, and which united to form a character, in which exces-sive energy, and the most meek submission to the will of Providence, were oddly enough combined. (357)

The West as adventure in Cooper is subordinated to the West as a les-son in humility. The trapper has learned limits: the limits of resources, the limits of action.

Finally, the Indians. Remember that Lewis and Clark and James not only traversed western landscapes, but they also wintered with the Mandans and Pawnees. Their journals have a wealth of information which cannot possibly be replaced, and Cooper's Indians, although they include some melodramatic characters, are thoroughly tribal. Their customs and religion are respected. Hard-heart is modeled on the Pawnee Petalasharoo, whom James had described in detail and whom Cooper had met in Washington before he sailed to Paris. Just as *The Prairie* uses western landscape to initiate us into human responsibility, not to take us away from it, it also uses Indians as an example of a dying civilization, not as natural men living a white fantasy of escape.

Cooper's Indians differ from the whites not by being perfectly natural, but by being humble. They acknowledge larger forces than themselves (the "Wahconda" deity of Lewis and Clark's journals appears throughout *The Prairie*) and they do not aspire to domination of the earth. Personal humility, which certainly appealed to Cooper's Christianity, is expressed in this book as a desert land ethic, and such humility defines the way in which the trapper is more red than white. After the trapper's speech on Yankee choppers reaching the Pacific and turning back to find "the madness of their waste," Ishmael Bush says to him, "Old man . . . to which people do you belong? You have the color and speech of a Christian, while it seems that your heart is with the red-skins" (82).

At the great meeting of La Balafre, the ancient and wise Indian, with the trapper—two men of different races and identical character—the connection of humility to land use is made clear. The white men are distinguished by greed expressed through "rapacious tempers," the Indians by humility expressed through restraint. La Balafre is nearly blind; approaching the trapper at the council fire he is "in doubt whether he addressed one like himself, or some wanderer of that race who, he had heard, were spreading themselves like hungry locusts throughout the land" (366). Finding that the trapper is white, La Balafre asks the question that lies at the center of the book, at the center of the great westward movement, at the center of our culture:

Then let my brother look at me. I am nigh him, and he can see that I am a foolish Red-man. Why cannot his people see everything, since they crave all? (366)

The trapper acknowledges to Balafre "the justice of your words," but says that for himself, he never "coveted more ground than the Lord has intended each man to fill." From awareness of a barren and fragile land, from fear of Europeans "spreading themselves like hungry locusts" throughout that land, Cooper has come to ethical land use as the primary virtue, and to land abuse as our primary greed. The land abuse comes from an expanding population using resources as if there were no limit. Cooper's view is not romantic. Cooper's view is not wrong.

Cooper's view is modern, and western. John Wesley Powell's 1877 "Report on the Lands of the Arid Region" has been called by Wallace Stegner, with admiration, "a denial of almost every cherished fantasy and myth associated with the Westward migration and the American dream of the Garden of the World." Powell stressed two factors: low rainfall (under twenty inches, the minimum for agriculture without irrigation) and variety, caused by variations in altitude, latitude, topography, climate, and soil. Except for parts of Spain, this aridity and variety distinguish the West from any other landscape in Europe, England, or America east of the Mississippi. These realities prompted Powell, like Cooper, to reexamine our conceptions of land productivity and ownership. He questioned surveying and owning by the rectangular grid system (developed in even-rainfall countries with homogenous topography, such as England) rather than by river systems, ridges, and valleys. He thought Americans out West would have to accept limits to their notions of progress.

Powell's approach was ecological, as was James's and Cooper's. Ecological thought questions progress for practical, not romantic, reasons. And that is a western tradition. No matter how pervasive the *myths* of pastoralism and primitivism out West, and no matter how silly the *expectations* of some of those who came, those who *stayed* soon learned to question the limits of progress on practical grounds.

We can define the European notion of "progress" as bettering one's lot through reason and science. A technological explosion, based on empirical method, accompanied the population explosion of Europe from 1500 to 1980. Those last 400 years of European civilization may have been quite odd in human history because ours was not simply another empire, taking from here to give to there. The rise of science and population—products and markets—coupled with the new exploitation of vast fossil fuel deposits, produced during that period a brief suspension of "necessity," both in the real world (we were indeed rich) and in the conceptual world (the temporary conditions of tremendous growth and resources, mistaken as permanent, created a myth of unlimited progress and manipulation of nature). This has nothing to do with the poverty and misery of many; a rational and charitable system could have distributed the wealth. Increasingly the poor have seen themselves not as doomed to poverty but as cut out of a good thing. They are right. The system is rich as long as energy and resources last, cheap labor is found, and earth, air, and water are usable. Each Third World country may come to enjoy this prosperity, for a while. Who is next after Japan and Korea?

During those 400 years of expansion in population and science, there were many critiques of "progress." Some critiques were dear to Americans: Jefferson, remember, directly opposed manufacturing in America; he had seen the "progress" of factories and believed them debilitating places to work. The common man would do better to stay on the farm. Nature itself, in its purity, beauty, and peace, was seen as a rebuke to cities.

Both the pastoral and the primitivist critiques of progress, as we saw in Chapter 2, assumed a split between man and nature. They provided the only discourse of dissent: to love nature is to distrust man and his works. The tremendous importance of the ecological movement in our intellectual history is that it constitutes the first critique of progress on empirical grounds. No split between man and nature need be assumed; the ecological movement accepts the empirical methods of science and reason and uses the tools of technology to define the practical limits of progress. Ecological dissent does not imply a rejection of society.

Note that "ecology," in its pure sense, is not the same as environmentalism, which is a political movement. Many environmentalists *are* primitivists, just as the lumber industry says they are. The lumber industry, unfortunately, just as often advocates short-term exploitation. Exploit ruthlessly for man, or preserve God's own against man. Those two nineteenth-century frontier choices are complementary opposites. The ecological movement proposes a different situation: man is nature, nature is man, they are one system, and if 90 percent of our body is water, the Indian statement that "The river is our brother" is not a quaint metaphor; it is an understatement, for the river is ourselves.

An ecologist, then, could be for abolishing every wilderness area in the United States, for he does not believe that nature is more precious without man. An ecologist would be likely to propose such abolition, however, *only if* men had demonstrated an ability to live in stable harmony within the natural system. Population stability, and resource stability, would be necessary prerequisites. Perhaps the greatest challenge facing capitalism is to convert from colonial and expansionist goals to steady-state goals, for the good of everyone on earth. Consumers should not encourage McDonald's to encourage Brazil to ravage the rain forest in order to grow cheap beef.

A shift in our way of looking at nature is particularly important to white Americans, for whom nature was always an identity as well as a resource. Who are we? Europeans with a whole lot of nature. So Americans, whenever they have felt inferior to Europe's civilization, cities, and art, have always praised the virtues of the natural world. Long before primitivism, the Reverend Samuel Sewell in New England suggested that being part of a beautiful nature could help save souls, and Thomas Jefferson pointed proudly to American birds and mammals as superior to European strains. Nature, in America, is a part of nationalism.

But we have also been, from the very beginning, those who manipulate nature to our own advantage. The shrewd Yankee, the industrious farmer are Europeans who go out and chop and burn and clear and build ships and dream up new uses for the trees and minerals, and who expand into new lands. So we have always had a double identity: we are the people who use up nature, and we are the people who have a lot of it left.

The real closing of the frontier, perhaps, came during our lives, since 1970. The Arab oil embargo made all the recent prophets of scarcity look believable, and by the end of the decade the RARE I and II surveys and the Alaska Lands Bill had a subtext sobering to all Americans: the wild is gone. Nothing is extra anymore. Not a single acre, even in Alaska, will be simply out there, unspoken for. It not only must be "owned" on paper, it will be used for something, perhaps aesthetic "non-use." In the 1980s this need to designate everything's use has reached our water too; in the West, instream reservations of "unused" water, for fish and flow, are being negotiated on every river. No longer is the water wild; the Blackfoot is not God's river. How many acre-feet has He reserved? Law is our logos now.

This hurts so because it changes our identity. Before the 1970s, we could have our cake and eat it too. We could exploit, expand, and still look west to the wild. The contradiction in our double identity made no difference. The first life of Daniel Boone, written in 1784 by John Filson, was an appendix to a real estate brochure. Filson was selling lots in Kentucky, and wanted to assure people that Boone had secured the territory against bears and Indians. The romance of the wild and free man in nature, and the reality of subdivisions and exploding populations, could coexist from 1620 to 1980. No more. Expand the picture to encompass the earth, include nuclear capability, and the same point appears in more chilling form. Everything lives at our discretion. We could poison the seas, the air. There is no wild; there is no part of nature beyond our power, divine in its divorce from man. Only a deliberate withholding of our power permits the system to continue. Everything, in a sense, is now within our imagination, within our culture. That was Cooper's prescient vision.

To my father, and many of his generation, the opposite of nature was not civilization but time. He was not alone in hoping that the natural world was eternal, beyond the ravages of change. At least spring returned the same each year. Nature's healing power, strength, and dependability functioned for all of us somewhat like idealized women in the nineteenth century, an opposite and counterforce to our growing industrialization. The ecological movement, or more properly the obvious environmental disasters we have brought upon ourselves, and the closing of the land frontier have forced on the American public the painful truth that Darwin had already asserted: nature occurs within time. In 1859 Darwin took nature out of the transcendental categories of the romantics—the sacred and the eternal—and made it part of our world of growth, change, decay. We are just beginning to work out the enormity of that shift, and to absorb the responsibility it places on a species capable of such radical change at a pace that leaves adaptation and natural selection behind.

We hear all this with fear because we all fear man. We would like to think there is something beyond. And that is part of the enduring appeal of Montana, mountains, the West; they give the impression of a whole lot beyond, greater than us, out of our control. But in a short-term physical sense, that is no longer true. Montana *could* be astro-domed for growing orchids. Behind our anger at this news is our fear of an exploding population and technology that seem to have run "wild," in a cruel parody of that term's reversal over the last 400 years. Fear of "progress." We all know the orchids would develop some new rot, and then where would we be?

Unlimited progress as it was conceived during the heyday of colonial expansion is outmoded, no matter how convenient it was for a time, especially for those of us in control. And strangely, our West, which often thinks of itself as backward—"what America was"—is in these matters forward. I am suggesting that at least since 1810, when whites left the prairie river bottoms, the American West has encouraged a critique of progress on practical grounds. That is the heritage of the Inland West, which appears in our literature as an overwhelming sense of land and weather and a commensurate humility about the human need to adjust. The philosophy found in Montana writers is not mainly manipulative; like the old trapper, they preach a chastened endurance.

Montana, then, and the Inland West have in the popular consciousness been centers of primitivist mythology, representing sacred space beyond human touch or control. That mythology is still powerful in a state where driving in winter can mean death by freezing, no accident at all. The heroes of that mythology are cowboys and mountain men, imagined to act quickly, violently, without a care, in a space with plenty of room and air. But beneath that mythology has always been another one, less publicized and more native to the West: a humble sense of fragile systems and practical limits to progress. Heroes of this mythology feel a responsibility to land, to stewardship. The central image of Montana art and literature from Lewis and Clark until 1970 was killing the grizzly; from 1970 to now, in Hugo, Welch, Doig, and most vividly in the final scene of the movie *Heartland*, it is pulling the calf.

The argument that gets us from primitivism to ecology, from Cooper to now, runs something like this:

1. Americans and especially westerners have always placed great importance on their relation to nature.

2. Romantic primitivism and pastoralism have been, until recently, the main *theories* available to us to understand our relation to nature.

3. Those theories are not adequate to describe our *actual* relation to nature.

4. Those theories make love of nature seem regressive, escapist, and antisocial.

5. But in fact, westerners have long feared and loved nature *not* for primitivist reasons, but for practical reasons.

6. Therefore we find the Inland West, though full of *primitivist myth*, actually offers early examples of *ecological thought*. Cooper is one example.

7. This *ecological thought* comes from a practical humility based on respect for an awesome but harsh and fragile land, and is apparent in much of the best contemporary Montana literature (such as Hugo, Welch, Maclean, Doig).

8. Such a practical, realistic appraisal of man's relation to nature in the semi-arid West is a major revision of standard western myths. Such revision has always been voiced (Native Americans, Cooper, J. W. Powell, Joe Howard, Wallace Stegner) but has seldom been heard.

This book has mentioned a number of revisions of western myths. I have criticized the pastoral and primitivist pursuits of innocence and their rejections of society, psychology, and experience; I have attacked myths of the rugged individual, especially conceived as the lone rogue male; and I have pointed out flaws, as they seemed to me, in cherished authors. The danger of reacting *against* material is of seeming negative.

But make no mistake: I believe that these criticisms clear the way, letting us see a West in which love of the land and respect for the earth are not equated with antisocial escape. These revisionist ideas *better* represent what has already been thought and felt by many westerners. What the literature does is voice our own life. Many a person, many a family, isolated and hard-worked in a vast land, never *lived* the old myths at all, but when they came to think of or describe their lives, only those pastoral, primitivist, and rugged-individual conceptions were available. The old myths were born of escapist European dreams; we need to listen to those who have lived here.

For example, scholars now point out the extent of alchoholism and wife-beating on the frontier. The evidence seems irrefutable that western humor about booze and violence, humor which many of us enjoy, has accompanied a situation in which freedom meant the freedom of a male to indulge himself without anyone telling him no. And if anyone did, punch. In the isolated hardships of frontier life, the only person saying "no," often to a drunk man, was his wife. Melody Graulich's excellent article in *The Women's West*, "Violence Against Women," uses novels by four western women, several about their own fathers, to show that abuse was blatant and in the eyes of those women and their mothers, common. Mary Austin warned us of this long ago. Marie Sandoz's portrait of her father, "Old Jules," the land locator in North Dakota, is frightening. Tillie Olsen's Anna "had questioned [her husband] timidly concerning his work; he struck her on the mouth with a bellow of "shut your damn trap." Then he thinks, "Just let her say one word to me and I'll bash her head in."

You know who it sounds like: Boone Caudill. And simply the existence of recent feminist critiques of the nineteenth-century Cult of True Womanhood, in which woman is the pure, ideal civilizing influence and recipient of chivalry, makes us reread *The Big Sky*. Remember how angry Boone was at Teal Eye's asking where he was going? And remember that his father was a child-abusing drunk with a frightened, timid wife? Guthrie has clearly joined both plots: Boone has all the earmarks of a self-indulgent wife-beater, but he has married the female ideal of goodness and passivity, and has been tamed. He kills his best friend but doesn't even strike Teal Eye.

I once received an excellent paper pointing out all the child and family abuse in our books: beatings by Boone's father and Garcia's father and by priests (all hated or feared), Loney's father giving him the gun for self-destruction with a grin. Violence between Charlie and Ruth in *This House of Sky*. Conscious abandonments by Nannie's mother, Loney's mother, Hugo's mother. The deaths of Doig's mother and the mother of the narrator of *Winter in the Blood*. The most powerful presentation of child abuse is out of print, in Grace Stone Coates's *Black Cherries*, but the first chapter is reprinted in *The Last Best Place*. All of these family disasters are not just mentioned, but functionally important in the books. Not a nuclear family on the list. Not a single *Little House on the Prairie*. Clearly we are rethinking the West, and the readers, as well as the writers, should ask what these books are really about.

Just for fun, let's apply these revisionist ideas to everyone's favorite subject, the cowboy. The cowboy has been seen from a primitivist point of view: wild, alone, antisocial. In fact he was just as plausibly an economic ideal: during a period of growing industrialization, of factories with workers as "wage slaves," the cowboy was a free worker who liked his work. Not because the job was easy or paid well, but because the job offered self-respect, rewarded skill and guts, could be done with pride. It reminds me of teaching. The cowboy was a free worker who was not alienated from his product. He was a nineteenth-century democratic and Jeffersonian alternative to the new degradation of workers; he was a poor man, uneducated, but he had freedom, dignity, and that ancient symbol of aristocracy: the horse. Which he rode, not walked behind. The bottom line of his freedom was always his potential to say, "Take this job and shove it."

And what does "cowboy" stand for around the world? Bill Finnegan, who recently wrote an award-winning book on South Africa, was in Missoula (where he once studied writing) describing his moral and passionate response to apartheid in South Africa. He had urged various individual blacks to do something. They seemed not to hear. Later, he found out that they were already involved in organized underground dissent; and who was he, just sailing in to change things alone? They called it a "cowboy" approach. "Cowboy" meant, to them, someone who thinks he can operate outside society, alone. I vote to keep the dream of working-class freedom and throw out the antisocial escapism and the innocence.

By questioning the old assumptions, we make room for the new. If freedom as license, if freedom to do whatever you wish without hassles, turned out to be a shallow ideal, we should say so and move on.

Freedom, after all, is our national project. We had better get it right. We don't always get it right in foreign policy, and we don't always get it right at home. If freedom should be defined as having meaningful choices to make, which for most of us implies society and family, then we had better be working on a society that extends as many meaningful choices as possible to all citizens. That's what Nannie was looking for; that's what Loney died for. Freedom occurs within a culture, not outside of it. Outside, is lonely.

Cultures change, as they say. Constructive criticism helps give us control of the change. As we go into the next century (and millennium), we won't save Montana or the West by calling it a remnant of our past, a museum of a Golden Age, a Paradise Lost. Those arguments are inaccurate as well as inexpedient. In the future, to love the land, to keep farms in family hands, to control progress and make it work for us, we in the West will have to advocate a theory of the future, not of escape from it, a theory of land planning, not of escape from it, a theory of society, not of escape from it. The essential western goals remain unchanged: opportunity, freedom, equality. But their naive "boosterism" connotations are changed by a literature stressing hardship, limited possibility, humility, and the realities of an all-too-often lonely and violent and drifting and careless populace.

The world has dreamed of the West. In Montana, at least, we still have enough of that beautiful world to feel some responsibility in caring for it. But the West is not a lost divinity or a shrinking wilderness; it is and always was a part of one culture or another, and what we do with it depends on cultural choices. We can keep the dream of freedom, for instance, and throw out the dream of escape. It can be done here. Where else in the world does an educated populace have so many advantages of both nature and industry? If the industrial revolution is going to work any better, it should be figured out in a place that has something to lose. A place that knows what clean air and water are, a place that knows what a sweet world it is without too many people. Not devoid of our species, mind you; just not too many. Missoula is about the size of Athens in the fifth century B.C.

Enough of this preaching. You can see that I have tried to be good. I *do* believe that hatred of one's own kind is not natural, that cities and societies do not have to be horrid, that the universe is not structured by inevitable decline and that we have to rewrite that story. But we can get sick of progressivism too. I don't trust social engineering— what I have really expressed in this book is a nationwide mood: we are fed up with irresponsible individualism from Boone to Boesky, from the plains to the stock exchange, fed up with a national vision of greed, fed up with destruction of our earth. But like most people I know, I also love the prickly, cantankerous, and potentially violent free individual, and I don't want to trade him in for goodness. Like most, I wouldn't mind a little reform, closer families, or a more just society, but I also like to walk into the Calf-A in Dell, Montana, for a chicken fried steak and see Ken's sign on the wall:

> $250 REWARD
> for enof information
> on the party who stole
> the old phonograph
> so that I can shoot
> the son of a bitch.
> Ken

When I was in Paris in 1982 working on Cooper and beginning this book, I kept a journal, and in one entry the dream of the West seemed very clear, to me as it did to Cooper, when seen from that international and urban center. I would like to conclude with that essay.

I am sitting in an apartment in Paris. Street sounds float up through windows which open, floor to ceiling, like double doors into the room. Thin white curtains move in the breeze. The sounds? Children shout,

taxis go and stop and go, the madame's "merci" in the bread shop below rings like the song of a bird. These are the same shouts, the same
chirps, the same windows and buildings that surrounded Cooper
when in the spring of 1827, a few blocks from here, he finished the
first great novel about the American West.

The West! The words cannot cross my mind without raising a whirr
of feelings. "What will the Yankee choppers say, when they have cut
their path from the eastern to the western waters. . . ." Cooper, living
in Paris with wife and children and society, imagined so vividly the
prairie: "Ay, you may travel for weeks and see it still the same." He
was obsessed, frightened, attracted. And I think I know why.

So far away. So far from this choked street in Paris, so far from
these sounds: the French and Arabic shouts from Tunesians watching
soccer in the bar below (Algeria is beating Germany—echoes of lost
empires in North Africa, echoes of revenge). So far from these smells:
every food in every stage from gross to fine to gross, hanging butch-
ered from the ceiling or wrapped in crisp white paper or simmering in
sauce or lying in the filthy street. Through these drifting curtains the
whole world crowds my senses. The West! In *Moby Dick*, when Ishmael found the world too much, when he tired of opening the paper
to read "Bloody Battle in Afghanistan—Ten Thousand Killed," he ran
off to sea. Others ran West. And now as then the world crowds us,
crowds us all. The ABC reporter who owns my apartment is at this
moment in Afghanistan to cover their latest bloody battle with the
Soviets. The West! Here Cooper sat, reading the journals of an 1819
expedition to the Rockies, here he sat listening to these shouts, and
dreaming of endless plains. And now, when these curtains move, I
suddenly remember a wind that Paris never knows, and I stare out
the window at our old pinto horse, head down, and two fence posts
fading in blowing snow. So far away.

I am sitting in a library in Paris. In front of me, Cooper's letters. He
describes his Paris street, his second-story apartment, his courtyard,
his meetings with Sir Walter Scott, Talleyrand, Lafayette, the Dauphine. Yet every morning he sat at his desk and pictured an old hunter
alone on the western prairie, and right at this second, if I raise my
eyes from the library table to the wall behind the card catalogue, I see

a painting of an old man and two companions, with pack horses, on a bare rise of the plains—they could be Cooper's hunter and friends, or Guthrie's Summers and Deakins and Boone beneath the Big Sky— and in the distance, I can see the Front Range or maybe it's the Little Rockies or Bear's Paws or the Crazies or Belts. The painting hanging here in Paris is by Charlie Russell, and beneath the three men are the words: "The World was all before Them."

That's it. "The World was all before Them." How often Europe, with so much world behind it, has dreamed of having so much world before. "In the beginning," as John Locke said, "all the world was America." Young, nothing but future in sight. How different, then, the European West from the Indian West, for the Indian West was not a new hope but an old home. Cooper felt both the dream, and the westerner's fear that the dream was not true.

Montana—in the heart of the West, old and new, Indian and white. Its writers speak very well for the high plains and northern Rockies, that area of beaver, gold, cattle, and cold that to the whole world is "The West." We are connected to Afghanistan, to Arab cries, to Paris papers, even by the myth that we are not. The dream of Montana as a fresh start was the dream of an old world.

Notes

Introduction

Because there are few college courses on the American West, there are few books of general overview or introduction to the material. A curious reader might begin, however, with two recent books and their bibliographical notes: *The Mythic West* by Robert G. Athearn (1986), focusing on the twentieth century, and *The Legacy of Conquest* by Patricia Limerick (1987), a readable overview of the West incorporating current revisionist history. To these discussions one could add two resource books, Howard Lamar's encyclopedia, *The American West* (1977), and Richard Etulain's *Bibliographic Guide to the Study of Western American Literature* (1982).

Two more specialized but interesting studies are William Goetzmann's *Exploration and Empire* (1966) and Robert Berkhofer's *The White Man's Indian* (1978), a review in one book of our political and conceptual treatment of Indians. Sandra Myres's *Westering Women and the Frontier Experience* (1982), and Susan Armitage and Elizabeth Jameson's collection of articles, *The Women's West* (1987), will bring you up to date on the expanding field of western women's studies. For currents in methodology and content within western history, try Michael Malone's anthology, *Historians and the American West* (1983), and Roger Nichols's *American Frontier and Western Issues* (1986).

Montana history is best approached through K. Ross Toole's lively and readable introduction, *Montana: An Uncommon Land* (1959), and Malone and Roeder's more thorough and accurate *Montana: A History of Two Centuries* (1976). A subscription to *Montana*, the excellent journal of the Montana Historical Society in Helena, will then keep you informed on future books.

Wallace Stegner's remarkable career includes history, criticism, and creative work. His novel, *The Big Rock Candy Mountain*, and his story of growing up on the plains, *Wolf Willow* (1962), along with his books on John Wesley Powell and *The Sound of Mountain Water* (1980), are especially concerned with this region and its culture. Richard Hugo's poetry and career are discussed in chapter 9.

The tradition of the personal essay in Montana is strong: Joseph Kinsey Howard, K. Ross Toole, and most recently, Bill Kittredge in *Owning It All* (1987), have written powerfully of western history and experience. Bill Kitt-

Notes

redge and Annick Smith are the senior editors of the anthology of Montana writings, *The Last Best Place* (Montana Historical Society, 1988).

The colonization of the West by the East certainly happened in several definable ways, and continues, and the more polemical historians such as K. Ross Toole have achieved some popularity by working the theme. However, recent historians question the importance of such colonization (Malone and Roeder) and point out the myriad ways in which the West was complicit with and dependent on federal handouts (Athearn, Limerick). Colonization seems to me a truth, and a sore one, which unfortunately happens to reinforce inaccurate and self-serving myths of western independence, rebellion, and disenfranchisement. It is a truth which obscures other truths, and thus makes scholars nervous. See Patricia Limerick (and Howard Lamar, on whom she draws), *The Legacy of Conquest*, chapter 3, for a recent discussion.

A number of excellent books on agrarianism, Jefferson, and western mythologies have appeared over the last generation. To the old standards—Leo Marx, *The Machine in the Garden* (1964), and Henry Nash Smith, *Virgin Land*—we might add Richard Slotkin, *Regeneration through Violence* (1973), and Drew McCoy, *The Elusive Republic: Political Economy in Jeffersonian America* (1980).

The nineteenth-century documents mentioned begin with the journals of Lewis and Clark, available in Biddle's 1814 journalistic editing, Coues's 1893 rewriting of the various journals (reprinted in Dover paperback), or the raw journals printed by Thwaites in 1904–5 and sometimes reprinted in part (as in Bernard DeVoto's edition). Osborne Russell's *Journal of a Trapper* in the 1840s (treated in chapter 3), is most readable and out in paper, as are Teddy Blue Abbott's *We Pointed Them North* (a better cowboy reminiscence than Andy Adams's *Log of a Cowboy*), and Granville Stuart's *Pioneering in Montana* and other memoirs. The quotation from Abbott's book is on page 5.

The Last Best Place gives some hint of the quality of out-of-print Montana material. Myron Brinig, with a number of his early books set in Butte, was a well-known writer in the 1930s, as was Grace Stone Coates, whose *Black Cherries* (1931) is an extraordinary tale of child abuse. Mildred Walker a decade later wrote numerous stories and books; the novels *Winter Wheat* (1944) and *If a Lion Could Talk* (1970) are among her best, one a story of ranching in the thirties and the other a historical novel of a missionary on Montana's Highline. The recent interest in women on the frontier should help bring Coates and Walker back into print.

Van Tilburg Clark's *The Ox-bow Incident* (1940) is one of the finest and earliest westerns of substance. He taught creative writing at UM in the fifties.

Linderman, Plenty-coups, Pretty-shield, McNickle, and Welch are all discussed in Part II.

Heartland was directed by Richard Pierce, written by Beth Ferris and Bill Kittredge, and produced by Annick Smith. Based on the letters of the homesteader Elinore Pruitt Stewart, the movie has won several prizes in Europe and America and is available on video cassette.

J. Malcolm Swan's *Montana: Let There Be Lit* (Montana Committee for the Humanities, 1988) is a resource book for teachers of Montana literature.

Chapter 1. Guthrie's Big Sky

The Big Sky goes in and out of print in various paper editions rather quickly. These page numbers refer to the Houghton Mifflin Sentry edition (1965), introduced by Wallace Stegner, 386 pages of text.

Treasure Island by Robert Louis Stevenson may be a fantasy of exotic adventure but it is well written, and his more realistic, autobiographical novel of California in 1880, *The Silverado Squatters*, might interest readers.

The quotations of Guthrie are from the author's tape, KUFM-Bevis, Montana Writers, UM archives, Missoula. Guthrie has made similar comments in many interviews; some may be found in Thomas Ford's *A. B. Guthrie, Jr.* (1981). Other local interviews are listed in *A Catalogue of Audio and Video Tapes of Montana Writers* (Western Studies Project, UM; Montana Committee for the Humanities, 1986). The criticism of Guthrie's work is not impressive, and may be found through the annual bibliographies of academic journals. Arnold Krupat has recently written interesting pieces on *The Big Sky* and on white and Native American autobiographies.

Bill Kittredge has written numerous popular novels in the Cord series, two books of short stories (*The Van Gogh Field* and *We Are Not in This Together*), a number of magazine articles, and a book of essays on growing up on a ranch in Oregon, *Owning It All* (1987). In many ways *Owning It All* updates Stegner's *Wolf Willow* as this generation's account of a western childhood. Kittredge teaches creative writing at the University of Montana.

The accounts of Guthrie's life are based mainly on Thomas Ford's book.

Hollywood westerns have been well covered in Cawelti's *The Six Gun Mystique* (1971), and are discussed in Athearn's *The Mythic West* (1986). Guthrie, DeVoto, Stegner, Van Tilburg Clark, and others were part of a consciously realistic revolt that had the weight and therefore the momentum of a movement. That is not to say, however, that they were the first or the only ones to treat western themes realistically. Linderman's trapper novel, *Lige Mounts* (1922), was in several ways a model for Guthrie's book, and H. L. Davis in Oregon, Willa Cather in Nebraska, Mari Sandoz, Vardis Fisher, and others wrote realistically of the West before the forties.

Joseph Kinsey Howard was a pioneering reporter and essayist, one of the first to vigorously oppose Anaconda Copper during the forties when The Company still dominated the state and its newspapers. *Montana, High, Wide and Handsome* (1943) developed the dark side of Montana's boom and bust history and corporate woes, and set the tone for Toole's histories. Howard's work on the Metis Indians, *Strange Empire* (1952), remains crucial on that subject, and his anthology *Montana Margins* (1946) is a fine collection of documentary writings. Other sources for Montana writings before *The Last Best Place* include Merriam's collections culled from *Frontier* magazine (roughly 1920–40): *Frontier Omnibus* and *Way Out West*. All four anthologies have excellent and differing material.

Chapter 2. Guthrie's Dream of the West

A popular summary and overview of European relations to nature may be found in Roderick Nash, *Wilderness and the American Mind* (1967), especially the first three chapters, and Hans Huth, *Nature and the American* (1957). Leo Marx, *The Machine in the Garden* (1964), remains a fine study of American pastoralism, along with Drew McCoy's *The Elusive Republic* (1980) on Jefferson. Contentious and interesting arguments on Jefferson, the frontier, and industrialization may be found in Richard Slotkin's *The Fatal Environment* (1985) as well as in his first and more trustworthy book on colonial America, *Regeneration through Violence* (1973). I have taken most quotations from Nash and Marx's widely available books.

Bradford and Petrarch are quoted in Nash, pages 24 and 20. The Kentucky professor was the late Clay Hunt of Williams College.

Jefferson's *Notes on the State of Virginia* and a few letters contain most of his famous remarks on farming versus industry, which are quoted in almost any discussion of Jeffersonian pastoralism. The Adams, Crèvecoeur, and Jefferson remarks may be found in Marx, pages 148, 115, 124, and 131 respectively; Chateaubriand is quoted by Nash on page 49, Bartram on page 55. Chateaubriand's French is in Hans Huth, page 50.

Readers who enjoy the French perceptions of America might look at full editions of Chateaubriand, including his romantic novels set in America, at Crèvecoeur's *Letters from an American Farmer*, and of course at De Toqueville's brilliant 1840 study, *Democracy in America*. The French connection to its partner in revolution is explored in the last chapter of this book, "Cooper: Then and Now."

The Lewis and Clark journals exist in many different and highly edited forms. I am using the Dover reprint of the Coues version, which collates several versions from the trip, following Biddle's original version of 1814. The latest discussion of Lewis and Clark scholarship, by editor Gary Moulton, appeared in *Montana*, Summer 1988.

Guthrie's speech in Jackson Hole, 1972, is quoted by Thomas Ford, *Guthrie*, page 53.

Chapter 3. Garcia's Tough Trip

Page numbers in the text refer to Garcia, *Tough Trip Through Paradise*, Ben Stein, ed. (Sausalito, Calif.: Comstock, 1967).

There is very little published criticism of Garcia's book, partly because it is presented as a reminiscence rather than a novel, partly because it is so zany, and partly because it might be a hoax. The original *New York Times* book review raised the issue of the work's authenticity, and I still find scholars at meetings and people all over Montana with inside theories on the manuscript. Someone may well know the truth; perhaps that person will now step forward.

The only interview I had with Ben Stein was over the telephone in 1978. The quotations are from notes I made as we talked.

Chapter 4. Alderson's Bride Goes West

Page numbers in the text refer to Alderson, *A Bride Goes West* (Lincoln: Univ. of Nebraska Press, 1942).

The cattle boom of the 1880s, the role of the railroads, and the slaughter of the buffalo are well documented in most contemporary histories. Malone and Roeder, *Montana: A History of Two Centuries* (1976), and Barsness, *The Bison in Art* (1977), contain most of the material used here.

The moral crisis concerning realism versus virtue at the end of the last century is summarized in just a few pages of Thomas Henry Huxley's essay, "Evolution and Ethics" (1893). Huxley wants to argue that evolution is a natural and nasty reality, and he is therefore driven to find that civilization and virtue, conversely, are unnatural idealisms. We must then oppose the ugly realities of the survival of the fittest in order to be civilized. Freud at the same time was discussing "civilization and its discontents," opposing the "natural" id to the "civilized" superego. A culture that believes the good is the opposite of the true is in trouble. The apologists for progress and unrestrained business opportunity often argued (and still do) for a nasty truth, versus virtue. Our models of the world, however, have changed significantly; there is no longer much reason to believe that isolated self-interest, rather than a community of species, is natural.

The 1882 Bozeman *Courier* remarks are from the original. The Schultz and

Joe Kipp observations on the disappearance of buffalo may be found in the recent (and not very satisfactory) biography, *The Life and Times of James Willard Schultz* (1986), by Warren Hanna. Other comments on the buffalo are in Malone and Roeder.

The reminiscence of Pearl Price Robertson appeared in *Frontier* magazine, 1933. Part is reprinted in *The Last Best Place*.

Railroad hype of the West is not as well documented in the Montana histories as one might wish. The Cooke brochure, undated, is titled *The Northern Pacific Railroad, its Route, Resources, Progress and Business*, "issued by Jay Cooke & Co." (University of Montana Archives 26146, pages 12–13).

Roberta Cheney wrote *Names on the Face of Montana* (1980), an excellent guide to Montana place names.

The 1887 law against foreign investment and the details of the winter of 1886–87 may be found in Malone and Roeder, pages 118 and 124 ff. Selections from a number of fine ranching memoirs appear in *The Last Best Place* and in *Cowboys and Cattlemen* (1964), by Michael Kennedy.

The Cheyenne side of the story is based, unless otherwise noted, on *Cheyenne Memories* by John Stands in Timber and Margot Liberty (1967), collated with the Montana histories. The actual burning of the cabin is on pages 243–45 of *Cheyenne Memories*. Teddy Blue Abbott in *We Pointed Them North* also describes the Cheyenne burning of the Alderson cabin, and its aftermath (reprinted in *The Last Best Place*).

The articles mentioned here on women in the West are collected in Armitage and Jameson, *The Women's West* (1987).

Chapter 5. Linderman and Plenty-coups

Page numbers in the text refer to Linderman, *Plenty-coups* (Lincoln: University of Nebraska Press, 1962), and *Pretty Shield* (Lincoln: University of Nebraska Press, 1974).

The film *Contrary Warriors* was made in 1985 by Beth Ferris et al., Rattlesnake Productions. Filmed on the Crow reservation, it tells the life of Robert Yellowtail and so tells much of the fortunes of the Crow tribe in this century. Chief Plenty-coups is prominent in Yellowtail's early life. It has been released on video cassette.

Russell, Schultz, Linderman, and Grinnell have received a good deal of attention but not nearly enough. We need biographies of the painter Russell and of Grinnell, whose work on Blackfeet and Cheyenne tales was influential, while the new biography of Schultz by Hanna is not satisfactory (a graduate student at the University of Montana, Celeste River, is working on a biography of Linderman). These men, and to a lesser extent Frederic Remington, are important as sympathetic whites drawn to the old West. They had enormous talents, led fascinating lives, and their blindnesses as well as perceptions could teach us much of who we were and are.

H. G. Merriam gives a complete list of Linderman's work in Appendix B of *Montana Adventure, The Recollections of Frank Linderman*, the unfinished autobiography which Merriam edited and published in 1968. The Linderman papers are at the UM archives. *Lige Mounts* was a predecessor and model for *The Big Sky*.

The Perkins, van de Water, and Day Child letters are quoted in Merriam, *Montana Adventure*, pages 211 and 207. Linderman's letter on his duty to preserve the West is on page 210.

The year after his interviews with Plenty-coups, Linderman was able to approach Pretty-shield, a Crow of the same age, for her story. These parallel tales of the same traditional plains tribe during the same years by a man and a woman form a unique pair of books. All of chapter 14 is fascinating. Other powerful memoirs by or of Indian women, including the Cheyenne Iron Teeth, may be found in *The Last Best Place*.

Chapter 6. McNickle: Homing In

Page numbers in the text refer to McNickle, *The Surrounded* (Albuquerque: University of New Mexico Press, 1964), and to *Wind from an Enemy Sky* (New York: Harper and Row, 1978). The University of New Mexico Press published a new edition of *Wind* in 1988.

D'Arcy McNickle was a member of the Salish-Kootenai tribe. McNickle was mixed blood Cree and Metis, adopted by the Salish.

There has been a great deal of discussion of Native American novelists recently. Readers could consult Kenneth Lincoln's *Native American Renaissance* (1983) and Swann and Krupat's two anthologies of criticism, *Smoothing the Ground* (1983) and *Recovering the Word* (1987). The North Dakota novels of the Chippewa-German-French Louise Erdrich are brilliant, and part of our growing Northern Plains heritage: *Love Medicine* (1984), *Beet Queen* (1986), and *Tracks* (1988).

The Last Best Place reprints McNickle's successive chapters on the Harvard Club and the vision quest.

The Lincoln quote is from *Native American Renaissance*, page 8.

The quote on money and land is from Harold Fey and D'Arcy McNickle, *Indians and Other Americans* (1959).

Notes

Chapter 7. Native Nature: Chickadee Jive

Discussions of the Native American relation to nature occur in many works. Joseph Eppes Brown's *Native American Religions* is a good place to start. Brown teaches at the University of Montana and edited *The Sacred Pipe* (1953), sequel to *Black Elk Speaks*.

Welch's quote on wanting to take tourists along the Highline is from his interview in *Dialogues with Northwest Writers* (1982), page 165.

For discussions of standard views of Indians, of whites looking at Indians, and for general satire of white theorizing, see Robert Berkhofer, *The White Man's Indian* (1978), and anything by Vine Deloria.

Chapter 8. Welch's Winters and Bloods

Dee McNamer's description of Cut Bank was in a paper on Welch for English 375. The degree of respect by Highliners for Welch's work is remarkable.

Excellent books concerning the Blackfeet include James Willard Schultz's tales of the 1880s, John C. Ewers's history of *The Blackfeet* (1958), William Farr's collection of photographs in *The Reservation Blackfeet* (1984), and Percy Bullchild's telling of traditional stories, *The Sun Came Down* (1985).

Welch's positive view of the end of *Loney* is recorded in his interview in *Dialogues*, page 126. Linda Weasel Head's remarks occurred in a paper for English 375. She has now published short stories and poems of her own.

Welch first read McNickle about 1977, after *Loney* was drafted.

Karl Kroeber's remarks on Indian dreaming are in *Smoothing the Ground*, pages 323 ff.

Dee Brown's review of *Fools Crow* appeared in *The Chicago Sun-Times*, Oct. 28, 1986. The Eskimo's statement to Rasmussen is quoted in *Smoothing the Ground*, page xiv.

Chapter 9. Hugo's Poetry

Page numbers of poems refer to *Making Certain It Goes On: The Collected Poems of Richard Hugo* (1984).

The first two quotations from Hugo and the Kittredge quote are from the Bevis-Hugo interview tape, KUFM-Bevis Course on Montana Writers, 1977. The third, on density and jazz, and the remark on Stafford, are from Jack Myers, ed., *A Trout in the Milk* (1982), pages 257 and 220. Hugo's statement that he burst loose when he quit drinking in 1971 appeared in *Dialogues with*

Northwest Writers, Northwest Review Books, vol. 20, no. 2–3 (1982), page 128. He compared himself to Leslie Howard in the interview in *Trout*, page 255, but he knew better.

The Moses Austin journal is quoted in Arthur K. Moore, *The Frontier Mind* (1957), page 26.

Hugo's memories of Seattle, and becoming a poet, and of endless spaces suiting his sensibilities, appear in *Trout*, pages 207 and 258, while Dave Smith's descriptions of him as bear-blunt and a meat-and-potatoes poet are in *Trout*, pages 289 and 281. A number of the Hugo interviews derive originally from the film on Hugo, *Kicking the Loose Gravel Home*, by Annick Smith, his friend who later made *Heartland*. Both films are available on video cassette.

A remarkable number of Montana writers have been influenced by Hugo's teaching, person, and no-nonsense, workingman's style. Although some writers such as Leslie Fiedler and Jesse Bier were established before Hugo arrived, many after 1964 owed much to him, including James Crumley, Bill Kittredge, Jon Jackson, Bob Reid, Robert Wrigley, Sandra Alcossar, Ralph Beer, Neil McMahon (aka Daniel Rhodes), Bryan DiSalvatore, Rick DeMarinis, Jim Welch —to name just a few and a lot of recent books. The Hugo issue of the UM literary magazine, *Cutbank* (#20), has some fine pieces and excerpts from the memorial service.

Other fine recent writing from this region would include Richard Ford, Tom McGuane, Louise Erdrich, Marilynne Robinson's brilliant *Housekeeping* (1981, set in northern Idaho), and Dee McNamer and Debra Earling's forthcoming first novels.

Chapter 10. Doig's House of Sky

The popularity of *This House of Sky* propelled Doig into full-time writing, and his current trilogy on Montana history is well publicized and well read. The concluding session of the Western Literature Association meeting in 1988 focused on Doig, and scholarship on his work increases each year.

Mary Blew has written a number of fine short stories since her book *Lambing Out*. She was on the editorial board of *The Last Best Place*. A new collection of stories, *Runaway*, is due out in 1990.

Kittredge's *Owning It All* speaks of his disillusionment with large-scale irrigation ranching in central Oregon.

A nice book of photographs on the Doigs' background, *Inside This House of Sky* by Duncan Kelso, came out from Atheneum in 1983.

Chapter 11. Maclean's River

The considerable popularity of *A River Runs Through It* will no doubt increase if and when Robert Redford completes the film of the book, to which he has bought the rights. The first version of the screenplay was written by Bill Kittredge and Annick Smith.

Walter Hesford has written on Maclean's religion, his piscatory prose, and his antinomian tendencies. His article and other excellent pieces by Wallace Stegner, Glen Love, Mary Blew, and others appear in McFarland and Nichols, eds., *Norman Maclean* (1988).

The complete transcript of the Maclean interview from which the National Public Radio piece was excerpted (1985) is at Bill Bevis, Western Studies, UM.

Many of my esteemed colleagues disagree with my reading of Maclean; for them the salvation works, and the book is nearly perfect. *A River Runs Through It* is immensely popular, sixth on the all-time best seller list from university presses. I have heard considerable disagreement and bitterness at conferences concerning attacks on the book, on the one hand, or on the other hand, the failure to see it as flawed. Why is Rawhide kicked, instead of Neal? Clearly the feeling on both sides points to a work so exceptionally beautiful and passionate that it creates its own force field; loyalty is commanded of some, while those who find flaws feel betrayed.

Chapter 12. Cooper: Then and Now

Page numbers in the text refer to Cooper, *The Prairie*, New York: Holt, Rinehart & Winston, 1950.

The quotations of French newspapers and pamphlets are from the originals at the Bibliothèque Nationale, Paris. The translations are mine. *The Prairie* quotations are from the Rinehart edition of 1950, introduced by Henry Nash Smith. Cooper had already written most of his eastern woodland Leatherstocking series.

All journal quotations from Lewis and Clark and the James expeditions may be found in the various editions by date or place of entry. Lewis and Clark entries are from the Coues edition. (Lewis and Clark scholarship is discussed in the Notes to the Introduction and to Chapter 2.) Some of Nicolas Point's observations are reprinted in *The Last Best Place*; a beautiful edition of his journals, including his own watercolor illustrations, is published by Holt, Rinehart & Winston under the title *Wilderness Kingdom*. Other early observers of the West such as Catlin and Audubon can be found in *The Last Best Place*.

The Stegner quotation is from his biography of Powell, *Beyond the Hundredth Meridian* (1954), page 212.

A fascinating history by Rudolph Kaiser of the bogus speech attributed to Chief Seattle, "The River Is Our Brother," appears in Krupat and Swann, *Recovering the Word*.

Select Bibliography

Abbott, E. C. (Teddy Blue), and Helena Huntington Smith. *We Pointed Them North*. 1939; rpt. Norman: University of Oklahoma Press, 1984.

Alderson, Nannie T., and Helena Huntington Smith. *A Bride Goes West*. Lincoln: University of Nebraska Press, 1942.

Armitage, Susan, and Elizabeth Jameson. *The Women's West*. Norman: University of Oklahoma Press, 1987.

Athearn, Robert G. *The Mythic West in Twentieth Century America*. Lawrence: University Press of Kansas, 1986.

Audubon, John James. Maria Audubon, ed. *Audubon and his Journals*. New York: Dover, 1960.

Barsness, Larry. *The Bison in Art*. Fort Worth: Amon Carter Museum Press, 1977.

Beer, Ralph. *The Blind Corral*. New York: Viking, 1986.

Berkhofer, Robert. *The White Man's Indian*. New York: Knopf, 1978.

Biddle, Nicolas. See Coues, Elliott.

Bier, Jesse. *A Hole in the Lead Apron*. New York: Harcourt, Brace, 1964.

———. *Year of the Cougar*. New York: Harcourt, Brace, 1976.

Billington, Ray Allen. *America's Frontier Heritage*. New York: Holt, Rinehart & Winston, 1966.

———. *Land of Savagery, Land of Promise*. New York: Norton, 1981.

Blew, Mary Clearman. *Lambing Out*. Columbia: University of Missouri Press, 1977.

———. *Runaway*. Lewiston, Idaho: Confluence Press, 1990.

Brinig, Myron. *Singermann*. New York: Farrar and Rinehart, 1929.

———. *Wide Open Town*. New York: Farrar and Rinehart, 1931.

Brown, Dee. *Bury My Heart at Wounded Knee*. New York: Henry Holt, 1971.

Bullchild, Percy. *The Sun Came Down*. San Francisco: Harper and Row, 1985.

Catlin, George. *Letters and Notes on the Manners, Customs, and Conditions of the North American Indians*. 1841; rpt. New York: Dover, 1973, 2 vol. paper.

Cawelti, John. *Six Gun Mystique*. Bowling Green, Ohio: Bowling Green University Press, 1971.

Cheney, Roberta. *Names on the Face of Montana*. Missoula: Mountain Press Publishing, 1983.

Clark, Walter Van Tilburg. *The Ox Bow Incident*. New York: Random House, 1940.

———. *The Track of the Cat*. New York: Random House, 1949.

Clark, William. See Coues, Elliott.

Coates, Grace Stone. *Black Cherries*. New York: Alfred A. Knopf, 1931.

Coburn, Walt. *Pioneer Cattleman in Montana: The Story of the Circle C Ranch*. Norman: University of Oklahoma Press, 1968.

Colonnese, Tom, and Louis Owens. *Native American Novelists: An Annotated Critical Bibliography*. New York: Garland, 1983.

Cooper, James Fenimore. *The Prairie*. 1827; rpt. New York: Holt, Rinehart & Winston, 1950.

Coues, Elliott, ed. *History of the Expedition under the Command of Lewis and Clark*. (Expanded version of Biddle, 1814.) 1893; rpt. New York: Dover, n.d. See also Notes, Chapter 2.

Crumley, James. *Dancing Bear*. New York: Random House, 1983.

De Crèvecouer, Hector St. John. *Letters from an American Farmer*. 1782; rpt. New Haven: Yale University Press, 1925.

DeFrees, Madeline. *When Sky Lets Go*. New York: Braziller, 1978.

Deloria, Vine. *The Nations Within: The Past and Future of American Indian Sovereignty*. New York: Pantheon, 1984.

De Toqueville, Alexis. *Democracy in America*. 1835; rpt. New York: Random House, 1981.

DeVoto, Bernard. *Across the Wide Missouri*. Boston: Houghton Mifflin, 1947.

Doig, Ivan. *This House of Sky*. New York: Harcourt, Brace, 1978.

———. *English Creek*. New York: Atheneum, 1984.

———. *Dancing at the Rascal Fair*. New York: Atheneum, 1987.

Drinnon, Richard. *Facing West: The Metaphysics of Indian-Hating and Empire-Building*. Minneapolis: University of Minnesota Press, 1980.

Eastlake, William. *The Bronc People*. Albuquerque: University of New Mexico Press. 1975.

Emmons, David. *The Butte Irish: Class and Ethnicity in an American Mining Town 1875–1925*. Urbana: University of Illinois Press, 1989.

Erdrich, Louise. *Love Medicine*. New York: Henry Holt, 1984.

———. *The Beet Queen*. New York: Henry Holt, 1986.

———. *Tracks*. New York: Henry Holt, 1988.

Etulain, Richard. *Bibliographical Guide to the Study of Western American Literature*. Lincoln: University of Nebraska Press, 1982.

———, and Michael Malone. *The American West: A Twentieth Century History*. Lincoln: University of Nebraska Press, 1989.

Ewers, John C. *The Blackfeet: Raiders on the Northwestern Plains*. Norman: University of Oklahoma Press, 1958.

Farr, William E. *The Reservation Blackfeet, 1882–1945.* Seattle: University of Washington Press, 1984.

Ferris, Beth. Screenplay for *Heartland.* Film and video. See Smith, Annick.

———. *Contrary Warriors: A Story of the Crow Tribe.* Coproduced by Pam Roberts, Connie Poten, and Beth Ferris. Written by Beth Ferris and Connie Poten. Edited by Jennifer Chinlund. Missoula: Rattlesnake Productions, 1985.

Fey, Harold, and D'Arcy McNickle. *Indians and Other Americans.* New York: Harper, 1959.

Ford, Richard. *Rock Springs.* New York: Random House, 1986.

Ford, Thomas W. *A. B. Guthrie, Jr.* Boston: Twayne, 1981.

Garcia, Andrew. *Tough Trip Through Paradise.* Bennett Stein, ed. Sausalito, Calif.: Comstock, 1967.

Goetzmann, William H. *Exploration and Empire.* New York: Knopf, 1966.

———, and William N. Goetzmann. *The West of the Imagination.* New York: Norton, 1986.

Grinnell, George B. *Blackfoot Lodge Tales.* 1892; rpt. Lincoln: University of Nebraska Press, 1962.

———. *The Fighting Cheyennes.* 1915; rpt. Norman: University of Oklahoma Press, 1985.

Guthrie, A. B., Jr. *The Big Sky.* 1947; rpt. New York: Houghton Mifflin, 1965.

———. *The Blue Hen's Chick.* New York: McGraw-Hill, 1965.

Hanna, Warren L. *The Life and Times of James Willard Schultz.* Norman: University of Oklahoma Press, 1986.

Hesford, Walter. "Fishing for the Words of Life." In McFarland and Nichols, *Maclean.*

Howard, Joseph Kinsey. *Montana, High, Wide, and Handsome.* New Haven: Yale University Press, 1943.

———. *Montana Margins.* New Haven: Yale University Press, 1946.

Huffman, L. A. "Last Busting at Bow-Gun." In Kittredge and Smith, *The Last Best Place.*

Hugo, Richard. *Making Certain It Goes On: The Collected Poems of Richard Hugo.* New York: Norton, 1984.

———. *The Real West Marginal Way.* New York: Norton, 1986.

Huth, Hans. *Nature and the American.* Berkeley: University of California Press, 1957.

James, Edwin. *Account of an Expedition from Pittsburgh to the Rocky Mountains.* 1823; rpt. Ann Arbor, University Microfilms, 1966.

Jameson, Elizabeth. See Armitage and Jameson.

Jefferson, Thomas. *Notes on the State of Virginia.* 1784; rpt. New York: Norton, 1972.

Johnson, Dorothy. *A Man Called Horse and Other Stories*. New York: Ballantine, 1977.

Jordan, Teresa. *Cowgirls: Women of the American West*. New York: Doubleday, 1982.

Josephy, Alvin, Jr. *The Nez Perce Indians and the Opening of the Northwest*. New Haven: Yale University Press, 1965.

———. *Now That the Buffalo's Gone: A Study of Today's American Indians*. New York: Knopf, 1982.

Kelso, Duncan. *Inside This House of Sky*. New York: Atheneum, 1983.

Kennedy, Michael S. *Cowboys and Cattlemen*. New York: Hastings House, 1964.

Kittredge, William. *The Van Gogh Field*. Columbia: University of Missouri Press, 1978.

———. *We Are Not in This Together*. Saint Paul, Minn.: Graywolf Press, 1984.

———, and Annick Smith, eds. *The Last Best Place: A Montana Anthology*. Helena: Montana Historical Society Press, 1988.

Krupat, Arnold. *For Those Who Come After: A Study of Native American Autobiography*. Berkeley: University of California Press, 1985.

———, and Brian Swann, eds. *Recovering the Word: Essays on Native American Literature*. Berkeley: University of California Press, 1987.

Lamar, Howard. *The Reader's Encyclopedia of the American West*. New York: Harper and Row, 1977.

Lang, William L., and Rex Myers, eds. *Montana: Our Land and People*. Boulder, Colo.: Pruett, 1979.

Lewis, Meriwether. See Coues, Elliott.

Liberty, Margo. See Stands in Timber, John.

Limerick, Patricia. *The Legacy of Conquest: The Unbroken Past of the American West*. New York: Norton, 1987.

Lincoln, Kenneth. *Native American Renaissance*. Berkeley: University of California Press, 1983.

Linderman, Frank. *Indian Why Stories*. New York: Scribners, 1915.

———. *Lige Mounts, Free Trapper*. New York: Scribners, 1922. (Later editions titled *Morning Light* and *Free Trapper*.)

———. *Plenty-coups*. 1930; rpt. Lincoln: University of Nebraska Press, 1962.

———. *Pretty Shield*. 1932; rpt. Lincoln: University of Nebraska Press, 1974.

Lynde, Stan. *A Month of Sundays: The Best of Rick O'Shay and Hipshot*. New York: Grosset and Dunlop, 1976.

McCoy, Drew. *The Elusive Republic: Political Economy in Jeffersonian America*. Chapel Hill: University of North Carolina Press, 1980.

McFarland, Ron, and Hugh Nichols, eds. *Norman Maclean*. Lewiston, Idaho: Confluence Press, 1988.

McGuane, Thomas. *Something to Be Desired*. New York: Random House, 1985.

Maclean, Norman. *A River Runs Through It*. Chicago: University of Chicago Press, 1977.

McNickle, D'Arcy. *The Surrounded*. 1936; rpt. Albuquerque: University of New Mexico Press, 1964.

———. *Wind from an Enemy Sky*. 1977; rpt. Albuquerque: University of New Mexico Press, 1988.

———. See also Fey and McNickle.

McRae, Wally. *Up North Is Down the Crick*. Bozeman, Mont.: Museum of the Rockies, 1985.

Malone, Michael. *The Battle for Butte*. Seattle: University of Washington Press, 1981.

———, and Richard Roeder. *Montana: A History of Two Centuries*. Seattle: University of Washington Press, 1976.

Malone, Michael, ed. *Historians and the American West*. Lincoln: University of Nebraska Press, 1983.

Malone, Michael, and Richard Etulain. *The American West: A Twentieth Century History*. Lincoln: University of Nebraska Press, 1989.

Marx, Leo. *The Machine in the Garden*. New York: Oxford University Press, 1964.

Merriam, H. G., ed. *Montana Adventure: The Recollections of Frank B. Linderman*. Lincoln: University of Nebraska Press, 1968.

———, ed. *Way out West*. Norman: University of Oklahoma Press, 1969.

———, ed. *Frontier Omnibus*. Missoula: University of Montana Press, 1962.

Milner, Clyde A., II, and Floyd O'Neal, eds. *Churchmen and the Western Indians*. Norman: University of Oklahoma Press, 1985.

Momaday, N. Scott. *House Made of Dawn*. 1969; rpt. New York: Harper and Row, 1977.

Moore, Arthur K. *The Frontier Mind*. Lexington: University of Kentucky Press, 1957.

Morris, Wright. *Ceremony in Lone Tree*. Lincoln: University of Nebraska Press, 1973.

Myers, Jack, ed. *A Trout in the Milk: A Composite Portrait of Richard Hugo*. Lewiston, Idaho: Confluence Press, 1982.

Myres, Sandra. *Westering Women and the Frontier Experience, 1800–1915*. Albuquerque: University of New Mexico Press, 1982.

Nash, Gerald D. *The American West in the Twentieth Century*. Englewood Cliffs, N.J.: Prentice-Hall, 1973.

Nash, Roderick. *Wilderness and the American Mind*. New Haven: Yale University Press, 1967.

Nichols, Roger L., ed. *American Frontier and Western Issues*. Westport, Conn: Greenwood Press, 1986.

Owens, Louis. See Colonnese and Owens.

Plenty-coups, Chief. *Plenty-coups*. See Linderman, F.

Point, Nicolas. *Wilderness Kingdom: Indian Life in the Rocky Mountains 1840–47, The Journals & Paintings of Nicolas Point, S.J.*, trans. J. P. Donnelly. New York: Holt, Rinehart & Winston, 1967.

Pretty-shield. *Pretty Shield*. See Linderman, F.

Robertson, Pearl Price. "Homestead Days in Montana." *Frontier* magazine, 1933; rpt. Howard, *Montana Margins*, and excerpts in Kittredge and Smith, *The Last Best Place*.

Roeder, Richard. *Montana: A History of Two Centuries*. See Malone and Roeder.

Russell, Charles M. *Trails Plowed Under*. New York: Doubleday, 1927.

Russell, Osborne. *Journal of a Trapper 1834–1843*. Lincoln: University of Nebraska Press, 1965.

Ruxton, G. F. *Life in the Far West*. 1848; rpt. Norman: University of Oklahoma Press, 1951.

Schultz, James Willard. *My Life as an Indian*. New York: Doubleday, Page and Co., 1907.

———. *Blackfeet and Buffalo*. Norman: University of Oklahoma Press, 1962.

Silko, Leslie. *Ceremony*. New York: Viking, 1977.

Slotkin, Richard. *Regeneration Through Violence*. Middletown: Wesleyan University Press, 1973.

Smith, Annick, ed., *The Last Best Place*. See Kittredge and Smith.

Smith, Annick, producer. *Richard Hugo: Kicking the Loose Gravel Home*. Film and video, with Beth Chadwick Ferris. 1977.

Smith, Annick, executive producer. *Heartland*. Film and video. Coproduced by Michael Hausman and Beth Ferris. Written by Beth Ferris with help from William Kittredge. 1979.

Smith, Helena Huntington. See Abbott, T. B., and Alderson, N.

Smith, Henry Nash. *Virgin Land*. Cambridge: Harvard University Press, 1950.

Stands In Timber, John, with Margot Liberty. *Cheyenne Memories*. 1967; rpt. Lincoln: University of Nebraska Press, 1972.

Stegner, Wallace. *The Sound of Mountain Water*. New York: Dutton, 1980.

———. *Beyond the Hundredth Meridian: John Wesley Powell and the Second Opening of the West*. 1954; rpt. Lincoln: University of Nebraska Press, 1982.

———. *Wolf Willow*. 1962; rpt. Lincoln: University of Nebraska Press, 1980.

Stein, Ben, ed. *Tough Trip through Paradise*. See Garcia, A.

Stewart, Elinore Pruitt. *Letters of a Woman Homesteader*. 1914; rpt. Boston: Houghton Mifflin, 1982.

Stuart, Granville. *Pioneering in Montana*. (Originally *Forty Years on the Frontier*) 1925; rpt. Lincoln: University of Nebraska Press, 1977.

Swann, Brian, ed. *Recovering the Word*. See Krupat, A.

Bibliography

Swann, J. Malcolm. *Montana: Let There be Lit*. Missoula: Montana Committee for the Humanities, 1988.

Toole, Ross K. *Montana: An Uncommon Land*. Norman: University of Oklahoma Press, 1959.

Van Cleve, Spike. *A Day Late and a Dollar Short*. Kansas City: Lowell Press, 1982.

Walker, Mildred. *Winter Wheat*. New York: Harcourt, Brace, 1944.

———. *The Curlew's Cry*. New York: Harcourt, Brace, 1955.

———. *If a Lion Could Talk*. New York: Harcourt, Brace, 1970.

Welch, James. *Winter in the Blood*. New York: Harper and Row, 1974.

———. *The Death of Jim Loney*. New York: Harper and Row, 1979.

———. *Fools Crow*. New York: Viking Penguin, 1986.

Index

Boldface numbers refer to main discussions.

Index

Index

Index

Index